Modern Critical Views

F. SCOTT FITZGERALD

Modern Critical Views

F. SCOTT FITZGERALD

Edited with an introduction by

Harold Bloom

Sterling Professor of the Humanities
Yale University

1985
CHELSEA HOUSE PUBLISHERS
New York

THE COVER:
This ironic, yet still tender cover represents Fitzgerald's characteristic metamorphoses of the Keatsian influence upon him, with *la belle dame san merci* transmogrified into a flapper.—H.B.

Cover illustration by Jennifer Caldwell

Printed and bound in the United States of America

10 9 8 7 6 5 4 3

Library of Congress Cataloging in Publication Data

F. Scott Fitzgerald.
(Modern critical views)
Bibliography: p.
Includes index.
1. Fitzgerald. F. Scott (Francis Scott), 1896–1940—
Criticism and interpretation—Addresses, essays,
lectures. I. Bloom, Harold. II. Series.
PS3511.I9Z6137 1985 813′.52 85–9606
ISBN 0–87754–650–9

Contents

Editor's Note

This volume attempts to give a representative selection of the best and most helpful literary criticism that the work of F. Scott Fitzgerald has received over the last sixty years. It is arranged in the chronological sequence of publication, beginning with Edmund Wilson's description of his friend's early fiction, in 1922. Lionel Trilling's elegiac estimate of 1945 is followed by Marius Bewley's shrewd reading of Fitzgerald's career as a catastrophe induced by the American dream of success. This is accompanied by the essays of Malcolm Cowley and Robert Ornstein, two other visions, from the same perspective of the 1950s, of Fitzgerald's "crack-up" as an episode in the American fable or romance of wealth.

Something of the cultural change transpiring in the 1960's can be observed in the essays by Millgate, Male, Mizener, and Gindin. Michael Millgate analyzes the unfinished Hollywood novel, *The Last Tycoon,* so as to uncover a fundamental dualism in Fitzgerald. Roy R. Male brings a Hawthornian ethos to a sympathetic study of Fitzgerald's most desolate and magnificent short story, "Babylon Revisited." A balanced defense of *Tender Is the Night* by Arthur Mizener precedes James Gindin's meditation on the problematics of the image of fatherhood in Fitzgerald's work.

With the essays by Mary E. Burton and David Parker, the very different emphasis of the 1970s gives us an examination of Dick Diver's victimage by the psychoanalytic counter-transference and a retrospective vision of the dialectics of heroism in *The Great Gatsby.* Three essays of the early 1980s complete the volume. Robert Roulston returns us to *The Last Tycoon* to uncover Fitzgerald's duality in his sense of the South (and of Zelda, as the last of the Southern belles), while Ronald J. Gervais analyzes Fitzgerald's political and social ambivalences. William E. Doherty considers the relation between Keats and Fitzgerald, with an emphasis upon dualism and estrangement. What has been consistent throughout sixty years of criticism is a deep awareness of how profoundly (and how fruitfully) Fitzgerald was divided against himself.

Introduction

I

It is difficult to imagine John Keats writing the fictions of Joseph Conrad, since there is nothing in common between the Great Odes and *The Secret Sharer* or *Heart of Darkness*. But such an imagining is not useless, since in some sense that was Scott Fitzgerald's accomplishment. *The Great Gatsby* does combine the lyrical sensibility of Keats and the fictive mode of Conrad, and makes of so odd a blending a uniquely American story, certainly a candidate for *the* American story of its time (1925). *Gatsby* has more in common with T.S. Eliot's "The Hollow Men," also published in 1925, than it does with such contemporary novels as the *Arrowsmith* of Sinclair Lewis or the *Manhattan Transfer* of John Dos Passos. Eliot's admiration for *The Great Gatsby* is understandable; the book, like the visionary lyric of Hart Crane, struggles against Eliot's conclusions while being compelled to appropriate Eliot's language and procedures. Fitzgerald, the American Keats, and Crane, even more the American Shelley, both sought to affirm a High Romanticism in the accents of a belated counter-tradition. The Keatsian belief in the holiness of the heart's affections is central to Fitzgerald, and *Tender Is the Night* owes more than its title to the naturalistic humanism of the Great Odes.

Fitzgerald's canonical status is founded more upon *Gatsby* and his best short stories, such as "Babylon Revisited," than it is upon the seriously flawed *Tender Is the Night*, let alone upon the unfinished *The Last Tycoon*. Oddly praised as "the best Hollywood novel," despite its manifest inferiority to Nathanael West's *The Day of the Locust*, *The Last Tycoon* is more an embryo than it is a torso. Edmund Wilson's affectionate overestimation of this fragment has been influential, but will fade away each time the book is actually read. *Tender Is the Night* demonstrates that Fitzgerald, unlike Conrad and Lawrence, cannot sustain too long a narrative. The book, though coming relatively late in his career, is Fitzgerald's *Endymion*, while *Gatsby* is, as it were, his *Fall of Hyperion*. Keats desired to write epic, but was more attuned to romance and to lyric. Fitzgerald desired to write novels on the scale of Thackeray and of Conrad, but his genius was more fitted to *Gatsby* as his mode of romance, and to "Babylon Revisited" as his version of the ode or of the reflective lyric.

The aesthetic of Scott Fitzgerald is quite specifically a personal revision of Keats's hope for Negative Capability, which Fitzgerald called "a romantic readiness" and attributed to his Gatsby. It is certainly part of the achievement of Fitzgerald's best novel that its hero possesses an authentic aesthetic dignity. By an effective troping of form, Fitzgerald made this a book in which nothing is aesthetically wasted, even as the narrative shows us everyone being humanly wasted. Edith Wharton rather nastily praised Fitzgerald for having created the "perfect Jew" in the gambler, Meyer Wolfsheim. Had she peered closer, she might have seen the irony of her patrician prejudice reversed in the ancient Jewish wisdom that even Wolfsheim is made to express:

> "Let us learn to show our friendship for a man when he is alive and not after he is dead," he suggested. "After that, my own rule is to let everything alone."

Whether Nick Carraway is capable of apprehending this as wisdom is disputable but Fitzgerald evidently could, since Wolfsheim is not wholly devoid of the dignity of grief. Lionel Trilling commended *The Great Gatsby* for retaining its freshness. After sixty years, it has more than retained its moral balance and affective rightness. Those qualities seem augmented through the perspective of lapsed time. What has been augmented also is the Eliotic phantasmagoria of the *Waste Land* imagery that is so effectively vivid throughout Fitzgerald's vision. Carraway begins by speaking of "what preyed on Gatsby, what foul dust floated in the wake of his dreams." These are also "the spasms of bleak dust," above which you perceive the blue and gigantic eyes of Doctor T.J. Eckleburg, which brood on over the dumping ground of the gray land. "My heart is a handful of dust," the monologist of Tennyson's *Maud* had proclaimed, in a great phrase stolen by Eliot for his *Waste Land*. Fitzgerald's dust is closer to Tennyson's heart than to Eliot's fear:

> . . . to where Myrtle Wilson, her life violently extinguished, knelt in the road and mingled her thick dark blood with the dust.
>
> Michaelis and this man reached her first, but when they had torn open her shirtwaist, still damp with perspiration, they saw that her left breast was swinging loose like a flap, and there was no need to listen for the heart beneath.

Fitzgerald's violence has that curious suddenness we associate with the same narrative quality in E.M. Forster. Something repressed in the phantasmagoria of the ordinary returns, all too often, reminding us that

Fitzgerald shares also in Conrad's sense of reality and its treacheries, particularly as developed in *Nostromo*, a novel that we know Fitzgerald rightly admired. *Heart of Darkness*, which Fitzgerald also admired, is linked to "The Hollow Men" by that poem's epigraph, and many critics have seen Carraway as Fitzgerald's version of Marlow, somewhat sentimentalized, but still an authentic secret sharer in Gatsby's fate. Like the Eliot of "The Hollow Men," Fitzgerald found in Conrad a seer of the contemporary abyss of:

> Shape without form, shade without color,
> Paralysed force, gesture without motion;

or, in the language of *Heart of Darkness*: "A vision of grayness without form."

II

Writing to his daughter about the "Ode on a Grecian Urn," Fitzgerald extravagantly observed that: "For awhile after you quit Keats all other poetry seems to be only whistling or humming." Fitzgerald's deepest affinity to Keats is in the basic stance of his work, at once rhetorical, psychological and even cosmological. In both Keats and Fitzgerald, the perpetual encounter is between the mortal poet or man-of-imagination (Gatsby, Diver) and an immortal or perpetually youthful goddess-woman. Fitzgerald's women—Daisy, Nicole, Rosemary—are not so much American dreams as they are Keatsian Lamias or perpetually virgin moon-maidens. "Virginity renews itself like the moon" is a Keatsian apothegm of Yeats's and the quester in Fitzgerald would have concurred. The murdered Gatsby is truly Daisy's victim; rather more grimly, Diver is emptied out by his relationship with Nicole, and to some degree, by his repetition of that pattern with Rosemary.

This has been read as misogyny in Fitzgerald but, as in Keats, it tends largely to be the reverse. Confronting his immortal women, the Keatsian quester seeks what at last Keats himself obtains from the harshly reluctant Muse, Moneta, in *The Fall of Hyperion*: recognition that he is *the* poet in and for his own time. "I sure should see/Other men here; but I am here alone." Fitzgerald was greatly ambitious, but his audacity did not extend quite that far. Yet his surrogates—Gatsby and Diver—are no more deceived than Keats's poets are deceived. Daisy, Nicole and Rosemary do not matter as personalities, not to us as readers and not much more to Gatsby or Diver. Gatsby, the more sublime quester, is allowed his famous touch of genius when he dismisses Daisy's love for her husband, the brutal Tom Buchanan: "In any case, it was just personal." Diver, less magnificently also knows better, but is just as doom-eager as Gatsby. The inadequacies of the actual women do not matter, because the drive is not for satisfaction or for happiness. It is Freud's uncanny death-drive, which replaces the drive for self-preservation, and exists in a dialectical balance with the libido. Gatsby somehow chooses to die in his own fashion, while Diver chooses the death-in-life of erotic and professional defeat.

Tender Is the Night survives the weakness of its characterizations and the clumsiness of its narrative structure precisely because of Diver's own fated sense that there are no accidents. His character is his fate, and his relationship with Nicole is not so much a failed counter-transference as it is another pathetic version of the sublime Romantic vision of sexual entropy set forth overtly in Blake's "The Mental Traveller" and implicitly in James's *The Sacred Fount*: "And she grows young as he grows old." For the Blakean "young" we can substitute "whole," yet for the "old" we cannot quite substitute "weak" but something closer to Fitzgerald's "interior laughter," the quality in Diver that drives him down and out until he ends up practicing medicine in progressively smaller towns in the Finger Lakes Section of the Western Reserve of New York State. The pathos of that dying fall is anything but Keatsian, and may have been Fitzgerald's trope for his own self-destructiveness.

III

A curious self-appropriation, or perhaps indeliberate self-repetition, links the close of *Tender Is the Night* to the close of "Babylon Revisited," which seems to me Fitzgerald's most impressive single short story. On the day before he leaves the Riviera for America, after his rejection by Nicole, Diver spends all his time with his children: "He was not young any more with a lot of nice thoughts and dreams to have about himself, so he wanted to remember them well." The penultimate sentence of "Babylon Revisited" is: "He wasn't young anymore, with a lot of nice thoughts and dreams to have about himself."

Whichever came first, the repetition is central to Fitzgerald. "Nice thoughts and dreams" are the essence, and Fitzgerald's regressive vision, like Gatsby's and Diver's and Charlie Wales's, is a Keatsian and Stevensian study of the nostalgias. Keats, staring at the face of the unveiled Moneta, prophesies the Stevens of *The Auroras of Autumn*, with his unabashed, Freudian celebration of the imago: "The mother's face, the purpose of the poem, fills the room." Charlie Wales, in "Babylon Revisited," longing for his daughter, remembers his dead wife as any man remembers his mother: "He was absolutely sure Helen wouldn't have wanted him to be so alone." As the last sentence of what may be Fitzgerald's most memorable story, it reverberates with a peculiar plangency in American Romantic tradition.

EDMUND WILSON

F. Scott Fitzgerald

It has been said by a celebrated person that to meet F. Scott Fitzgerald is to think of a stupid old woman with whom someone has left a diamond; she is extremely proud of the diamond and shows it to everyone who comes by, and everyone is surprised that such an ignorant old woman should possess so valuable a jewel; for in nothing does she appear so inept as in the remarks she makes about the diamond.

The person who invented this simile did not know Fitzgerald very well and can only have seen him, I think, in his more diffident or uninspired moods. The reader must not suppose that there is any literal truth in the image. Scott Fitzgerald is, in fact, no old woman, but a very good-looking young man, nor is he in the least stupid, but, on the contrary, exhilaratingly clever. Yet there *is* a symbolic truth in the description quoted above: it is true that Fitzgerald has been left with a jewel which he doesn't know quite what to do with. For he has been given imagination without intellectual control of it; he has been given the desire for beauty without an aesthetic ideal; and he has been given a gift for expression without very many ideas to express.

Consider, for example, the novel—*This Side of Paradise*—with which he founded his reputation. It has almost every fault and deficiency that a novel can possibly have. It is not only highly imitative but it imitates an inferior model. Fitzgerald, when he wrote the book, was drunk with Compton Mackenzie, and it sounds like an American attempt to rewrite *Sinister Street*. Now, Mackenzie, in spite of his gift for picturesque and comic invention and the capacity for pretty writing that he says he learned from Keats, lacks both the intellectual force and the emotional imagination to give body and outline to the material which he secretes in such enormous abundance. With the seeds he took from Keats's garden, one of the best-arranged gardens in England, he exfloreated so profusely that he blotted out the path of his own. Michael Fane, the hero of *Sinister Street*, was swamped in the forest of description; he was smothered by creepers and columbine. From the time he went up to Oxford, his personality began to grow dimmer, and, when he last turned up (in Belgrade) he seemed quite to have lost his identity. As a consequence, Amory Blaine, the hero of *This Side of Paradise*, had a very poor chance of coherence: Fitzgerald did endow him, to be sure, with a certain emotional life which the phantom Michael Fane lacks; but he was quite as much a wavering quantity in a phantasmagoria of incident that had no dominating intention to endow it with unity and force. In short, one of the chief weaknesses of *This Side of Paradise* is that it is really not *about* anything: its intellectual and moral content amounts to little more than a gesture—a gesture of indefinite revolt. The story itself, furthermore, is very immaturely imagined: it is always just verging on the ludicrous. And, finally, *This Side of Paradise* is one of the most illiterate books of any merit ever published (a fault which the publisher's proofreader seems to have made no effort to remedy). Not only is it ornamented with bogus ideas and faked literary references, but it is full of literary words tossed about with the most reckless inaccuracy.

I have said that *This Side of Paradise* commits almost every sin that a novel can possibly commit: but it does not commit the unpardonable sin: it does not fail to live. The whole preposterous farrago is animated with life. It is rather a fluttering and mercurial life: its emotions do not move you profoundly; its drama does not make you hold your breath; but its gaiety and color and movement did make it come as something exciting after the realistic heaviness and dinginess of so much serious American fiction. If one recalls the sort of flavorless fodder of which Ernest Poole's *The Harbor* was an example, one can understand the wild enthusiasm with which *This Side of Paradise* was hailed. The novel was also well-written—well-written in spite of its illiteracies. It is true, as I have said above, that Fitzgerald mishandles words; his works are full of malapropisms of the most disconcerting kind. You will find: "Whatever your flare [sic] proves to be—religion, architecture, literature"; "the Juvenalia of my collected editions"; "There were nice things in it [the room] . . . offsprings of a vicarious [vagarious] impatient taste"; "a mind like his, lucrative in intelligence, intuition and lightning decision"; etc., etc. It reminds one rather of:

Agib, who could readily, at sight,
Strum a march upon the loud Theodolite.
  He would diligently play
  On the Zoetrope all day,
And blow the gay Pantechnicon all night.

It is true that Scott Fitzgerald plays the language entirely by ear. But his instrument, for all that, is no mean one. He has an instinct for graceful and vivid prose that some of his more pretentious fellows might envy.

In regard to the man himself, there are perhaps two things worth knowing, for the influence they have had on his work. In the first place, he comes from the Middle West—from St. Paul, Minnesota. Fitzgerald is as much of the Middle West of large cities and country clubs as Sinclair Lewis is of the Middle West of the prairies and little towns. What we find in him is much what we find in the more prosperous strata of these cities: sensitivity and eagerness for life without a sound base of culture and taste; a structure of millionaire residences, brilliant expensive hotels and exhilarating social activities built not on the eighteenth century but simply on the flat Western land. And it seems to me rather a pity that he has not written more of the West: it is perhaps the only milieu that he thoroughly understands. When Fitzgerald approaches the East, he brings to it the standards of the wealthy West—the preoccupation with display, the appetite for visible magnificence and audible jamboree, the vigorous social atmosphere of amiable flappers and youths comparatively untainted as yet by the snobbery of the East. In *The Beautiful and Damned*, for example, we feel that he is moving in a vacuum; the characters have no real connection with the background to which they have been assigned; they are not part of the organism of New York as the characters, in, say, the short story *Bernice Bobs Her Hair* are a part of the organism of St. Paul. Surely F. Scott Fitzgerald should some day do for Summit Avenue what Lewis has done for Main Street.

But you are not to suppose from all this that the author of *This Side of Paradise* is merely a typical well-to-do Middle Westerner, with correct clothes and clear skin, who has been sent to the East for college. The second thing one should know about him is that Fitzgerald is partly Irish and that he brings both to life and to fiction certain qualities that are not Anglo-Saxon. For, like the Irish, Fitzgerald is romantic, but also cynical about romance; he is bitter as well as ecstatic; astringent as well as lyrical. He casts himself in the role of playboy, yet at the playboy he incessantly mocks. He is vain, a little malicious, of quick intelligence and wit, and has an Irish gift for turning language into something iridescent and surprising. He often reminds one, in fact, of the description that a great

Irishman, Bernard Shaw, has written of the Irish: "An Irishman's imagination never lets him alone, never convinces him, never satisfies him; but it makes him that he can't face reality nor deal with it nor handle it nor conquer it: he can only sneer at them that do . . . and imagination's such a torture that you can't bear it without whisky. . . . And all the while there goes on a horrible, senseless, mischievous laughter."

For the rest, F. Scott Fitzgerald is a rather childlike fellow, very much wrapped up in his dream of himself and his projection of it on paper. For a person of his mental agility, he is extraordinarily little occupied with the general affairs of the world: like a woman, he is not much given to abstract or impersonal thought. Conversations about politics or general ideas have a way of snapping back to Fitzgerald. But this seldom becomes annoying; he is never pretentious or boring. He is quite devoid of affectation and takes the curse off his relentless egoism by his readiness to laugh at himself and his boyish uncertainty of his talent. And he exhibits, in his personality as well as in his writings, a quality rare today among even the youngest American writers: he is almost the only one among them who is capable of lighthearted high spirits. Where a satirist like Sinclair Lewis would stew "the Problem of Salesmanship" in acrid rancorous fumes, Fitzgerald, in *The Beautiful and Damned*, has made of it hilarious farce. His characters—and he—are actors in an elfin harlequinade; they are as nimble, as gay and as lovely—and as hardhearted—as fairies: Columbine elopes with Harlequin on a rope ladder dropped from the Ritz and both go morris-dancing amuck on a case of bootleg liquor; Pantaloon is pinked with an epigram that withers him up like a leaf; the Policeman is tripped by Harlequin and falls into the Pulitzer Fountain. Just before the curtain falls, Harlequin puts on false whiskers and pretends to be Bernard Shaw; he gives reporters an elaborate interview on politics, religion and history; a hundred thousand readers see it and are more or less impressed; Columbine nearly dies laughing; Harlequin sends out for a case of gin.

Let me quote a characteristic incident in connection with *The Beautiful and Damned.* Since writing *This Side of Paradise*—on the inspiration of Wells and Mackenzie—Fitzgerald has become acquainted with a different school of fiction: the ironical-pessimistic. In college, he had supposed that the thing to do was to write biographical novels with a burst of ideas toward the close; since his advent in the literary world, he has discovered that another genre has recently come into favor: the kind which makes much of the tragedy and what Mencken has called "the meaninglessness of life." Fitzgerald had imagined, hitherto, that the thing to do in a novel was to bring out a meaning in life; but he now set bravely about it to contrive a shattering tragedy that should be, also, a hundred-percent meaningless. As a result of this determination, the first version of *The Beautiful and Damned* culminated in an orgy of horror for which the reader was imperfectly prepared. Fitzgerald destroyed his characters with a succession of catastrophes so arbitrary that, beside them, the perversities of Hardy seemed the working of natural laws. The heroine was to lose her beauty at a prematurely early age, and her character was to go to pieces with it; Richard Carmel, a writer of promise, was to lose his artistic ideals and prostitute himself to the popular taste; and the wealthy Anthony Patch was not only to lose his money but, finding himself unable to make a living, abjectly to succumb to drink and eventually to go insane. But the bitterest moment of the story was to come at the very end, when Anthony was to be wandering the streets of New York in an attempt to borrow some money. After several humiliating failures, he finally approaches an old friend whom he sees with an elegant lady just getting into a cab. This is the brilliant Maury Noble, a cynic, an intellectual and a man of genuine parts. Maury cuts Anthony dead and drives away in the taxi. "But," the author explains, "he really had not seen Anthony. For Maury had indulged his appetite for alcoholic beverage once too often: he was now stone-blind!" But the point of my story is this: though Fitzgerald had been perfectly serious in writing this bathetic passage, he did not hesitate, when he heard people laugh at it, to laugh about it himself, and with as much surprise and delight as if he had just come across it in Max Beerbohm. He at once improvised a burlesque: "It seemed to Anthony that Maury's eyes had a fixed glassy stare; his legs moved stiffly as he walked and when he spoke his voice was lifeless. When Anthony came nearer, he saw that Maury was dead."

To conclude, it would be quite unfair to subject Scott Fitzgerald, who is still in his twenties and has presumably most of his work before him, to a rigorous overhauling. His restless imagination may yet produce something durable. For the present, however, this imagination is certainly not seen to the best advantage: it suffers badly from lack of discipline and poverty of aesthetic ideas. Fitzgerald is a dazzling extemporizer, but his stories have a way of petering out: he seems never to have planned them completely or to have thought out his themes from the beginning. This is true even of some of his most successful fantasies, such as *The Diamond as Big as the Ritz* or his comedy, *The Vegetable*. On the other hand, *The Beautiful and Damned*, imperfect though it is, marks an advance over *This Side of Paradise*: the style is more nearly mature and the subject more solidly unified, and there are scenes that are more convincing than any in his previous fiction.

But, in any case, even the work that Fitzgerald has done up to date has a certain moral importance. In his very expression of the anarchy by which he finds himself bewildered, of his revolt which cannot fix on an object, he is typical of the war generation—the generation so memorably described on the last page of *This Side of Paradise* as "grown up to find all gods dead, all wars fought, all faiths in men shaken." There is a moral in *The Beautiful and Damned* that the author did not perhaps intend to point. The hero and the heroine of this giddy book are creatures without method or purpose: they give themselves up to wild debaucheries and do not, from beginning to end, perform a single serious act; yet somehow you get the impression that, in spite of their fantastic behavior, Anthony and Gloria Patch are the most rational people in the book. Wherever they come in contact with institutions, with the serious life of their time, these are made to appear ridiculous, they are subjects for scorn or mirth. We see the army, finance and business successively and casually exposed as completely without point or dignity. The inference we are led to draw is that, in such a civilization as this, the sanest and most honorable course is to escape from organized society and live for the excitement of the moment. It cannot be merely a special reaction to a personal situation which gives rise to the paradoxes of such a book. It may be that we cannot demand too high a degree of moral balance from young men, however able or brilliant, who write books in the year 1921: we must remember that they have had to grow up in, that they have had to derive their chief stimulus from the wars, the society and the commerce of the Age of Confusion itself.

LIONEL TRILLING

F. Scott Fitzgerald

" 'So be it! I die content and my destiny is fulfilled,' said Racine's Orestes; and there is more in his speech than the insanely bitter irony that appears on the surface. Racine, fully conscious of this tragic grandeur, permits Orestes to taste for a moment before going mad with grief the supreme joy of a hero; to assume his *exemplary* role." The heroic awareness of which André Gide speaks in his essay on Goethe was granted to Scott Fitzgerald for whatever grim joy he might find in it. It is a kind of seal set upon his heroic quality that he was able to utter his vision of his own fate publicly and aloud and in *Esquire* with no lessening of his dignity, even with an enhancement of it. The several essays in which Fitzgerald examined his life in crisis have been gathered together by Edmund Wilson—who is for many reasons the most appropriate editor possible—and published, together with Fitzgerald's notebooks and some letters, as well as certain tributes and memorabilia, in a volume called, after one of the essays, *The Crack-Up*. It is a book filled with the grief of the lost and the might-have-been, with physical illness and torture of mind. Yet the heroic quality is so much here, Fitzgerald's assumption of the "exemplary role" is so proper and right that it occurs to us to say, and not merely as a piety but as the most accurate expression of what we really do feel, that

> Nothing is here for tears, nothing to wail
> Or knock the breast, no weakness, no contempt,
> Dispraise, or blame, nothing but well and fair,
> And what may quiet us in a death so noble.

This isn't what we may fittingly say on all tragic occasions, but the original occasion for these words has a striking aptness to Fitzgerald. Like Milton's Samson, he had the consciousness of having misused the power with which he had been endowed. "I had been only a mediocre caretaker . . . of my talent," he said. And the parallel carries further, to the sojourn among the Philistines and even to the maimed hero exhibited and mocked for the amusement of the crowd—on the afternoon of September 25, 1936, the New York *Evening Post* carried on its front page a feature story in which the triumphant reporter tells how he managed to make his way into the Southern nursing home where the sick and distracted Fitzgerald was being cared for and there "interviewed" him, taking all due note of the contrast between the present humiliation and the past glory. It was a particularly gratuitous horror, and yet in retrospect it serves to augment the moral force of the poise and fortitude which marked Fitzgerald's mind in the few recovered years that were left to him.

The root of Fitzgerald's heroism is to be found, as it sometimes is in tragic heroes, in his power of love. Fitzgerald wrote much about love, he was preoccupied with it as between men and women, but it is not merely where he is being explicit about it that his power appears. It is to be seen where eventually all a writer's qualities have their truest existence, in his style. Even in Fitzgerald's early, cruder books, or even in his commercial stories, and even when the style is careless, there is a tone and pitch to the sentences which suggest his warmth and tenderness, and, what is rare nowadays and not likely to be admired, his gentleness without softness. In the equipment of the moralist and therefore in the equipment of the novelist, aggression plays an important part, and although it is of course sanctioned by the novelist's moral intention and by whatever truth of moral vision he may have, it is often none the less fierce and sometimes even cruel. Fitzgerald was a moralist to the core and his desire to "preach at people in some acceptable form" is the reason he gives for not going the way of Cole Porter and Rogers and Hart—we must always remember in judging him how many real choices he was free and forced to make—and he was gifted with the satiric eye; yet we feel that in his morality he was more drawn to celebrate the good than to denounce the bad. We feel of him, as we cannot feel of all moralists, that he did not attach himself to the good because this attachment would sanction his fierceness toward the bad—his first impulse was to love the good, and we know this the more surely because we perceive that he loved the good not only with his mind but also with his quick senses and his youthful pride and desire.

He really had but little impulse to blame, which is the more remarkable because our culture peculiarly honors the act of blaming, which it takes as the sign of virtue and intellect. "Forbearance, good word," is one of the jottings in his notebook. When it came to blame, he preferred, it seems, to blame himself. He even did not much want to blame the world. Fitzgerald knew where "the world" was at fault. He knew that it was the condition, the field, of tragedy. He is conscious of "what preyed on Gatsby, what foul dust floated in the wake of his dreams." But he never made out that the world imposes tragedy, either upon the heroes of his novels, whom he called his "brothers," or upon himself. When he speaks of his own fate, he does indeed connect it with the nature of the social world in which he had his early flowering, but he never finally lays it upon that world, even though at the time when he was most aware of his destiny it was fashionable with minds more pretentious than his to lay all personal difficulty whatever at the door of the "social order." It is, he feels, *his* fate—and as much as to anything else in Fitzgerald, we respond to the delicate tension he maintained between his idea of personal free will and his idea of circumstance: we respond to that moral and intellectual energy. "The test of a first-rate intelligence," he said, "is the ability to hold two opposed ideas in the mind, at the same time, and still retain the ability to function."

The power of love in Fitzgerald, then, went hand in hand with a sense of personal responsibility and perhaps created it. But it often happens that the tragic hero can conceive and realize a love that is beyond his own prudence or beyond his powers of dominance or of self-protection, so that he is destroyed by the very thing that gives him his spiritual status and stature. From Proust we learn about a love that is destructive by a kind of corrosiveness, but from Fitzgerald's two mature novels, *The Great Gatsby* and *Tender Is the Night*, we learn about a love—perhaps it is peculiarly American—that is destructive by reason of its very tenderness. It begins in romance, sentiment, even "glamour"—no one, I think, has remarked how innocent of mere "sex," how charged with sentiment is Fitzgerald's description of love in the jazz age—and it takes upon itself reality, and permanence, and duty discharged with an almost masochistic scrupulousness of honor. In the bright dreams begins the responsibility which needs so much prudence and dominance to sustain; and Fitzgerald was anything but a prudent man and he tells us that at a certain point in his college career "some old desire for personal dominance was broken and gone." He connects that loss of desire for dominance with his ability to write; and he set down in his notebook the belief that "to record one must be unwary." Fitzgerald, we may say, seemed to feel that both love and art needed a sort of personal defenselessness.

The phrase from Yeats, the derivation of the "responsibility" from the "dreams," reminds us that we must guard against dismissing, with easy words about its immaturity, Fitzgerald's preoccupation with the bright charm of his youth. Yeats himself, a wiser man and wholly fulfilled in his art, kept to the last of his old age his connection with his youthful vanity. A writer's days must be bound each to each by his sense of his life, and Fitzgerald the undergraduate was father of the best in the man and the novelist.

His sojourn among the philistines is always much in the mind of everyone who thinks about Fitzgerald, and indeed it was always much in his own mind. Everyone knows the famous exchange between Fitzgerald and Ernest Hemingway—Hemingway refers to it in his story, "The Snows of Kilimanjaro" and Fitzgerald records it in his notebook—in which, to Fitzgerald's remark, "The very rich are different from us," Hemingway replied, "Yes, they have more money." It is usually supposed that Hemingway had the better of the encounter and quite settled the matter. But we ought not to be too sure. The novelist of a certain kind, if he is to write about social life, may not brush away the reality of the differences of class, even though to do so may have the momentary appearance of a virtuous social avowal. The novel took its rise and its nature from the radical revision of the class structure in the eighteenth century, and the novelist must still live by his sense of class differences, and must be absorbed by them, as Fitzgerald was, even though he despise them, as Fitzgerald did.

No doubt there was a certain ambiguity in Fitzgerald's attitude toward the "very rich"; no doubt they were for him something more than the mere object of his social observation. They seem to have been the nearest thing to an aristocracy that America could offer him, and we cannot be too simple about what a critic has recently noted, the artist's frequent "taste for aristocracy, his need—often quite open—of a superior social class with which he can make some fraction of common cause—enough, at any rate, to account for his own distinction." Every modern reader is by definition wholly immune from all ignoble social considerations, and, no matter what his own social establishment or desire for it may be, he knows that in literature the interest in social position must never be taken seriously. But not all writers have been so simple and virtuous—what are we to make of those risen gentlemen, Shakespeare and Dickens, or those fabricators of the honorific "de," Voltaire and Balzac? Yet their snobbery—let us call it that—is of a large and generous kind and we are not entirely wrong in connecting their peculiar energies of mind with whatever it was they wanted from gentility or aristocracy. It is a common habit of writers to envision an actuality of personal life which shall have the freedom and the richness of detail and the order of form that they desire in art. Yeats, to mention him again, spoke of the falseness of the belief that the "inherited glory of the rich" really holds richness of life. This, he said, was a mere dream; and yet, he goes on, it is a necessary illusion—

> Yet Homer had not sung
> Had he not found it certain beyond dreams
> That out of life's own self-delight had sprung
> That abounding glittering jet. . . .

And Henry James, at the threshold of his career, allegorized in his story "Benvolio" the interplay that is necessary for some artists between their creative asceticism and the bright, free, gay life of worldliness, noting at the same time the desire of worldliness to destroy the asceticism.

With a man like Goethe the balance between the world and his asceticism is maintained, and so we forgive him his often absurd feelings—but perhaps absurd as well as forgivable only in the light of our present opinion of his assured genius—about aristocracy. Fitzgerald could not always keep the balance true; he was not, as we know, a prudent man. And no doubt he deceived himself a good deal in his youth, but certainly his self-deception was not in the interests of vulgarity, for aristocracy meant to him a kind of disciplined distinction of personal existence which, presumably, he was so humble as not to expect from his art. What was involved in that notion of distinction can be learned from the use which Fitzgerald makes of the word "aristocracy" in one of those serious moments which occur in his most frivolous *Saturday Evening Post* stories; he says of the life of the young man of the story, who during the war was on duty behind the lines, that "it was not so bad—except that when the infantry came limping back from the trenches he wanted to be one of them. The sweat and mud they wore seemed only one of those ineffable symbols of aristocracy that were forever eluding him." Fitzgerald was perhaps the last notable writer to affirm the Romantic fantasy, descended from the Renaissance, of personal ambition and heroism, of life committed to, or thrown away for, some ideal of self. To us it will no doubt come more and more to seem a merely boyish dream; the nature of our society requires the young man to find his distinction through cooperation, subordination, and an expressed piety of social usefulness, and although a few young men have made Fitzgerald into a hero of art, it is likely that even to these admirers the whole nature of his personal fantasy is not comprehensible, for young men find it harder and harder to understand the youthful heroes of Balzac and Stendhal, they increasingly find reason to blame the boy whose generosity is bound up with his will and finds its expression in a large, strict, personal demand upon life.

I am aware that I have involved Fitzgerald with a great many great names and that it might be felt by some that this can do him no service, the disproportion being so large. But the disproportion will seem large only to those who think of Fitzgerald chiefly through his early public legend of heedlessness. Those who have a clear recollection of the mature work or who have read *The Crack-Up* will at least not think of the disproportion as one of kind. Fitzgerald himself did not, and it is by a man's estimate of himself that we must begin to estimate him. For all the engaging self-depreciation which was part of his peculiarly American charm, he put himself, in all modesty, in the line of greatness, he judged himself in a large way. When he writes of his depression, of his "dark night of the soul" where "it is always three o'clock in the morning," he not only derives the phrase from St. John of the Cross but adduces the analogous black despairs of Wordsworth, Keats, and Shelley. A novel with Ernest Hemingway as the model of its hero suggests to him Stendhal portraying the Byronic man, and he defends *The Great Gatsby* from some critical remark of Edmund Wilson's by comparing it with *The Brothers Karamazov*. Or again, here is the stuff of his intellectual pride at the very moment that he speaks of giving it up, as years before he had given up the undergraduate fantasies of valor: "The old dream of being an entire man in the Goethe-Byron-Shaw tradition . . . has been relegated to the junk heap of the shoulder pads worn for one day on the Princeton freshman football field and the overseas cap never worn overseas." And was it, that old dream, unjustified? To take but one great name, the one that on first thought seems the least relevant of all—between Goethe at twenty-four the author of *Werther*, and Fitzgerald, at twenty-four the author of *This Side of Paradise*, there is not really so entire a difference as piety and textbooks might make us think; both the young men so handsome, both winning immediate and notorious success, both rather more interested in life than in art, each the spokesman and symbol of his own restless generation.

It is hard to overestimate the benefit which came to Fitzgerald from his having consciously placed himself in the line of the great. He was a "natural," but he did not have the contemporary American novelist's belief that if he compares himself with the past masters, or if he takes thought—which, for a writer, means really knowing what his predecessors have done—he will endanger the integrity of his natural gifts. To read

Fitzgerald's letters to his daughter—they are among the best and most affecting letters I know—and to catch the tone in which he speaks about the literature of the past, or to read the notebooks he faithfully kept, indexing them as Samuel Butler had done, and to perceive how continuously he thought about literature, is to have some clue to the secret of the continuing power of Fitzgerald's work.

The Great Gatsby, for example, after a quarter-century is still as fresh as when it first appeared; it has even gained in weight and relevance, which can be said of very few American books of its time. This, I think, is to be attributed to the specifically intellectual courage with which it was conceived and executed, a courage which implies Fitzgerald's grasp—both in the sense of awareness and of appropriation—of the traditional resources available to him. Thus, *The Great Gatsby* has its interest as a record of contemporary manners, but this might only have served to date it, did not Fitzgerald take the given moment of history as something more than a mere circumstance, did he not, in the manner of the great French novelists of the nineteenth century, seize the given moment as a moral fact. The same boldness of intellectual grasp accounts for the success of the conception of its hero—Gatsby is said by some to be not quite credible, but the question of any literal credibility he may or may not have becomes trivial before the large significance he implies. For Gatsby, divided between power and dream, comes inevitably to stand for America itself. Ours is the only nation that prides itself upon a dream and gives its name to one, "the American dream." We are told that "the truth was that Jay Gatsby of West Egg, Long Island, sprang from his Platonic conception of himself. He was a son of God—a phrase which, if it means anything, means just that—and he must be about His Father's business, the service of a vast, vulgar, and meretricious beauty." Clearly it is Fitzgerald's intention that our mind should turn to the thought of the nation that has sprung from its "Platonic conception" of itself. To the world it is anomalous in America, just as in the novel it is anomalous in Gatsby, that so much raw power should be haunted by envisioned romance. Yet in that anomaly lies, for good or bad, much of the truth of our national life, as, at the present moment, we think about it.

Then, if the book grows in weight of significance with the years, we can be sure that this could not have happened had its form and style not been as right as they are. Its form is ingenious—with the ingenuity, however, not of craft but of intellectual intensity. The form, that is, is not the result of careful "plotting"—the form of a good novel never is—but is rather the result of the necessities of the story's informing idea, which require the sharpness of radical foreshortening. Thus, it will be observed, the characters are not "developed": the wealthy and brutal Tom Buchanan, haunted by his "scientific" vision of the doom of civilization, the vaguely guilty, vaguely homosexual Jordan Baker, the dim Wolfsheim, who fixed the World Series of 1919, are treated, we might say, as if they were ideographs, a method of economy that is reinforced by the ideographic use that is made of the Washington Heights flat, the terrible "valley of ashes" seen from the Long Island Railroad, Gatsby's incoherent parties, and the huge sordid eyes of the oculist's advertising sign. (It is a technique which gives the novel an affinity with *The Waste Land*, between whose author and Fitzgerald there existed a reciprocal admiration.) Gatsby himself, once stated, grows only in the understanding of the narrator. He is allowed to say very little in his own person. Indeed, apart from the famous "Her voice is full of money," he says only one memorable thing, but that remark is overwhelming in its intellectual audacity: when he is forced to admit that his lost Daisy did perhaps love her husband, he says, "In any case it was just personal." With that sentence he achieves an insane greatness, convincing us that he really is a Platonic conception of himself, really some sort of Son of God.

What underlies all success in poetry, what is even more important than the shape of the poem or its wit of metaphor, is the poet's voice. It either gives us confidence in what is being said or it tells us that we do not need to listen; and it carries both the modulation and the living form of what is being said. In the novel no less than in the poem, the voice of the author is the decisive factor. We are less consciously aware of it in the novel, and, in speaking of the elements of a novel's art, it cannot properly be exemplified by quotation because it is continuous and cumulative. In Fitzgerald's work the voice of his prose is of the essence of his success. We hear in it at once the tenderness toward human desire that modifies a true firmness of moral judgment. It is, I would venture to say, the normal or ideal voice of the novelist. It is characteristically modest, yet it has in it, without apology or self-consciousness, a largeness, even a stateliness, which derives from Fitzgerald's connection with tradition and with mind, from his sense of what has been done before and the demands which this past accomplishment makes. ". . . I became aware of the old island here that flowered once for Dutch sailors' eyes—a fresh green breast of the new world. Its vanished trees, the trees that had made way for Gatsby's house, had once pandered in whispers to the last and greatest of all human dreams; for a transitory and enchanted moment man must have held his breath in the presence of this continent, compelled into an aesthetic contemplation he neither understood nor desired, face to face for the last time in history with something commensurate to his capacity for wonder."

Here, in the well-known passage, the voice is a little dramatic, a little *intentional*, which is not improper to a passage in climax and conclusion, but it will the better suggest in brief compass the habitual music of Fitzgerald's seriousness.

Fitzgerald lacked prudence, as his heroes did, lacked that blind instinct of self-protection which the writer needs and the American writer needs in double measure. But that is all he lacked—and it is the generous fault, even the heroic fault. He said of his Gatsby, "If personality is an unbroken series of successful gestures, there was something gorgeous about him, some heightened sensitivity to the promises of life, as if he were related to one of those intricate machines that register earthquakes ten thousand miles away. This responsiveness had nothing to do with that flabby impressionability which is dignified under the name of 'the creative temperament'—it was an extraordinary gift for hope, a romantic readiness such as I have never found in any other person and which it is not likely I shall ever find again." And it is so that we are drawn to see Fitzgerald himself as he stands in his exemplary role.

MARIUS BEWLEY

Scott Fitzgerald and the Collapse of the American Dream

To say that Scott Fitzgerald's stories are uneven is not to say that he has not written some of the greatest ones in American literature. 'The Diamond as Big as the Ritz' is a story of very genuine originality, and I can think of no classic American writer with whose work to associate it with the possible exception of Hawthorne in some of his short stories. There are aspects of it that make one think of 'My Kinsman, Major Molineux'. Hawthorne's story gives us a dramatic parable of how the English and the New World traditions coalesce in the young hero, Robin, under the impact of the American Revolution, to produce a new type—the first American. It seems to me indubitably the greatest of Hawthorne's stories. I did not discuss it in the relevant chapter here because Q.D. Leavis's essay, to which I have already referred on several occasions, rescued the story from the oblivion into which critics had allowed it to fall, and gave it definitive treatment. The hero of Scott Fitzgerald's story, John T. Unger, enacts the parable of the young American who awakes from the American Dream. To suggest a tentative alignment with 'My Kinsman, Major Molineux', may be more misleading than useful in the end, however. The subject-matter of the two stories distantly relate, but there are important differences. Hawthorne's subject-matter is far more complicated in its political and historical ramifications; his theme is positive, and it is the greatest specifically American theme that a writer could discover. Hawthorne's mastery of it is so great that I am not sure that I wouldn't prefer doing without *The Scarlet Letter* to

---

doing without 'My Kinsman, Major Molineux'. Moreover, Hawthorne has been able to confer a dimension of tragic greatness on Robin and Major Molineux which is no part of Fitzgerald's intention here, although it becomes so in *The Great Gatsby*. As the title of 'The Diamond as Big as the Ritz' suggests, it is in the tradition of the Western tall tale, and its Montana setting underlines this; but this is important only as supplying a traditional mould for a meaning and a seriousness that far exceed anything the genre had ever held before. There is a story called 'Absolution' which Scott Fitzgerald said that he had originally meant to form a kind of introductory piece for *The Great Gatsby*. Fortunately he saw in time the delimiting effect the story would have if it were to be appended to his novel, and he abstained. However, 'The Diamond as Big as the Ritz' is, from one point of view, an excellent introduction to *Gatsby*, and I should like to treat it so here, even though Fitzgerald didn't intend it. It will help to clarify the nature and the extent of Scott Fitzgerald's critical approach to the American experience, which is sometimes not admitted even though it is the first, the most obvious thing, that one ought to take from his art.

But before considering 'The Diamond as Big as the Ritz' in detail, I should like to digress for a few pages and consider Scott Fitzgerald's work in general, and how it stands in relation to the work of the other American novelists I have treated. More than with any other writer in the American tradition, Scott Fitzgerald's novels have been based on a concept of class. In this respect he far exceeds James whose characters, if they belong to an upper class, belong to one which is, as we have seen, strangely disembodied, and not really related to any economic structure at all—at least until his late years. Even then, the recognition was one of pained, shrinking, and rather superficial acknowledgement. The class role of Fitzgerald's characters is possible because he instinctively realized the part that money played in creating and supporting a way of life focused in the Ivy League universities, country clubs, trips to the Riviera, and the homes of the wealthy. He is the first American writer who seems to have discovered that such a thing as American class *really* existed—American class as an endemic growth, to be distinguished from James's delightfully mild Newport cosmopolities, united in the common circumstance of their having more or less lived in Europe. Fitzgerald was enabled to make this discovery because he was almost preternaturally aware of the reality that gold lent to the play of appearances he loved so much. Because he immersed himself so completely in this play of appearances—in swank parties, jazz tunes, alcohol, and coloured lights—many have questioned the fineness and the discrimination of his intelligence. But what he immersed himself in *was* the America of his time (and almost as much, perhaps, of ours), and just because he was as intelligent as any of the novelists treated here, he ended by making an evaluation of the life and wealth he seemed to love that was deeper, more richly informed, and at least as sensitive, as any ever made by James. The charge that Fitzgerald was 'taken in' by wealth is as irritating as it is untrue. There is a radical difference between coveting a 'tony' life that can only be supported by money—lots of money—and being critically and morally unable to assess the conditions under which the money must be acquired or its ultimate effects on character. As an artist, Scott Fitzgerald knew the worst there was to know about all these things, and he knew it with an inwardness and a profoundness. One admires James's instinctive recoil in the presence of the American economic age which the Republicans had fostered so neatly, but when one reads Scott Fitzgerald's treatment of it one is greatly relieved that he had found, in his better informed state, a more effective way of dealing with it than by Spencer Brydon's fainting fit.

I said that Scott Fitzgerald was the first of the great American writers to have found that a 'treatable' class, with its accompanying manners, really did exist in America—to have found it sufficiently, at any rate, to have been able to create characters who are representative of a socially solid and defined group rather than symbolic embodiments of the ultimate American solitude, or two-dimensional figures in the American morality play. As I shall point out later, Gatsby is an exception to this. He is a mythic embodiment in the great American tradition of Natty Bumpo and Huck Finn and Ishmael; but Fitzgerald's stories are populated by a type of rich or popular young man who, in a way that never really had happened in American literature before, carries a weight of representativeness. His manners, attitudes, and ideals, are shared by a large and important group, and have the admiring support of the influential members of the older generation. One may not like the group; its civilization may be a far cry from what one finds in Jane Austen's class structure (perhaps not if one looks into the fortunes of the great Whig peers who stood at the top of that structure), but one has to admit its existence, and its demands for 'treatment'. As the class had its origins in wealth, as its manners and way of life were nourished by gold, it was Fitzgerald's sense of, his feeling for, money, that enabled him not only to appreciate the surfaces, but to penetrate to the heart of the structure. But if that had been all it would certainly not have been enough. If Scott Fitzgerald loved wealth he was not taken in by it, and some of his gaudiest celebrations of it are simultaneously the most annihilating criticisms. And Scott Fitzgerald's rich young men *are* representative; they are representative in a way that Biron, Longaville, and Dumain were representative of the rich young men of Shakespeare's day; they are representative in a way that Hemingway's unpleasant tough young men are not. They may sometimes be a little silly or undiscriminating, but transposed to the level of actual living, they are no sillier than Bernard Longmore or White-Mason (who was, after all, forty-eight years old); and as for Roderick Hudson, he would certainly have preferred their company to Rowland Mallett's. To this extent at least, Scott Fitzgerald had begun to break through the abstracting and inhibiting American tradition, and this may have been one of the things that T.S. Eliot was thinking of when he wrote to Fitzgerald that he had taken the first important step in the American novel since James.

But to return to 'The Diamond as Big as the Ritz', this story is one in which Fitzgerald's attitude to wealth as a constituent part of the American dream is most clearly revealed. John T. Unger, the very young hero—just sixteen—is enrolled at St. Midas's School, half an hour from Boston, 'the most expensive and the most exclusive boys' preparatory school in the world'. But John T. Unger comes from Hades on the Mississippi, where his father 'held the amateur golf championship' and his mother played at politics. Although the story is fantasy, the overstatement given the native background is maintained at exactly the right pitch. It never balloons too high to miss the authentic note. At school John forms a friendship with an aloof and uncommunicative boy who asks John to spend the summer vacation with him at his home 'in the West'. John accepts, and during the long train trip into a remote part of Montana the dream quality that has been present from the first is intensified. The form of the story just a little resembles *Through the Looking-Glass*. We don't quite know when the dream begins, but we are there for the awakening on the last page:

> 'It *was* a dream,' said John quietly. 'Everybody's youth is a dream, a form of chemical madness.'

But certainly the dream has begun by the opening of Part II when the Transcontinental Express stops at the forlorn village of Fish:

> The Montana sunset lay between two mountains like a gigantic bruise from which dark arteries spread themselves over a poisoned sky. An immense distance under the sky crouched the village of Fish, minute, dismal, and forgotten. There were twelve men, so it was said, in the village of Fish, twelve sombre and inexplicable souls who sucked a lean milk from the almost literally bare rock upon which a mysterious populatory force had begotten them. They had become a race apart, these twelve men of Fish, like some species developed by an early whim of nature, which on second thought had abandoned them to struggle and extermination.

> Out of the blue-black bruise in the distance crept a long line of moving lights upon the desolation of the land, and the twelve men of Fish gathered like ghosts at the shanty depot to watch the passing of the seven o'clock train, the Transcontinental Express from Chicago. Six times or so a year the Transcontinental Express, through some inconceivable jurisdiction, stopped at the village of Fish, and when this occurred a figure or so would disembark, mount into a buggy that always appeared from out of the dusk, and drive off toward the bruised sunset. The observation of this pointless and preposterous phenomenon had become a sort of cult among the men of Fish. To observe, that was all; there remained in them none of the vital quality of illusion which would make them wonder or speculate, else a religion might have grown up around these mysterious visitations. But the men of Fish were beyond all religion—the barest and most savage tenets of even Christianity could gain no foothold on that barren rock—so there was no altar, no priest, no sacrifice; only each night at seven the silent concourse by the shanty depot, a congregation who lifted up a prayer of dim, anaemic wonder.

These two paragraphs are strangely impressive, not only because they create the atmosphere of dream, but because the twelve men of Fish seem, in their shadowy way, to embody meanings that, as in a dream, are both insistent and elusive. The Christian implications of the fish symbol are certainly intended by Fitzgerald, and these are enforced by the twelve solitary men who are apostles 'beyond all religion'. These grotesque and distorted Christian connotations are strengthened by their dream-like relation to Hades on the Mississippi where John was born. What we are given in these paragraphs is a queerly restless and troubled sense of a religion that is sick and expressing itself in disjointed images and associations, as if it were delirious. The landscape imagery helps build up this atmosphere. The religious imagery in these paragraphs is emphatic, but it stands here for spiritual desiccation, for the absence of any religion at all—even for the absence of the possibility of any religion. 'There was no altar, no priest, no sacrifice'. But even for the twelve spiritually dead Americans of Fish, a persistent capacity for wonder still survives, and the observation carries us to the great concluding page of *Gatsby* in which Nick Carraway thinks of those early Dutch sailors who must have held their breath in the presence of this continent, 'face to face for the last time in history with something commensurate to their capacity for wonder'. But no commensurate objects survive in the American world, for the American dream could feed only on material, and therefore exhaustible, possibilities. It was, as Scott Fitzgerald (a former Catholic who was never wholly at ease in his separation) very well knew, incompatible with any form of Christianity. The implicit contrast between the eternal promises of the old religion and the material promises of the American dream that had so largely taken the place of any orthodoxy in America provided the most dramatic and sinister note for Fitzgerald to strike as Percy and John descended from the Transcontinental Express at the forlorn, symbolic village of Fish.

What we have to bear in mind is that this story is an attack on that American dream which critics have so often imagined Fitzgerald was engaged in celebrating throughout his writings. The fevered religious imagery of the passage I have quoted presents it, in the very beginning, as a kind of gaudy substitute for a sterile orthodoxy whose promises cannot compete with the infinite material possibilities that the dream seems to hold out to the faithful Americans. This intitial religious note indicates how deeply Fitzgerald understood the American tradition of which he was so profoundly a part. But having sounded it once, he moves on through the rest of the story to analyse those material possibilities on the secular level at which Americans have believed Heaven to be attainable. Before considering the story farther I should like to pause for a moment's reflection on just what, historically, this American dream is.

Essentially, the phrase represents the romantic enlargement of the possibilities of life on a level at which the material and the spiritual have become inextricably confused. As such, it led inevitably towards the problem that has always confronted American artists dealing with American experience—the problem of determining the hidden boundary in the American vision of life at which the reality ends and the illusion begins. Historically, the American dream is anti-Calvinistic—in rejecting man's tainted nature it is even anti-Christian. It believes in the goodness of nature and man. It is accordingly a product of the frontier and the West rather than of the New England and Puritan traditions. Youth of the spirit—youth of the body as well—is a requirement of its existence; limit and deprivation are its blackest devils. But it shows an astonishing incapacity to believe in them:

> I join you . . . in branding as cowardly the idea that the human mind is incapable of further advances. This is precisely the doctrine which the present despots of the earth are inculcating, and their friends here re-echoing; and applying especially to religion and politics; 'that it is not probable that anything better will be discovered than what was known to our fathers' . . . But thank heaven the American mind is already too much opened to these impostures, and while the art of printing is left to us, science can never be retrograde. . . . To preserve the freedom of the human mind . . . every spirit should be ready to devote itself to martyrdom. . . . But that the enthusiasm which characterizes youth should lift

its parricide hands against freedom and science would be such a monstrous phenomenon as I could not place among the possible things in this age and country.

That is the hard kernel, the seed from which the American dream would grow into unpruned luxuriance, to become brutalized at last under the grossly acquisitive spirit of the Gilded Age and Republican capitalism. Jefferson's voice in the above passage is not remote from many European voices of his time, but it stands in unique relation to the country to whom he spoke. That attitude was bred into the bone of America, and in various, often distorted and corrupted ways, it has lasted. Perhaps this is where the trouble begins, for if the virtues of the American imagination which Jefferson singles out have the elements of greatness in them, they call immediately for discriminating and practical correctives. The reality in such an attitude lies in its faith in present life; the illusion lies in the undiscriminating multiplication of its material possibilities. The New England and puritan traditions saved Hawthorne and James from the pitfalls of the American dream, but in James we often feel that he would have believed in it if he could, and in the persons of Christopher Newman and Adam Verver he came dangerously close to doing so. *The Great Gatsby* is Scott Fitzgerald's great exploration of this theme, but first of all he explored its more degraded aspects as they had come to exist in the 'twenties in 'The Diamond as Big as the Ritz'.

From the moment that Percy and John leave the shanty depot of Fish in a buggy driven by a negro 'which had obviously appeared from nowhere', to the time they reach Percy's father's fantastic concealed chateau on the diamond mountain that makes him the richest man in the world, the imagery gradually changes in quality. The sick and portentous undertones that were struck by the twelve men of Fish, waiting under the poisoned sunset, give way to a riotous fantasy in a style that can only be called Babylonian-Hollywood. The implicit presence throughout of Hollywood criteria of values and taste (and Hollywood in its most barbaric age) is the technical means by which Fitzgerald makes his final point, and presses his condemnation. The boys change from the buggy into an immense limousine with jewel encrusted wheels, and in which 'the upholstery consisted of a thousand minute and exquisite tapestries of silk, woven with jewels and embroideries, and set upon a background of cloth of gold. The two armchair seats in which the boys luxuriated were covered with stuff that resembled duvetyn, but seemed woven in numberless colours of the ends of ostrich feathers'. The limousine is at last lifted by cables and cranes over a high ridge of rock into the little secret kingdom of Percy's father (a direct descendant of George Washington and Lord Baltimore). From this secret kingdom he sends out a discreet number of diamonds chipped from the mountain to be sold on the world market—not enough to flood it and lower the price, but enough to open up to him and his family all the material possibilities of life. By various fantastic means, Percy's father, Braddock Washington, has kept his diamond mountain a secret from the world so that it doesn't even appear on the official government maps of the area. Here, in this little circle of land that is quite literally out of the world, the Washington family lead a life as unrelated to any possible form of reality as the American dream itself.

The major part of the story is concerned with giving us a series of glimpses of life in this American dream—a fantasy on the theme of material possibilities run wild. Fitzgerald's treatment of the theme is completely successful. The sense of a colossal Hollywood movie set, and a 'plot' that unwinds along the lines of an old time movie scenario, keeps the question of reality implicitly to the fore of the reader's mind. In fact, the total effect of the story duplicates the odd ambivalence of response that one brings to the moving pictures of the period—disbelief neatly balanced by exhilarated acceptance. To have been able to do this is no small technical achievement, and in effect it adds up to a devastating comment on the experience it is presenting us in such an orgy of glamour. Here, for example, is a description of Percy's home and his mother as John first sees them as the limousine drives up:

> Full in the light of the stars, an exquisite chateau rose from the borders of the lake, climbed in marble radiance half the height of an adjoining mountain, then melted in grace, in perfect symmetry, in translucent feminine languor, into the massed darkness of a forest of pine. The many towers, the slender tracery of the sloping parapets, the chiselled wonder of a thousand yellow windows with their oblongs and hectagons and triangles of golden light, the shattered softness of the intersecting planes of star-shine and blue shade, all trembled on John's spirit like a chord of music. On one of the towers, the tallest, the blackest at its base, an arrangement of exterior lights at the top made a sort of floating fairy-land—and as John gazed up in warm enchantment, the faint acciaccare sound of violins drifted down in a rococo harmony that was like nothing he had ever heard before. Then in a moment the car stopped before the wide, high marble steps around which the night air was fragrant with a host of flowers. At the top of the stairs two great doors swung silently open and amber light flooded out upon the darkness, silhouetting the figure of an exquisite lady with black, high-piled hair, who held out her arms toward them.
>
> 'Mother,' Percy was saying, 'this is my friend, John Unger, from Hades.'

It is indeed the American dreamer's idea of Heaven, and Hades is where all this is not. The implicit moving picture imagery, as I have already said, opens on to the question of appearance and reality, and relates in its own way to Hawthorne's search for the inner sphere and James's search for life. What Fitzgerald is intent on here is a revelation of the emptiness of those so-called values by which the American world lived, and he makes it by revealing the grotesquerie in which its implications, if extended far enough, would inevitably end.

The grotesquerie, and also the inhumanity. The American dream which had started innocently enough when there had been a vast unexploited continent to support the possibilities it seemed to promise, had become brutalized as the only means of realizing them had more and more centred in money with the passing of the frontier and the advent of the Gilded Age. The Washingtons maintain their Hollywood existence on the diamond mountain only at the price of the freedom of others who have been unfortunate enough to stumble by accident into this 'forbidden paradise'. And John learns that the friends they invite must at last be put to death, lest returning to the world of reality they betray what they have seen. Thus, in a literal sense the American dream becomes the American nightmare with naked negro executioners chasing John through the Babylonian-Hollywood corridors. The tempo quickens, as in an ancient scenario, and United States bombers arrive in the nick of time.

The scene in which Braddock Washington attempts to bribe God on the mountainside to withhold the impending destruction with a gigantic diamond held by two negro slaves, brings the dream sequence to its conclusion. Its symbolism is obvious enough—too obvious to require comment; but it is a strong scene, and visually impressive. This morning scene, during which the giant diamond catches the first yellow light of the sun, balances the sunset scene in the first two paragraphs of Part II. Whether it was explicitly intended or not—perhaps not—it is appropriate that the American dream (the particular dream of John T. Unger) which began under a poisoned sky, should dissolve in the clear light of day, and that the ominous note in the religious imagery of the opening should reach its climax in the blasphemous prayer of Braddock Washington.

Having 'escaped' the destruction of the diamond mountain, John 'awakens' on the hillside with his two companions, Kasmine and Jasmine, daughters of Braddock Washington who have figured largely in the dream. The descent here is from the 'unrealistic' heights of the American dream towards the banality of the typical American romance. John's last words are:

> 'At any rate, let us love for awhile, for a year or so, you and me. That's a form of divine drunkenness that we can all try. There are only diamonds in the whole world, diamonds and perhaps the shabby gift of disillusion. Well, I have that last and I will make the usual nothing of it.' He shivered. 'Turn up your coat collar, little girl, the night's full of chill and you'll get pneumonia. His was a great sin who first invented consciousness. Let us lose it for a few hours.'
>
> So wrapping himself in his blanket he fell off to sleep.

The sentimentality is mawkish, almost aggressive, but it is redeemed by being played off against the 'sentimentality' of the sequence of dream images to which we have just been exposed. Fitzgerald equates the emotional extravagance of the dream with the emotional cheapness of the romance—they are both equally the products of the same sensibility. In *The Great Gatsby*, the tawdry romance with Daisy, as we shall see, is the means Fitzgerald uses to show Gatsby the intolerable cheapness of his dream and illusion. Fitzgerald has sometimes been criticized for the inadequacy of his treatment of love, but on this point it would be difficult to find any writer in the American tradition who has treated the subject better, or even as well. Among the artists treated here, Cooper and Melville automatically exclude themselves; Hawthorne has given us moral parables in which the 'love interest', in so far as it can be said to exist at all, is incidental to the moral theme; and James, in his American novels particularly, seems to me to give the whole subject the lightest 'treatment'. Where the sentimentality and cheapness of the romance are most blatant, as here, they are used structurally (and perhaps not even with Fitzgerald's fullest consciousness) to illuminate the final meaning.

II

The Great Gatsby is an exploration of the American dream as it exists in a corrupt period, and it is an attempt to determine that concealed boundary that divides the reality from the illusions. The illusions seem more real than the reality itself. Embodied in the subordinate characters in the novel, they threaten to invade the whole of the picture. On the other hand, the reality is embodied in Gatsby; and as opposed to the hard, tangible illusions, the reality is a thing of the spirit, a promise rather than the possession of a vision, a faith in the half-glimpsed, but hardly understood, possibilities of life. In Gatsby's America, the reality is undefined to itself. It is inarticulate and frustrated. Nick Carraway, Gatsby's friend and Fitzgerald's narrator, says of Gatsby:

> Through all he said, even through his appalling sentimentality, I was reminded of something—an elusive rhythm, a fragment of lost words, that I had heard somewhere a long time ago. For a moment a phrase tried to take shape in my mouth and my lips parted like a dumb man's, as though there was more struggling upon them than a wisp of startled air. But they made no sound, and what I had almost remembered was incommunicado forever.

This is not pretentious phrase-making performing a vague gesture towards some artificial significance. It is both an evocative and an exact description of that unholy cruel paradox by which the conditions of American history have condemned the grandeur of the aspiration and vision to expend itself in a waste of shame and silence. But the reality is not entirely lost. It ends by redeeming the human spirit, even though it live in a wilderness of illusions, from the cheapness and vulgarity that encompass it. In this novel, the illusions are known and condemned at last simply by the rank complacency with which they are content to be themselves. On the other hand, the reality is in the energy of the spirit's resistance, which may not recognize itself as resistance at all, but which can neither stoop to the illusions nor abide with them when they are at last recognized. Perhaps it is really nothing more than ultimate immunity from the final contamination, but it encompasses the difference between life and death. Gatsby never succeeds in seeing through the sham of his world or his acquaintances very clearly. It is of the essence of his romantic American vision that it should lack the seasoned powers of discrimination. But it invests those illusions with its own faith, and thus it discovers its projected goodness in the frauds of its crippled world. *The Great Gatsby* becomes the acting out of the tragedy of the American vision. It is a vision totally untouched by the scales of values that order life in a society governed by traditional manners; and Fitzgerald knows that although it would be easy to condemn and 'place' the illusions by invoking these outside values, to do so would be to kill the reality that lies beyond them, but which can sometimes only be reached through them.

For example, Fitzgerald perfectly understood the inadequacy of Gatsby's romantic view of wealth. But that is not the point. He presents it in Gatsby as a romantic baptism of desire for a reality that stubbornly remains out of his sight. It is as if a savage islander, suddenly touched with Grace, transcended in his prayers and aspirations the grotesque little fetish in which he imagined he discovered the object of his longing. The scene in which Gatsby shows his stacks of beautiful imported shirts to Daisy and Nick has been mentioned as a failure of Gatsby's, and so of Fitzgerald's, critical control of values. Actually, the shirts are sacramentals, and it is clear that Gatsby shows them, neither in vanity nor in pride, but with a reverential humility in the presence of some inner vision he cannot consciously grasp, but toward which he desperately struggles in the only way he knows.

In an essay called 'Myths for Materialists' Mr. Jacques Barzun once wrote that figures, whether of fact or fiction, in so far as they express destinies, aspirations, attitudes typical of man or particular groups, are invested with a mythical character. In this sense Gatsby is a 'mythic' character, and no other word will define him. Not only is he an embodiment (as Fitzgerald makes clear at the outset) of that conflict between illusion and reality at the heart of American life; he is an heroic personification of the American romantic hero, the true heir of the American dream. 'There was something gorgeous about him,' Nick Carraway says, and although 'gorgeous' was a favourite word with the 'twenties, Gatsby wears it with an archetypal American elegance.

One need not look far in earlier American literature to find his forebears. Here is the description of a young bee hunter from *Col. David Crockett's Exploits and Adventures in Texas*, published in 1836:

> I thought myself alone in the street, where the hush of morning was suddenly broken by a clear, joyful, and musical voice, which sang. . . .
>
> I turned toward the spot whence the sounds proceeded, and discovered a tall figure leaning against the sign post. His eyes were fixed on the streaks of light in the east, his mind was absorbed, and he was clearly unconscious of anyone being near him. He continued his song in so full and clear a tone, that the street re-echoed. . . .
>
> I now drew nigh enough to see him distinctly. He was a young man, not more than twenty-two. His figure was light and graceful at the same time that it indicated strength and activity. He was dressed in a hunting shirt, which was made with uncommon neatness, and ornamented tastily with fringe. He held a highly finished rifle in his right hand, and a hunting pouch, covered with Indian ornaments, was slung across his shoulders. His clean shirt collar was open, secured only by a black riband around his neck. His boots were polished, without a soil upon them; and on his head was a neat fur cap, tossed on in a manner which said, 'I don't give a d—n' just as plainly as any cap could speak it. I thought it must be some popinjay on a lark, until I took a look at his countenance. It was handsome, bright, and manly. There was no mistake in that face. From the eyes down to the breast he was sunburnt as dark as mahogany while the upper part of his high forehead was as white and polished as marble. Thick clusters of black hair curled from under his cap. I passed on unperceived, and he continued his song. . . .

This young dandy of the frontier, dreaming in the dawn and singing to the morning, is a progenitor of Gatsby. It is because of such a traditional American ancestry that Gatsby's romanticism transcends the limiting glamour of the Jazz Age.

But such a romanticism is not enough to 'mythicize' Gatsby. Gatsby, for all his shimmer of representative surfaces, is never allowed to become soiled by the touch of realism. In creating him, Fitzgerald observed as high a decorum of character as a Renaissance playwright: for although Gatsby's parents were shiftless and unsuccessful farm people, Gatsby really 'sprang from his Platonic conception of himself. He was a son of God—a phrase which, if it means anything, means just that—and he must be about His Father's business, the service of a vast, vulgar, meretricious beauty.'

Fitzgerald created Gatsby with a sense of his own election; but the beauty it was in his nature to serve had already been betrayed by history. Even in the midst of the blighted earthly paradise of West Egg, Long Island, Gatsby bore about him the marks of his birth. He is a kind of exiled Duke in disguise. We know him by his bearing, the decorous pattern of his speech. Even his dress invariably touches the imagination: 'Gatsby in a white flannel suit, silver shirt, and gold coloured tie. . . .' There is something dogmatically Olympic about the combination. After Gatsby's death when his pathetic old father journeys east for the funeral, one feels that he is only the kindly shepherd who once found a baby on the cold hillside.

But so far I have been talking in general terms. This beautiful control of conventions can be studied more closely in the description of Gatsby's party at which (if we except that distant glimpse of him at the end of Chapter I, of which I shall speak later) we encounter him for the first time. We are told later that Gatsby was gifted with a 'hint of the unreality of reality, a promise that the rock of the world was founded securely on a fairy's wing'. Fitzgerald does not actually let us meet Gatsby face to face until he has concretely created this fantastic world of Gatsby's vision, for it is the element in which we must meet Gatsby if we are to understand his impersonal significance:

> There was music from my neighbour's house through the summer nights. In his blue gardens men and girls came and went like moths among the whisperings and the champagne and the stars. At high tide in the afternoon I watched his guests diving from the tower of his raft, or taking the sun on the hot sand of his beach while his two motor-boats slit the waters of the Sound, drawing aquaplanes over cataracts of foam. On week-ends his Rolls-Royce became an omnibus, bearing parties to and from the city between nine in the morning and long past midnight, while his station wagon scampered like a brisk yellow bug to meet all

> trains. And on Mondays eight servants, including an extra gardener, toiled all day with mops and scrubbing-brushes and hammers and garden-shears, repairing the ravages of the night before.

The nostalgic poetic quality, which tends to leave one longing for sterner stuff, is, in fact, deceptive. It is Gatsby's ordeal that he must separate the foul dust that floated in the wake of his dreams from the reality of the dream itself: that he must find some vantage point from which he can bring the responsibilities and the possibilities of life into a single focus. But the 'ineffable gaudiness' of the world to which Gatsby is committed is a fatal deterrent. Even within the compass of his paragraph we see how the focus has become blurred: how the possibilities of life are conceived of in material terms. But in that heroic list of the vaster luxury items—motor-boats, aquaplanes, private beaches, Rolls-Royces, diving towers—Gatsby's vision maintains its gigantic unreal stature. It imposes a rhythm on his guests which they accept in terms of their own tawdry illusions, having no conception of the compulsion that drives him to offer them the hospitality of his fabulous wealth. They come for their week-ends as George Dane in Henry James's *The Great Good Place* went into his dream retreat. But the result is not the same: 'on Mondays eight servants, including an extra gardener, toiled all day with mops and scrubbing-brushes and hammers and garden-shears, repairing the ravages of the night before'. That is the most important sentence in the paragraph, and despite the fairy-story overtone, it possesses an ironic nuance that rises towards the tragic. And how fine that touch of the extra gardener is—as if Gatsby's guests had made a breach in nature. It completely qualifies the over-fragility of the moths and champagne and blue gardens in the opening sentences.

This theme of the relation of his guests to Gatsby is still further pursued in Chapter IV. The cataloguing of American proper names with poetic intention has been an ineffectual cliché in American writing for many generations. But Fitzgerald uses the convention magnificently:

> Once I wrote down on the empty spaces of a time-table the names of those who came to Gatsby's house that summer. It is an old time-table now, disintegrating at its folds, and headed 'This schedule in effect July 5th, 1922'. But I can still read the grey names, and they will give you a better impression than my generalities of those who accepted Gatsby's hospitality and paid him the subtle tribute of knowing nothing about him.

The names of these guests could have been recorded nowhere else as appropriately as in the margins of a faded timetable. The embodiments of illusions, they are as ephemeral as time itself; but because their illusions represent the distortions and shards of some shattered American dream, the timetable they adorn is 'in effect July 5th'—the day following the great national festival when the exhausted holiday crowds, as spent as exploded fire-crackers, return to their homes. The list of names which Fitzgerald proceeds to enumerate conjures up with remarkable precision an atmosphere of vulgar American fortunes and vulgar American destinies. Those who are familiar with the social registers, business men's directories, and movie magazines of the 'twenties might be able to analyse the exact way in which Fitzgerald achieves his effect, but it is enough to say here that he shares with Eliot a remarkable clairvoyance in seizing the cultural implications of proper names. After two pages and more, the list ends with the dreamily elegiac close: 'All these people came to Gatsby's house in the summer.'

Why did they come? There is the answer of the plotted story—the free party, the motor-boats, and private beach, the endless flow of cocktails. But in the completed pattern of the novel one knows that they came for another reason—came blindly and instinctively—illusions in pursuit of a reality from which they have become historically separated, but by which they might alone be completed or fulfilled. And why did Gatsby invite them? As contrasted with them, he alone has a sense of the reality that hovers somewhere out of sight in this nearly ruined American dream; but the reality is unintelligible until he can invest it again with the tangible forms of his world, and relate it to the logic of history. Gatsby and his guests feel a mutual need of each other, but the division in American experience has widened too far, and no party, no hospitality however lavish, can heal the breach. The illusions and the reality go their separate ways. Gatsby stands at the door of his mansion, in one of the most deeply moving and significant paragraphs of the novel, to wish his guests good-bye:

> The caterwauling horns had reached a crescendo and I turned away and cut across the lawn toward home. I glanced back once. A wafer of a moon was shining over Gatsby's house, making the night fine as before, and surviving the laughter and the sound of his still glowing garden. A sudden emptiness seemed to flow now from the windows and the great doors, endowing with complete isolation the figure of the host, who stood on the porch, his hand up in a formal gesture of farewell.

If one turns back to Davy Crockett's description of the elegant young bee hunter, singing while the dawn breaks in the east, and thinks of it in relation with this midnight picture of Gatsby, 'his hand up in a formal gesture of farewell', while the last guests depart through the debris of the finished party, the quality of the romanticism seems much the same, but the situation is exactly reversed; and from the latter scene there opens a perspective of profound meaning. Suddenly Gatsby is not merely a likeable, romantic hero; he is a creature of myth in whom is incarnated the aspiration and the ordeal of his race.

'Mythic' characters are impersonal. There is no distinction between their public and their private lives. Because they share their meaning with everyone, they have no secrets and no hidden corners into which they can retire for a moment, unobserved. An intimacy so universal stands revealed in a ritual pattern for the inspection and instruction of the race. The 'mythic' character can never withdraw from that air which is his existence—that is to say, from that area of consciousness (and hence of publicity) which every individual shares with the members, both living and dead, of his group or race. Gatsby is a 'mythic' character in this sense—he has no private life, no meaning or significance that depends on the fulfilment of his merely private destiny, his happiness as an individual in a society of individuals. In a transcendent sense he touches our imaginations, but in this smaller sense—which is the world of the realistic novel—he even fails to arouse our curiosity. At this level, his love affair with Daisy is too easily 'placed', a tawdry epic 'crush' of no depth or interest in itself. But Gatsby not only remains undiminished by what is essentially the meanness of the affair: his stature grows, as we watch, to the proportions of a hero. We must inquire how Fitzgerald managed this extraordinary achievement.

Daisy Buchanan exists at two well-defined levels in the novel. She is what she is—but she exists at the level of Gatsby's vision of her. Even Fitzgerald's admirers regard Daisy as rather a good, if somewhat silly, little thing; but Fitzgerald knew that at its most depraved levels the American dream merges with the American debutante's dream—a thing of deathly hollowness. Fitzgerald faces up squarely to the problem of telling us what Daisy has to offer in a human relationship. At one of Gatsby's fabulous parties—the one to which Daisy brings her husband, Tom Buchanan—Gatsby points out to Daisy and Tom, among the celebrated guests, one particular couple:

> 'Perhaps you know that lady,' Gatsby indicated a gorgeous, scarcely human orchid of a woman who sat in state under a white-plum tree. Tom and Daisy stared, with that peculiarly unreal feeling that accompanies the recognition of a hitherto ghostly celebrity of the movies.
>
> 'She's lovely,' said Daisy.
>
> 'That man bending over her is her director.'

Superficially, the scene is highly civilized. One fancies one has seen it in Manet. But in the contest we know that it has no reality whatever—the star and her director can get no nearer reality than by rehearsing a scene. Our attention is then taken up by other scenes at the party, but by suddenly returning to this couple after an interval of two pages to make his point, Fitzgerald achieves a curious impression of static or arrested action. We have the feeling that if we walked behind the white-plum tree we should only see the back of a canvas screen:

> Almost the last thing I remember was standing with Daisy and watching the moving-picture director and his Star. They were still under the white-plum tree and their faces were touching except for a pale, thin ray of moonlight between. It occurred to me that he had been very slowly bending toward her all evening to attain this proximity, and even while I watched I saw him stoop one ultimate degree and kiss at her cheek.
>
> 'I like her,' said Daisy, 'I think she's lovely.'
>
> But the rest offended her—and inarguably, because it wasn't a gesture but an emotion.

Daisy likes the moving-picture actress because she has no substance. She is a gesture that is committed to nothing more real than her own image on the silver screen. She has become a gesture divorced forever from the tiresomeness of human reality. In effect, this passage is Daisy's confession of faith. She virtually announces here what her criteria of human emotions and conduct are. Fitzgerald's illustration of the emptiness of Daisy's character—an emptiness that we see curdling into the viciousness of a monstrous moral indifference as the story unfolds—is drawn with a fineness and depth of critical understanding, and communicated with a force of imagery so rare in modern American writing, that it is almost astonishing that he is often credited with giving in to those very qualities which *The Great Gatsby* so effectively excoriates.

But what is the basis for the mutual attraction between Daisy and Gatsby? In Daisy's case the answer is simple. We remember that Nick Carraway has described Gatsby's personality as an 'unbroken series of successful gestures'. Superficially, Daisy finds in Gatsby, or thinks she finds, that safety from human reality which the empty gesture implies. What she fails to realize is that Gatsby's gorgeous gesturings are the reflex of an aspiration towards the possibilities of life, and this is something entirely different from those vacant images of romance and sophistication that fade so easily into the nothingness from which they came. But in a sense, Daisy is safe enough from the reality she dreads. The true question is not what Gatsby sees in Daisy, but the direction he takes from her, what he sees *beyond* her; and that has, despite the immaturity intrinsic in

Gatsby's vision, an element of grandeur in it. For Gatsby, Daisy does not exist in herself. She is the green light that signals him into the heart of his ultimate vision. *Why* she should have this evocative power over Gatsby is a question Fitzgerald faces beautifully and successfully as he recreates that milieu of uncritical snobbishness and frustrated idealism—monstrous fusion—which is the world in which Gatsby is compelled to live.

Fitzgerald, then, has a sure control when he defines the quality of this love affair. He shows it in itself as vulgar and specious. It has no possible interest in its own right, and if it did have the pattern of the novel would be ruined. Our imagination would be fettered in those details and interests which would detain us on the narrative level where the affair works itself out as human history, and Gatsby would lose his 'mythic' quality. But the economy with which Gatsby is presented, the formal and boldly drawn structural lines of his imagination, lead us at once to a level where it is obvious that Daisy's significance in the story lies in her failure to constitute the objective correlative of Gatsby's vision. And at the same time, Daisy's wonderfully representative quality as a creature of the Jazz Age relates her personal failure to the larger failure of Gatsby's society to satisfy his need. In fact, Fitzgerald never allows Daisy's failure to become a human or personal one. He maintains it with sureness on a symbolic level where it is identified with and reflects the failure of Gatsby's decadent American world. There is a famous passage in which Gatsby sees Daisy as an embodiment of the glamour of wealth. Nick Carraway is speaking first to Gatsby:

> 'She's got an indiscreet voice,' I remarked. 'It's full of—' I hesitated.
>
> 'Her voice is full of money,' he said suddenly.
>
> That was it. I'd never understood before. It was full of money—that was the inexhaustible charm that rose and fell in it, the jingle of it, the cymbals' song of it. . . . High in a white palace the king's daughter, the golden girl. . . .

Gatsby tries to build up the inadequacy of each value by the support of the other; but united they fall as wretchedly short of what he is seeking as each does singly. Gatsby's gold and Gatsby's girl belong to the fairy story in which the Princess spins whole rooms of money from skeins of wool. In the fairy story, the value never lies in the gold but in something beyond. And so it is in this story. For Gatsby, Daisy is only the promise of fulfilment that lies beyond the green light that burns all night on her dock.

This green light that is visible at night across the bay from the windows and lawn of Gatsby's house is the central symbol in the book.

Significantly, our first glimpse of Gatsby at the end of Chapter I is related to it. Nick Carraway, whose modest bungalow in West Egg stands next to Gatsby's mansion, returning from an evening at the Buchanans', while lingering on the lawn for a final moment under the stars, becomes aware that he is not alone:

> . . . fifty feet away a figure had emerged from the shadow of my neighbour's mansion and was standing with his hands in his pockets regarding the silver pepper of the stars. Something in his leisurely movements and the secure position of his feet upon the lawn suggested that it was Mr. Gatsby himself, come out to determine what share was his of our local heavens.
>
> I decided to call to him. . . . But I didn't . . . for he gave a sudden intimation that he was content to be alone—he stretched out his arms toward the dark water in a curious way, and, as far as I was from him, I could have sworn he was trembling. Involuntarily I glanced seaward—and distinguished nothing except a single green light, minute and far away, that might have been the end of a dock. When I looked once more for Gatsby he had vanished, and I was alone again in the unquiet darkness.

It is hardly too much to say that the whole being of Gatsby exists only in relation to what the green light symbolizes. This first sight we have of Gatsby is a ritualistic tableau that literally contains the meaning of the completed book, although the full meaning of what is implicit in the symbol reveals itself slowly, and is only finally rounded out on the last page. We have a fuller definition of what the green light means in its particular, as opposed to its universal, signification in Chapter V. Gatsby is speaking to Daisy as they stand at one of the windows of his mansion:

> 'If it wasn't for the mist we could see your home across the bay,' said Gatsby. 'You always have a green light that burns all night at the end of your dock.'
>
> Daisy put her arm through his abruptly, but he seemed absorbed in what he had just said. Possibly it had occurred to him that the colossal significance of that light had now vanished forever. Compared to the great distance that had separated him from Daisy it had seemed very near to her, almost touching her. It had seemed as close as a star to the moon. Now it was again a green light on dock. His count of enchanted objects had diminished by one.

Some might object to this symbolism on the grounds that it is easily vulgarized, but if studied carefully in its full context it represents a convincing achievement. The tone or pitch of the symbol is exactly adequate to the problem it dramatizes. Its immediate function is that it signals Gatsby into his future, away from the cheapness of his affair with

Daisy which he has vainly tried (and desperately continues trying) to create in the image of his vision. The green light is successful because, apart from its visual effectiveness as it gleams across the bay, it embodies the profound naïveté of Gatsby's sense of the future, while simultaneously suggesting the historicity of his hope. This note of historicity is not fully apparent at this point, of course. The symbol occurs several times, and most notably at the end:

> Gatsby believed in the green light, the orgastic future that year by year recedes before us. It eluded us then, but that's no matter—tomorrow we will run faster, stretch out our arms farther. . . . And one fine morning—
>
> So we beat on, boats against the current, borne back ceaselessly into the past.

Thus the American dream, whose superstitious valuation of the future began in the past, gives the green light through which alone the American returns to his traditional roots, paradoxically retreating into the pattern of history while endeavouring to exploit the possibilities of the future. There is a suggestive echo of the past in Gatsby's sense of Daisy. He had known her, and fallen in love with her, five years before the novel opens. During that long interval while they had disappeared from each other's sight, Daisy has become a legend in Gatsby's memory, a part of his private past which (as a 'mythic' character) he assimilates into the pattern of that historic past through which he would move into the historic future. But the legendary Daisy, meeting her after five years, has dimmed a little in lustre:

> 'And she doesn't understand,' he said. 'She used to be able to understand. We'd sit for hours—'
>
> He broke off and began to walk up and down a desolate path of fruit rinds and discarded favours and crushed flowers.
>
> 'I wouldn't ask too much of her,' I ventured. 'You can't repeat the past.'
>
> 'Can't repeat the past?' he cried incredulously. 'Why of course you can!'
>
> He looked around him wildly, as if the past were lurking here in the shadow of his house, just out of reach of his hand.

By such passages Fitzgerald dramatizes Gatsby's symbolic role. The American dream, stretched between a golden past and a golden future, is always betrayed by a desolate present—a moment of fruit rinds and discarded favours and crushed flowers. Imprisoned in his present, Gatsby belongs even more to the past than to the future. His aspirations have been rehearsed, and his tragedy suffered, by all the generations of Americans who have gone before. His sense of the future, of the possibilities of life, he has learned from the dead.

If we return to the passage in which, linked arm in arm, Gatsby and Daisy stand at the window looking towards the green light across the bay, it may be possible to follow a little more sympathetically that quality of disillusion which begins to creep into Gatsby's response to life. It does not happen because of the impoverished elements of his practical romance; it happens because Gatsby is incapable of compromising with his inner vision. The imagery of this particular passage, as I suggested, is gauged to meet the requirements of Gatsby's young romantic dream. But two pages later Fitzgerald takes up the theme of Gatsby's struggle against disenchantment once again, and this time in an imagery that suggests how much he had learned from *The Waste Land*:

> When Klipspringer had played 'The Love Nest' he turned around on the bench and searched unhappily for Gatsby in the gloom.
>
> 'I'm all out of practice, you see. I told you I couldn't play. I'm all out of prac—'
>
> 'Don't talk so much, old sport,' commanded Gatsby. 'Play!'
>
> In the morning,
> In the evening,
> Ain't we got fun—
>
> Outside the wind was loud and there was a faint flow of thunder along the Sound. All the lights were going on in West Egg now; the electric trains, men-carrying, were plunging home through the rain from New York. It was the hour of a profound human change, and excitement was generating on the air.
>
> One thing's sure and nothing's surer
> The rich get richer and poor get—children.
> In the meantime,
> In between time—
>
> As I went over to say good-bye I saw that the expression of bewilderment had come back into Gatsby's face, as though a faint doubt had occurred to him as to the quality of his present happiness. Almost five years! There must have been moments even that afternoon when Daisy tumbled short of his dreams—not through her own fault, but because of the colossal vitality of his illusion. It had gone beyond her, beyond everything. He had thrown himself into it with a creative passion, adding to it all the time, decking it out with every bright feather that drifted his way. No amount of fire or freshness can challenge what a man can store up in his ghostly heart.

In view of such writing it is absurd to argue that Fitzgerald's art was a victim of his own attraction to the Jazz Age. The snatches of song that

Klipspringer sings evoke the period with an immediacy that is necessary if we are to understand the peculiar poignancy of Gatsby's ordeal. But the songs are more than evocative. They provide the ironic musical prothalamion for Gatsby's romance, and as Gatsby listens to them an intimation of the practical truth presses in on him. The recognition is heightened poetically by that sense of the elements, the faint flow of thunder along the Sound, which forms the background of those artificial little tunes. And it is not odd that this evocation of the outdoor scene, while Klipspringer pounds at the piano inside, sustains in the imagination the image of that green light, symbol of Gatsby's faith, which is burning across the bay. This scene draws on the 'violet hour' passage from 'The Fire Sermon' in which 'the human engine waits Like a taxi throbbing waiting. . . .' It is the hour of a profound human change, and in the faint stirrings of Gatsby's recognition there is for a moment, perhaps, a possibility of his escape. But the essence of the American dream whose tragedy Gatsby is enacting is that it lives in a past and a future that never existed, and is helpless in the present that does.

Gatsby's opposite number in the story is Daisy's husband, Tom Buchanan, and Gatsby's stature—his touch of doomed but imperishable spiritual beauty, if I may call it so—is defined by his contrast with Tom. In many ways they are analogous in their characteristics—just sufficiently so to point up the differences. For example, their youth is an essential quality of them both. But Tom Buchanan was 'one of those men who reach such an acute limited excellence at twenty-one that everything afterward savours of anti-climax'. Even his body—'a body capable of enormous leverage'—was 'a cruel body'. In the description of Tom we are left physically face to face with a scion of those ruthless generations who raised up the great American fortunes, and who now live in uneasy arrogant leisure on their brutal acquisitions. But Gatsby's youth leaves an impression of interminability. Its climax is always in the future, and it gives rather than demands. Its energy is not in its body, but in its spirit, and meeting Gatsby for the first time, one seizes, as Nick Carraway did, this impression in his smile:

> It was one of those rare smiles with a quality of eternal reassurance in it, that you may come across four or five times in life. It faced—or seemed to face—the whole eternal world for an instant, and then concentrated on *you* with an irresistible prejudice in your favour. It understood you just as far as you wanted to be understood, believed in you as you would like to believe in yourself, and assured you that it had precisely the impression of you that, at your best, you hoped to convey. Precisely at that point it vanished—and I was looking at an elegant young rough-

neck, a year or two over thirty, whose elaborate formality of speech just missed being absurd.

This passage is masterly in the way in which it presents Gatsby to us less as an individual than as a projection, or mirror, of our ideal selves. To do that is the function of all 'mythic' characters. Gatsby's youth is not simply a matter of three decades that will quickly multiply themselves into four or five. It is a quality of faith and hope that may be betrayed by history, may be killed by society, but that no exposure to the cynical turns of time can reduce to the compromises of age.

Again, Gatsby and Tom are alike in the possession of a certain sentimentality, but Tom Buchanan's is based on depraved self-pity. He is never more typical than when coaxing himself to tears over a half-finished box of dog biscuits that recalls a drunken and illicit day from his past, associated in memory with his dead mistress. His self-pity is functional. It is sufficient to condone his most criminal acts in his own eyes as long as the crimes are not imputable. But Gatsby's sentimentality exists in the difficulty of expressing, in the phrases and symbols provided by his decadent society, the reality that lies at the heart of his aspiration. 'So he waited, listening for a moment longer to the tuning fork that had been struck upon a star'—Gatsby's sentimentality (if it *is* sentimentality, and I rather doubt it) is as innocent as that. It has nothing of self-pity or indulgence in it—it is all aspiration and goodness; and it must be remembered that Fitzgerald himself is *outside* Gatsby's vocabulary, using it with great mastery to convey the poignancy of the situation.

Tom Buchanan and Gatsby represent antagonistic but historically related aspects of America. They are related as the body and the soul when a mortal barrier has risen up between them. Tom Buchanan is virtually Gatsby's murderer in the end, but the crime that he commits by proxy is only a symbol of his deeper spiritual crime against Gatsby's inner vision. Gatsby's guilt, in so far as it exists, is radical failure—a failure of the critical faculty that seems to be an inherent part of the American dream—to understand that Daisy is as fully immersed in the destructive elements of the American world as Tom himself. After Daisy, while driving Gatsby's white automobile, has killed Mrs. Wilson and, implicitly at least, left Gatsby to shoulder the blame, Nick Carraway gives us a crucial insight into the spiritual affinity of the Buchanan couple, drawing together in their callous selfishness in a moment of guilt and crisis:

> Daisy and Tom were sitting opposite each other at the kitchen table, with a plate of cold fried chicken between them, and two bottles of ale. He was talking intently across the table at her, and in his earnestness his

> hand had fallen upon and covered her own. Once in a while she looked up at him and nodded in agreement.
>
> They weren't happy, and neither of them had touched the chicken or the ale—and yet they weren't unhappy either. There was an unmistakable air of natural intimacy about the picture, and anybody would have said that they were conspiring together.

They instinctively seek out each other because each recognizes the other's strength in the corrupt spiritual element they inhabit.

There is little point in tracing out in detail the implications of the action any further, although it could be done with an exactness approaching allegory. That it is not allegory is owing to the fact that the pattern emerges from the fullness of Fitzgerald's living experience of his own society and time. In the end the most that can be said is that *The Great Gatsby* is a dramatic affirmation in fictional terms of the American spirit in the midst of an American world that denies the soul. Gatsby exists in, and for, that affirmation alone.

When, at the end, not even Gatsby can hide his recognition of the speciousness of his dream any longer, the discovery is made in universalizing terms that dissolve Daisy into the larger world she has stood for in Gatsby's imagination:

> He must have looked up at an unfamiliar sky through frightening leaves and shivered as he found what a grotesque thing a rose is and how raw the sunlight was upon the scarcely created grass. A new world, material without being real, where poor ghosts, breathing dreams like air, drifted fortuitously about. . . .

'A new world, material without being real'. Paradoxically, it was Gatsby's dream that conferred reality upon the world. The reality was in his faith in the goodness of creation, and in the possibilities of life. That these possibilities were intrinsically related to such romantic components limited and distorted his dream, and finally left it helpless in the face of the Buchanans, but it did not corrupt it. When the dream melted, it knocked the prop of reality from under the universe, and face to face with the physical substance at last, Gatsby realized that the illusion was *there*—there where Tom and Daisy, and generations of small-minded, ruthless Americans had found it—in the dreamless, visionless complacency of mere matter, substance without form. After this recognition, Gatsby's death is only a symbolic formality, for the world into which his mere body had been born rejected the gift he had been created to embody—the traditional dream from which alone it could awaken into life.

As the novel closes, the experience of Gatsby and his broken dream explicitly becomes the focus of that historic dream for which he stands. Nick Carraway is speaking:

> Most of the big shore places were closed now and there were hardly any lights except the shadowy, moving glow of a ferryboat across the Sound. And as the moon rose higher the inessential houses began to melt away until gradually I became aware of the old island here, that flowered once for Dutch sailors' eyes—a fresh, green breast of the new world. Its vanished trees, the trees that had once made way for Gatsby's house, had once pandered in whispers to the last and greatest of all human dreams; for a transitory enchanted moment man must have held his breath in the presence of this continent, compelled into an aesthetic contemplation he neither understood nor desired, face to face for the last time in history with something commensurate to his capacity for wonder.

It is fitting that this, like so many of the others in *Gatsby*, should be a moonlight scene, for the history and the romance are one. Gatsby fades into the past for ever to take his place with the Dutch sailors who had chosen their moment in time so much more happily than he.

We recognize that the great achievement of this novel is that it manages, while poetically evoking a sense of the goodness of that early dream, to offer the most damaging criticism of it in American literature. The astonishing thing is that the criticism—if indictment wouldn't be the better word—manages to be part of the tribute. Gatsby, the 'mythic' embodiment of the American dream, is shown to us in all his immature romanticism. His insecure grasp of social and human values, his lack of critical intelligence and self-knowledge, his blindness to the pitfalls that surround him in American society, his compulsive optimism, are realized in the text with rare assurance and understanding. And yet the very grounding of these deficiencies is Gatsby's goodness and faith in life, his compelling desire to realize all the possibiliites of existence, his belief that we can have an Earthly Paradise populated by Buchanans. A great part of Fitzgerald's achievement is that he suggests effectively that these terrifying deficiencies are not so much the private deficiencies of Gatsby, but are deficiencies inherent in contemporary manifestations of the American vision itself—a vision no doubt admirable, but stupidly defenceless before the equally American world of Tom and Daisy. Gatsby's deficiencies of intelligence and judgment bring him to his tragic death—a death that is spiritual as well as physical. But the more important question that faces us through our sense of the immediate tragedy is where they have brought America.

MALCOLM COWLEY

Fitzgerald: The Romance of Money

Those who were lucky enough to be born a little before the end of the last century, in any of the years from 1895 to 1900, went through much of their lives with a feeling that the new century was about to be placed in their charge; it was like a business in financial straits that could be rescued by a timely change in management. As Americans and optimists, they believed that the business was fundamentally sound. They identified themselves with the century; its teens were their teens, troubled but confident; its World War, not yet known as the First, was theirs to fight on the winning side; its reckless twenties were their twenties. As they launched into their careers, they looked about for spokesmen, and the first one they found—though soon they would have doubts about him—was F. Scott Fitzgerald.

Among his qualifications for the role was the sort of background that his generation regarded as typical. Scott was a Midwestern boy, born in St. Paul on September 24, 1896, to a family of Irish descent that had some social standing and a very small fortune inherited by the mother. The fortune kept diminishing year by year, and the Fitzgeralds, like all families in their situation, had to think a lot about money. When the only son was eleven they were living in Buffalo, where the father was working for Procter and Gamble. "One afternoon," Fitzgerald told a reporter thirty years later, ". . . the phone rang and my mother answered it. I didn't

---

understand what she said, but I felt that disaster had come to us. My mother, a little while before, had given me a quarter to go swimming. I gave the money back to her. I knew something terrible had happened and I thought she couldn't spare the money now. 'Dear God,' I prayed, 'please don't let us go to the poorhouse.'

"A little later my father came home. I had been right. He had lost his job." More than that, as Fitzgerald said, "He had lost his essential drive, his immaculateness of purpose." The family moved back to St. Paul, where the father worked as a wholesale grocery salesman, earning hardly enough to pay for his desk space. It was help from a pious aunt that enabled Scott to fulfill his early ambition of going to an Eastern preparatory school, then going to Princeton.

In 1917 practically the whole student body went off to war. Fitzgerald went off in style, having received a provisional commission as second lieutenant in the regular army. Before leaving Princeton in November, he ordered his uniform at Brooks Brothers and gave the manuscript of a first novel to his faculty mentor, Christian Gauss, not yet dean of the college, but a most persuasive teacher of European literature. Gauss, honest as always, told him that it wasn't good enough to publish. Not at all discouraged, Fitzgerald reworked it completely, writing twelve hours a day during his weekends at training camp and his first furlough. When the second draft was finished, he sent it to Shane Leslie, the Irish man of letters, who had shown some interest in his work. Leslie spent ten days correcting and punctuating the script, then sent it to Scribners, his own publishers. "Really if Scribner takes it," Fitzgerald said in a letter to Edmund Wilson, "I know I'll wake some morning and find that the debutantes have made me famous overnight. I really believe that no one else could have written so searchingly the story of the youth of our generation."

Scribners sent back the novel, rightly called *The Romantic Egotist*, while expressing some regret, and Maxwell Perkins, who was still too young to be the senior editor, suggested revisions that might make it acceptable. Fitzgerald tried to follow the suggestions and resubmitted the manuscript that summer. In August it was definitely rejected, and Fitzgerald then asked Perkins as a favor to submit it to two other publishers, one radical and one conservative. His letter was dated from Camp Sheridan, in Alabama, where he was soon to be named aide-de-camp to Major General J.A. Ryan. It was at a dance in Montgomery that he fell in love with a judge's daughter, Zelda Sayre, whom he described to his friends as "the most beautiful girl in Alabama *and* Georgia"; one state wasn't big enough to encompass his admiration. "I didn't have the two top things:

great animal magnetism or money," he wrote years afterward in his notebook. "I had the two second things, though: good looks and intelligence. So I always got the top girl."

He was engaged to the judge's daughter, but they couldn't marry until he was able to support her. After being discharged from the army—without getting overseas, as I noted—he went to New York and looked for a job. Neither the radical nor the conservative publisher had shown interest in his novel. All his stories were coming back from the magazines, and at one time he had 122 rejection slips pinned in a frieze around his cheap bedroom on Morningside Heights. The job he found was with an advertising agency and his pay started at $90 a month, with not much chance of rapid advancement; the only praise he received was for a slogan written for a steam laundry in Muscatine, Iowa: "We keep you clean in Muscatine." He was trying to save money, but the girl in Alabama saw that the effort was hopeless and broke off the engagement on the score of common sense. Fitzgerald borrowed from his classmates, stayed drunk for three weeks, and then went home to St. Paul to write the novel once again, this time with another ending and a new title, *This Side of Paradise*. Scribners accepted it on that third submission. The book was so different from other novels of the time, Max Perkins wrote him, "that it is hard to prophesy how it will sell, but we are all for taking a chance and supporting it with vigor."

This Side of Paradise, published at the end of March 1920, is a very young man's novel and memory book. The author put into it samples of everything he had written until that time—short stories, essays, poems, prose poems, sketches, and dialogues—and he also put himself into it, after taking a promotion in social rank. The hero, Amory Blaine, instead of being a poor relative has been reared as the heir of millions, but he looks and talks like Fitzgerald, besides reading the same books (listed in one passage after another) and falling in love with the same girls. The story told in the novel, with many digressions, is how Amory struggles for self-knowledge and for less provincial standards than those of the Princeton eating clubs. "I know myself," he says at the end, "but that is all." Fitzgerald passed a final judgment on the novel in 1938, when he said in a letter to Max Perkins, "I think it is now one of the funniest books since *Dorian Gray* in its utter spuriousness—and then, here and there, I find a page that is very real and living."

Some of the living pages are the ones that recount the eating-club elections, the quarrel between Amory and his first flame, Isabelle—Fitzgerald would always be good on quarrels—the courting of Rosalind Connage, and Amory's three-weeks drunk when Rosalind throws him over. Besides having a spurious and imitative side, the novel proved that Fitzgerald had started with gifts of his own, which included an easy narrative style rich with images, a sense of comedy, and a natural ear for dialogue. Its memorable feature, however, was that it announced a change in standards. "Here was a new generation," Fitzgerald or his hero, it isn't clear which, says in the last chapter, "shouting the old cries, learning the old creeds, through a revery of long days and nights; destined finally to go out into that dirty gray turmoil to follow love and pride; a new generation dedicated more than the last to the fear of poverty and the worship of success; grown up to find all gods dead, all wars fought, all faiths in man shaken." With energy, candor, and a sort of innocence, Fitzgerald (or the hero) was speaking for his contemporaries. They recognized the voice as their own, and his elders listened.

Suddenly the magazines were eager to print Fitzgerald's stories and willing to pay high prices for them. The result shows in his big ledger: in 1919 he earned $879 by his writing; in 1920 he earned $18,850—and managed to end the year in debt. Early success and princely spending had been added to everything else that made him stand out as a representative of his generation; and Fitzgerald was beginning to believe in his representative quality. He was learning that when he wrote truly about his dreams and misadventures and discoveries, other people recognized themselves in the picture.

The point has to be made that Fitzgerald wasn't "typical" of his own period or any other. He lived harder than most people have ever lived and acted out his dreams with an extraordinary intensity of emotion. The dreams themselves were not at all unusual: in the beginning they were dreams of becoming a football star and a big man in college, of being a hero on the battlefield, of winning through to financial success, and of getting the top girl. They were the commonplace visions shared by almost all the young men of his age and background, especially by those who were forging ahead in the business world; in many ways Fitzgerald was closer to them than he was to the other serious writers of his generation. It was the emotion he put into his dreams, and the honesty with which he expressed the emotion, that made them seem distinguished. By feeling intensely he made his readers believe in the unique value of the world in which they lived. He was to say later, writing in the third person, that he continued to feel grateful to the Jazz Age because "It bore him up, flattered him and gave him more money than he had dreamed of, simply for telling people that he felt as they did."

At the beginning of April 1920, Zelda came to New York and they were married in the rectory of St. Patrick's Cathedral—although Zelda's family was Episcopalian and Scott had ceased to be a good Catholic. They set up housekeeping at the Biltmore. To their bewilderment they found themselves adopted not as a Midwesterner and a Southerner respectively, not even as detached observers, but—Scott afterward wrote—"as the arch type of what New York wanted." A new age was beginning, and Scott and Zelda were venturing into it innocently, hand in hand. Zelda said, "It was always tea-time or late at night." Scott said, "We felt like children in a great bright unexplored barn."

II

Scott also said, "America was going on the greatest, gaudiest spree in history and there was going to be plenty to tell about it." There is still plenty to tell about it, in the light of a new age that continues to be curious about the 1920s and usually misjudges them. The gaudiest spree in history was also a moral revolt, and beneath the revolt were social transformations. The 1920s were the age when puritanism was under attack, with the Protestant churches losing their dominant position. They were the age when the country ceased to be English and Scottish and when the children of later immigrations moved forward to take their places in the national life. Theodore Dreiser, whom Fitzgerald regarded as the greatest living American writer, was South German Catholic by descent, H.L. Mencken, the most influential critic, was North German Protestant, and Fitzgerald did not forget for a moment that one side of his own family was "straight potato-famine Irish." Most of his heroes have Irish names and all except Gatsby are city-bred, thus reflecting another social change. The 1920s were the age when American culture became urban instead of rural and when New York set the social and intellectual standards of the country, while its own standards were being set by transplanted Southerners and Midwesterners like Zelda and Scott.

More essentially the 1920s were the age when a production ethic—of saving and self-denial in order to accumulate capital for new enterprises—gave way to a consumption ethic that was needed to provide markets for the new commodities that streamed from the production lines. Instead of being exhorted to save money, more and more of it, people were being exhorted in a thousand ways to buy, enjoy, use once and throw away, in order to buy a later and more expensive model. They followed the instructions, with the result that more goods were produced and consumed or wasted and money was easier to earn or borrow than ever in the past. Foresight went out of fashion. "The Jazz Age," Fitzgerald was to say, "now raced along under its own power, served by great filling stations full of money. . . . Even when you were broke you didn't worry about money, because it was in such profusion around you."

Young men and women in the 1920s had a sense of reckless confidence not only about money but about life in general. It was part of their background: they had grown up in the years when middle-class Americans read Herbert Spencer and believed in the doctrine of automatic social evolution. The early twentieth century seemed to confirm the doctrine. Things were getting better each year: more grain was reaped, more iron was smelted, more rails were laid, more profits earned, more records broken, as new cities were founded and all cities grew, as the country grew, as the world apparently grew in wealth and wisdom toward the goal of universal peace—and those magical results were obtained, so it seemed, by each man's seeking his private interest. After 1914 the notion of automatic progress lost most of its support in events, but retained its place in the public mind. Young men and women of Fitzgerald's time, no matter how rebellious and cynical they thought of themselves as being, still clung to their childhood notion that the world would improve without their help; that was one of the reasons why most of them felt excused from seeking the common good. Plunging into their personal adventures, they took risks that didn't impress them as being risks because, in their hearts, they believed in the happy ending.

They were truly rebellious, however, and were determined to make an absolute break with the standards of the prewar generation. The distinction between highbrow and lowbrow (or liberal and conservative) was not yet sharp enough to divide American society; the gulf was between the young and the old. The younger set paid few visits to their parents' homes and some of them hardly exchanged a social word with men or women over forty. The elders were straitlaced or stuffy, and besides they had made a mess of the world; they were discredited in younger eyes not only by the war and what followed it—especially Prohibition—but also, after 1923, by the scandals that clustered round Teapot Dome and the little green house on K Street, in Washington, where members of President Harding's Cabinet, and sometimes the President himself, played their cozy games of poker with the oil barons. So let the discredited elders keep to themselves; the youngsters would then have a free field in which to test their standards of the good life.

Those standards were elementary and close to being savage. Rejecting almost everything else, the spokesmen for the new generation celebrated the value of simple experiences such as love, foreign travel, good food, and drunkenness. "Immortal drunkenness!" Thomas Wolfe was to exclaim in a novel, interrupting the adventures of his hero. "What tribute can we ever pay, what song can we ever sing, what swelling praise can ever be sufficient to express the joy, the gratefulness and love which we, who have known youth and hunger in America, have owed to alcohol? . . . You came to us with music, poetry, and wild joy when we were twenty, when we reeled home at night through the old moon-whitened streets of Boston and heard our friend, our comrade and our dead companion, shout through the silence of the moonwhite square: 'You are a poet and the world is yours.' " Others besides Wolfe heard the voice repeating "You are a poet!" and they hastened to enjoy their birthday-present world by loving, traveling, eating, drinking, dancing all night, and writing truthfully about their mornings after. They all recognized the value of being truthful, even if it hurt their families or their friends and most of all if it hurt themselves; almost any action seemed excusable and even admirable in those days if one simply told the truth about it, without boasting, without shame.

They liked to say yes to every proposal that suggested excitement. Will you take a new job, throw up the job, go to Paris and starve, travel round the world in a freighter? Will you get married, leave your husband, spend a weekend for two in Biarritz? Will you ride through Manhattan on the roof of a taxi and then go bathing in the Plaza fountain? "WYBMADIITY?" read a sign on the mirror behind the bar of a popular speakeasy, the Dizzy Club. Late at night you asked the bartender what it meant, and he answered, "Will You Buy Me A Drink If I Tell You?" The answer was yes, always yes, and the fictional heroine of the 1920s was Serena Blandish, the girl who couldn't say no. Or the heroine was Joyce's Molly Bloom as she dreamed about the days when she was being courted: ". . . and I thought as well him as another and then I asked him with my eyes to ask again yes and then he asked me would I yes to say yes my mountain flower and first I put my arms around him yes and drew him down to me so he could feel my breasts all perfume yes and his heart was going like mad and yes I said yes I will Yes."

The masculine ideal of the 1920s was what Fitzgerald called "the old dream of being an entire man in the Goethe-Byron-Shaw tradition, with an opulent American touch, a sort of combination of J.P. Morgan, Topham Beauclerk and St. Francis of Assisi." The entire man would be one who "did everything," good and bad, who realized all the potentialities of his nature and thereby acquired wisdom. The entire man, in the 1920s, was one who followed the Rule of the Thelemites as revealed by Rabelais: *Fais ce que vouldras*, "Do what you will!" But that rule implied a second imperative like an echo: "Will!" To be admired by the 1920s young men had to will all sorts of actions and had to possess enough energy and boldness to carry out even momentary wishes. They lived in the moment with what they liked to call "an utter disregard of consequences." In spirit they all made pilgrimages to the abbey of the Thelemites, where they consulted the Oracle of the Divine Bottle and received for answer the one word *Trinc.* They obeyed the oracle and drank, in those days of the Volstead Act when drinking was a rite of comradeship and an act of rebellion. As Fitzgerald said at the time, they drank "cocktails before meals like Americans, wines and brandies like Frenchmen, beer like Germans, whiskey-and-soda like the English . . . this preposterous mélange that was like a gigantic cocktail in a nightmare."

But the 1920s were not so much a drinking as a dancing age—the Jazz Age, in the phrase that Fitzgerald made his own. In those days one heard jazz everywhere—from orchestras in ballrooms, from wind-up phonographs in the parlor, from loudspeakers blaring in variety stores, lunch wagons, even machine shops—and jazz wasn't regarded as something to listen to and be cool about, without even tapping one's feet; jazz was music with a purpose, *Gebrauchsmusik*; it was music to which you danced:

I met her in Chicago and she was married.
   Dance all day,
leave your man, Sweet Mamma, and come away;
manicured smiles and kisses, to dance all day, all day.
   How it was sad.

Please, Mr. Orchestra, play us another tune.
My daddy went and left me and left the cupboard bare.
Who will pay the butcher bill now Daddy isn't there?
   Shuffle your feet.
Found another daddy and he taught me not to care,
   and how to care.
Found another daddy that I'll follow anywhere.
Shuffle your feet, dance,

dance among the tables, dance across the floor,
slip your arm around me, we'll go dancing out the door,
Sweet Mamma, anywhere, through any door.
Wherever the banjos play is Tennessee.

Jazz carried with it a constant message of change, excitement, violent escape, and an undertone of sadness, but with a promise of enjoyment somewhere around the corner of next week, perhaps at midnight in a distant country. The young men heard the message and followed it anywhere, through any door, even the one that led into what was then, for Americans, the new world of difficult art. They danced too much, they drank too much, but they also worked, with something of the same desperation; they worked to rise, to earn social rank, to sell, to advertise, to organize, to invent gadgets, and to create enduring works of literature. In ten years, before losing their first vitality, they gave a new tempo to American life.

Fitzgerald not only represented the age but came to suspect that he had helped to create it, by setting forth a pattern of conduct that would be followed by persons a little younger than himself. That it was a dangerous pattern was something he recognized almost from the beginning. "If I had anything to do with creating the manners of the contemporary American girl I certainly made a botch of the job," he said in a 1925 letter. In a notebook he observed that one of his relatives was still a flapper in the 1930s. "There is no doubt," he added, "that she originally patterned herself upon certain immature and unfortunate writings of mine, so that I have a special fondness for——as for one who has lost an arm or a leg in one's service." When he was living at La Paix, a brown wooden late-Victorian lodge on a thirty-acre estate near Baltimore, a drunken young man teetered up to his door and said, "I had to see you. I feel I owe you more than I can say. I feel that you formed my life." It was not the young man—later a widely read novelist and an alcoholic—but Fitzgerald himself who became the principal victim of his capacity for creating fictional types in life. "Sometimes," he told another visitor to La Paix, late at night, "I don't know whether Zelda and I are real or whether we are characters in one of my novels."

That was in the spring of 1933, a few weeks after the banks had closed all over the country. It seemed then that the whole generation of the 1920s had been defeated by life, and yet, in their own defeat, Scott and Zelda were still its representative figures.

III

Fitzgerald never lost a quality that very few writers are able to acquire: a sense of living in history. Manners and morals were changing all through his life and he set himself the task of recording the changes. These were revealed to him, not by statistics or news reports, but in terms of living characters, and the characters were revealed by gestures, each appropriate to a certain year. He wrote: "One day in 1926 we"—meaning the members of his generation—"looked down and found we had flabby arms and a fat pot and we couldn't say boop-boop-a-doop to a Sicilian. . . . By 1927 a widespread neurosis began to be evident, faintly signaled, like a nervous beating of the feet, by the popularity of cross-word puzzles. . . . By this time"—also in 1927—"contemporaries of mine had begun to disappear into the dark maw of violence. . . . By 1928 Paris had grown suffocating. With each new shipment of Americans spewed up by the boom the quality fell off, until towards the end there was something sinister about the crazy boatloads."

He tried to find the visible act that revealed the moral quality inherent in a certain moment of time. He was haunted by time, as if he wrote in a room full of clocks and calendars. He made lists by the hundred, including lists of the popular songs, the football players, the top debutantes (with the types of beauty they cultivated), the hobbies, and the slang expressions of a given year; he felt that all those names and phrases belonged to the year and helped to reveal its momentary color. "After all," he said in an otherwise undistinguished magazine story, "any given moment has its value; it can be questioned in the light of after-events, but the moment remains. The young prince in velvet gathered in lovely domesticity around the queen amid the hush of rich draperies may presently grow up to be Pedro the Cruel or Charles the Mad, but the moment of beauty was there."

Fitzgerald lived in his great moments, and lived in them again when he reproduced their drama, but he also stood apart from them and coldly reckoned their causes and consequences. That is his doubleness or irony, and it is one of his distinguishing marks as a writer. He took part in the ritual orgies of his time, but he kept a secretly detached position, regarding himself as a pauper living among millionaires, a Celt among Sassenachs, and a sullen peasant among the nobility; he said that his point of vantage "was the dividing line between two generations," prewar and postwar. Always he cultivated a double vision. In his novels and stories he was trying to intensify the glitter of life in the Princeton eating clubs, on the north shore of Long Island, in Hollywood, and on the Riviera; he surrounded his characters with a mist of admiration, and at the same time he kept driving the mist away. He liked to know "where the milk is watered and the sugar sanded, the rhinestone passed for the diamond and the stucco for stone." It was as if all his fiction described a big dance to which he had taken, as he once wrote, the prettiest girl:

There was an orchestra—Bingo-Bango
Playing for us to dance the tango
And the people all clapped as we arose
For her sweet face and my new clothes—

and as if he stood at the same time outside the ballroom, a little Midwestern boy with his nose to the glass, wondering how much the tickets cost and who paid for the music. But it was not a dance he was watching so much as it was a drama of conflicing manners and aspirations in which he was both the audience and the leading actor. As audience he kept a cold eye on the actor's performance. He wrote of himself when he was twenty, "I knew that at bottom I lacked the essentials. At the last crisis, I knew that I had no real courage, perseverance or self-respect." Sixteen years later he was just as critical, and he said to a visitor at La Paix, "I've got a very limited talent. I'm a workman of letters, a professional. I know when to write and when to stop writing." It was the maximum of critical detachment, but it was combined with the maximum of immersion in the drama. He said in his notebook, and without the least exaggeration, "Taking things hard, from Ginevra to Joe Mankiewicz," mentioning the names of his first unhappy love and of the Hollywood producer who, so he thought, had ruined one of his best scripts: "That's the stamp that goes into my books so that people read it blind like Braille."

The drama he watched and in which he overplayed a leading part was a moral drama leading to rewards and punishments. "Sometimes I wish I had gone along with that gang," he said in a letter that discussed musical comedies and mentioned Cole Porter and Rodgers and Hart; "but I guess I am too much a moralist at heart and want to preach at people in some acceptable form, rather than to entertain them." The morality he wanted to preach was a simple one, in the midst of the prevailing confusion. Its four cardinal virtues were Industry, Discipline, Responsibility (in the sense of meeting one's social and financial obligations), and Maturity (in the sense of learning to expect little from life while continuing to make one's best efforts). Thus, his stories had a way of becoming fables. For virtues they displayed or failed to display, the characters were rewarded or punished in the end.

The handle by which he took hold of the characters was their dreams. These, as I said, might be commonplace or even cheap, but usually Fitzgerald managed to surround them with an atmosphere of the mysterious and illimitable or of the pitifully doomed. His great scenes were, so to speak, played to music: sometimes the music from a distant ballroom, sometimes that of a phonograph braying out a German tango, sometimes the wind in the leaves, sometimes the stark music of the heart. When there was no music, at least there were pounding rhythms: "The city's quick metropolitan rhythm of love and birth and death that supplied dreams to the unimaginative"; "The rhythm of the week-end, with its birth, its planned gaieties and its announced end"; "New York's flashing, dynamic good looks, its tall man's quick-step." Fitzgerald's dream of his mature years, after he had outgrown the notion of becoming a big man in college, was also set to music, perhaps to the *Unfinished Symphony*; it was the dream of becoming a great writer, specifically a great novelist who would do for American society in his time what Turgenev, for example, had done for the old regime in Russia.

It was not his dream to be a poet, yet that was how he started and in some ways he remained a poet primarily. He noted, "The talent that matures early is usually of the poetic type, which mine was in large part." His favorite author was Keats, not Turgenev or Flaubert. "I suppose I've read it a hundred times," he said of the "Ode on a Grecian Urn." "About the tenth time I began to know what it was about, and caught the chime in it and the exquisite inner mechanics. Likewise with the 'Nightingale,' which I can never read without tears in my eyes; likewise 'The Pot of Basil,' with its great stanzas about the two brothers. . . . Knowing these things very young and granted an ear, one could scarcely ever afterwards be unable to distinguish between gold and dross in what one read." When his daughter was learning to be a writer he advised her to read Keats and Browning and try her hand at a sonnet. He added, "The only thing that will help you is poetry, which is the most concentrated form of style."

Fitzgerald himself was a poet who never learned some of the elementary rules for writing prose. His grammar was shaky and his spelling definitely bad: for example, he wrote, "ect." more often than "etc." and misspelled the name of his friend Monsignor Fay on the dedication page of *This Side of Paradise*. In his letters he always misspelled the given names of his first and last loves. He was not a student, for all the books he read; not a theoretician and perhaps one should flatly say, not a thinker. He counted on his friends to do much of his thinking for him; at Princeton it was John Peale Bishop who, he said, "made me see, in the course of a couple of months, the difference between poetry and non-poetry." Twenty years later, at the time of his crack-up, he re-examined his scale of values and found thinking incredibly difficult; he compared it to "the moving about of great secret trunks." He was then forced to the conclusion "That I had done very little thinking, save within the problems of my craft. For twenty years a certain man had been my intellectual conscience. That man was Edmund Wilson." Another contemporary "had been an artistic conscience to me. I had not imitated his infectious style, because my own style, such as it was, was formed before he published anything, but there was an awful pull towards him when I was on the spot."

Fitzgerald was making the confession in order to keep straight with himself, not to forestall any revelation that might have been made by his critics. The critics would have said that there was little of Wilson's influence perceptible in his work and still less of Hemingway's, although he once wrote a story about two dogs, "Shaggy's Morning," that is a delicate and deliberate pastiche of the Hemingway manner. By listening hard one can overhear a few, a very few suggestions by Hemingway in the dialogue of other stories, especially the later ones, but Fitzgerald was faithful to his own vision of the world and his way of expressing it. His debt to Wilson and Hemingway is real, but hard to define. In essence they were two older-brother figures (though Hemingway was younger than Fitzgerald); two different models of literary conduct. Though his style of life bore no resemblance to either of theirs, he used them to test and define his moral attitude toward the problems of his craft.

IV

There was one respect in which Fitzgerald, much as he regarded himself as a representative figure of the age, was completely different from most of its serious writers. In that respect he was, as I said, much closer to the men of his college year who were trying to get ahead in the business world; like them he was fascinated by the process of earning and spending money. The young businessmen of his time, much more than those of a later generation, had been taught to measure success, failure, and even virtue in pecuniary terms. They had learned in school and Sunday school that virtue was rewarded with money and vice punished by the loss of money; apparently their one aim should be to earn lots of it fast. Yet money was only a convenient and inadequate symbol for what they dreamed of earning. The best of them were like Jay Gatsby in having "some heightened sensitivity to the promise of life"; or they were like another Fitzgerald hero, Dexter Green of "Winter Dreams," who "wanted not association with glittering things and glittering people—he wanted the glittering things themselves." Their real dream was that of achieving a new status and a new essence, of rising to a loftier place in the mysterious hierarchy of human worth.

The serious writers also dreamed of rising to a loftier status, but—except for Fitzgerald—they felt that moneymaking was the wrong way to rise. They liked money if it reached them in the form of gifts or legacies or publishers' advances; they would have liked it in the form of prizes or fellowships, though there were few of these to be had in the 1920s; but they were afraid of high earned incomes because of what the incomes stood for: obligations, respectability, time lost from their essential work, expensive habits that would drive them to seek still higher incomes—in short, a series of involvements in the commercial culture that was hostile to art. "If you want to ruin a writer," I used to hear some of them saying, "just give him a big magazine contract or a job at ten thousand a year." Many of them tried to preserve their independence by earning only enough to keep them alive while writing; a few regarded themselves as heroes of poverty and failure. "Now I can write," Faulkner said when his third novel was turned down and he thought he would never be published again.

A disdainful attitude toward money went into the texture of Faulkner's work, as into that of many others. The work was noncommercial in the sense of being written in various new styles that the public was slow to accept. It was an age of literary experiment when young writers were moving in all directions simultaneously. They were showing the same spirit of adventure and exploration in fiction that their contemporaries were showing in the business world. That spirit made them part of the age, but at the same time they were trying to stand apart from it, and some of them looked back longingly to other ages when, so they liked to think, artists had wealthy patrons and hence were able to live outside the economic system.

Fitzgerald immersed himself in the age and always remained close to the business world which they were trying to evade. That world was the background of his stories, and these performed a business function in themselves, by supplying the narrative that readers followed like a thread through the labyrinth of advertising in the slick-paper magazines. He did not divorce himself from readers by writing experimental prose or refusing to tell a story. His very real originality was a matter of mood and subject and image rather than of structure, and it was more evident in his novels than in his stories, good as the stories often were. Although he despised the trade of writing for magazines—or despised it with part of his mind—he worked at it honestly. It yielded him a large income that he couldn't have earned in any other fashion, and the income was necessary to his self-respect.

Fitzgerald kept an accurate record of his earnings—in the big ledger in which he also kept a record of his deeds and misdeeds, as if to strike a bookkeeper's balance between them—but he was vague about his expenditures and usually vague about his possessions, including his balance in the bank. Once he asked a cashier, "How much money have I got?" The cashier looked in a big book and answered without even scowling, "None." Fitzgerald resolved to be more thrifty, knowing he would break the resolution. "All big men have spent money freely," he explained in a letter to his mother. "I hate avarice or even caution." He had little interest in the physical objects that money could buy. On the other hand, he had a great interest in earning money, lots of it fast, because that was a gold medal offered with the blue ribbon for competitive achievement. Once the money was earned, he and Zelda liked to spend lots of it fast, usually for impermanent things: not for real estate, fine motorcars, or furniture, but for traveling expenses, the rent of furnished houses, the wages of nurses and servants; for parties, party dresses, and feather fans of five colors. Zelda was as proudly careless about money as an eighteenth-century nobleman's heir. Scott was more practical and had his penny-pinching moments, as if in memory of his childhood, but at other times he liked to spend without counting in order to enjoy a proud sense of potency.

In his attitude toward money he revealed the new spirit of an age when conspicuous accumulation was giving way to conspicuous earning and spending. It was an age when gold was melted down and became fluid; when wealth was no longer measured in possessions—land, houses, livestock, machinery—but rather in dollars per year, as a stream is measured by its flow; when for the first time the expenses of government were being met by income taxes more than by property and excise taxes; and when the new tax structure was making it somewhat more difficult to accumulate a stable and lasting fortune. Such fortunes still existed at the hardly accessible peak of the social system, which young men dreamed of reaching like Alpinists, but the romantic figures of the age were not capitalists properly speaking. They were salaried executives and advertising men, they were promoters, salesmen, stock gamblers, or racketeers, and they were millionaires in a new sense—not men each of whom owned a million dollars' worth of property, but men who lived in rented apartments and had nothing but stock certificates and insurance policies (or nothing but credit and the right connections), while spending more than the income of the old millionaires.

The change went deep into the texture of American society and deep into the feelings of Americans as individuals. Fitzgerald is its most faithful recorder, not only in the stories that earned him a place in the new high-income class, but also in his personal confessions. He liked to describe his vitality and his talent in pecuniary terms. When both of them temporarily disappeared, in his crack-up of the years 1935–36, he pictured the event as a sort of financial bankruptcy. He wrote (but without my italics), "I began to realize that for two years my life had been a *drawing on resources* that I did not possess, that I had been *mortgaging myself* physically and spiritually up to the hilt." Again he wrote, "When a new sky cut off the sun last spring, I didn't at first relate it to what had happened fifteen or twenty years ago. Only gradually did a certain family resemblance come through—an over-extension of the flank, a burning of the candle at both ends; a call upon physical resources that I did not command, *like a man overdrawing at his bank. . . .* There were plenty of *counterfeit coins* around that I could pass off instead of these"—that is, in spite of the honest emotions he had lost—"and I knew where I could get them at *a nickel on the dollar.*"

"Where was the leak," Fitzgerald asked, "through which, unknown to myself, my enthusiasm and my vitality had been steadily and prematurely trickling away?" Vitality was something liquid and it was equated with money, which was also liquid. The attitude was different from that which prevailed before World War I, when people spoke of saving money as "piling up the rocks," instead of filling the reservoir, and when the millionaire in the funny papers was "Mr. Gotrocks." In Freud's great system, which is based on his observation of nineteenth-century types, money is something solid, gold or silver, and the bodily product it suggests is excrement. Thus, the pursuit of money for its own sake develops from anal eroticism, and Freud maintains that the miser is almost always a constipated man. I doubt whether recent analysts have observed how money is losing its old symbolic value and how, in the American subconscious, it tends to be identified with other bodily products such as urine ("I just pee'd it away"), blood, sperm, or milk.

Fitzgerald was more closely involved with contemporary values than most of the professional analysts. He uses the new imagery in much of his confessional writing, and it becomes especially clear in a free-verse poem, "Our April Letter," which he wrote during his crack-up. Three lines of the poem read:

> *I have asked a lot of my emotions—one hundred and twenty stories. The price was high, right up with Kipling, because there was one little drop of something—not blood, not a tear, not my seed, but me more intimately than these, in every story, it was the extra I had. Now it has gone and I am just like you now.*
>
> *Once the phial was full—here is the bottle it came in.*
>
> *Hold on, there's a drop left there. . . . No, it was just the way the light fell.*

Note that the something more intimate than blood or tears or sperm—though suggested by all of these—had a monetary value and was being sold to the magazines at a price right up with what Kipling had been paid. Note also that in its absence Fitzgerald was no longer able to write salable stories, so that he came to identify emotional with financial bankruptcy. In that black year 1936 he was earning very little money and owed more than forty thousand dollars, but he kept a careful record of his debts and later paid off most of them, by living in a modest fashion even during the months when he was earning a big salary in Hollywood. He never became solvent, but his financial obligations were not so pressing at the end of his life, and he was doing some of his best work.

In writing about the romance of money, as he did in most of his earlier novels and stories, he was dealing not only with an intimate truth but also with what seemed to him the central truth of his American age. "Americans," he liked to say, "should be born with fins and perhaps they were—perhaps money was a form of fin."

V

One of his remarks about himself has often puzzled his critics. "D.H. Lawrence's great attempt to synthesize animal and emotional—things he left out," Fitzgerald wrote in his notebook, then added the comment, "Essential pre-Marxian. Just as I am essentially Marxian." He was never Marxian in any sense of the word that Marxians of whatever school would be willing to accept. It is true that he finally read well into *Das Kapital* and was impressed by "the terrible chapter," as he called it, "on 'The Working Day' "; but it left in him no trace of Marx's belief in the mission of the proletariat.

His picture of proletarian life was of something alien to his own background, mysterious and even criminal. It seems to have been symbolized in some of his stories—notably in "Winter Dreams" and "A Short Trip Home"—by the riverfront strip in St. Paul that languished in the shadow of the big houses on Summit Avenue; he described the strip as a gridiron of mean streets where consumptive or pugilistic youths lounged in front of poolrooms, their skins turned livid by the neon lights. In *The Great Gatsby* he must have been thinking about the lower levels of American society when he described the valley of ashes between West Egg and New York—"A fantastic farm," he calls it, "where ashes grow like wheat into ridges and hills and grotesque gardens; where ashes take the forms of houses and chimneys and rising smoke and, finally, with a transcendent effort, of men who move dimly and always crumbling through the powdery air." One of his early titles for the novel was "Among Ash Heaps and Millionaires"—as if he were setting the two against each other while suggesting a vague affinity between them. Tom Buchanan, the brutalized millionaire, finds a mistress in the valley of ashes.

In Fitzgerald's stories there can be no real struggle between this dimly pictured ash-gray proletariat and the bourgeoisie. On the other hand, there can be a different struggle that the author must have regarded, for a time, as essentially Marxian. It is the struggle I have already suggested, between wealth as fluid income and wealth as an inherited and solid possession—or rather, since Fitzgerald is not an essayist but a storyteller, it is between a man and a woman as representatives of the new and the old moneyed classes.

We are not allowed to forget that they are representatives. The man comes from a family with little or no money, but he manages to attend an Eastern university—most often Yale, to set a distance between the hero and the Princeton author. He then sets out to earn a fortune equal to that of his wealthy classmates. Usually what he earns is not a fortune but an impressively large income, after he has risen to the top of his chosen profession—which may be engineering or architecture or advertising or the laundry business or bootlegging or real estate or even, in one story, frozen fish; the heroes are never novelists, although one of them is said to be a successful playwright. When the heroes are halfway to the top, they fall in love.

The woman—or rather the girl—in a Fitzgerald story is as alluring as the youngest princess in a fairy tale. "In children's books," he says when presenting one heroine, "forests are sometimes made out of all-day suckers, boulders out of peppermints and rivers out of gently flowing, rippling molasses taffy. Such . . . localities exist, and one day a girl, herself little more than a child, sat dejected in the middle of one. It was all hers, she owned it; she owned Candy Town." Another heroine "was a stalk of ripe corn, but bound not as cereals are but as a rare first edition, with all the binder's art. She was lovely and expensive and about nineteen." Of still another heroine Fitzgerald says when she first appears that "Her childish beauty was wistful and sad about being so rich and sixteen." Later, when her father loses his money, the hero pays her a visit in London. "All around her," Fitzgerald says, "he could feel the vast Mortmain fortune melting down, seeping back into the matrix whence it had come." The hero thinks she might marry him, now that she has fallen almost to his financial level; but he finds that the Mortmain (or deadhand) fortune, even though lost, is still a barrier between them. Note that the man is not attracted by the fortune in itself. He is not seeking money so much as position at the peak of the social hierarchy, and the girl becomes the symbol of that position, the incarnation of its mysterious power. That is Daisy Buchanan's charm for the great Gatsby and the reaon why he directs his whole life toward winning back her love.

"She's got an indiscreet voice," Nick Carraway says of her. "It's full of—" and he hesitates.

"Her voice is full of money," Gatsby says.

And Nick, the narrator, thinks to himself, "That was it. I'd never understood before. It was full of money—that was the inexhaustible charm that rose and fell in it, the cymbals' song of it. . . . High in a white palace the king's daughter, the golden girl."

In Fitzgerald's stories a love affair is like secret negotiations between the diplomats of two countries which are not at peace and not quite at war. For a moment they forget their hostility, find it transformed into mutual inspection, attraction, even passion (though the passion is not physical); but the hostility will survive even in marriage, if marriage is to be their future. I called the lovers diplomats, ambassadors, and that is another way of saying that they are representatives. When they meet it is as if they were leaning toward each other from separate high platforms—the man from a platform built up of his former poverty, his ambition, his competitive triumphs, his ability to earn and spend always more, more; the girl from another platform covered with cloth of gold and feather fans of many colors, but beneath them a sturdy pile of stock certificates testifying to the ownership of mines, forests, factories, villages—all of Candy Town.

She is ownership embodied, as can be seen in one of the best of Fitzgerald's early stories, "Winter Dreams." A rising young man named Dexter Green takes home the daughter of a millionaire for whom he used to be a caddy. She is Judy Jones, "a slender enamelled doll in cloth of gold: gold in a band at her head, gold in two slipper points at her dress's hem." The rising young man stops his coupé "in front of the great white bulk of the Mortimer Jones house, somnolent, gorgeous, drenched with the splendor of the damp moonlight. Its solidity startled him. The strong walls, the steel of the girders, the breadth and beam and pomp of it were there only to bring out the contrast with the young beauty beside him. It was sturdy to accentuate her slightness—as if to show what a breeze could be generated by a butterfly's wing." In legends butterflies are symbols of the soul. The inference is clear that, holding Judy in his arms, Dexter Green is embracing the spirit of a great fortune.

Nicole Warren, the heroine of *Tender Is the Night*, embodies the spirit of an even greater fortune. Fitzgerald says of her, in a familiar passage:

> Nicole was the product of much ingenuity and toil. For her sake trains began their run at Chicago and traversed the round belly of the continent to California; chicle factories fumed and link belts grew link by link in factories; men mixed toothpaste in vats and drew mouthwash out of copper hogs-heads; girls canned tomatoes quickly in August or worked rudely at the Five-and-Tens on Christmas Eve; half-breed Indians toiled

> on Brazilian coffee plantations and dreamers were muscled out of patent rights in new tractors—these were some of the people who gave a tithe to Nicole, and as the whole system swayed and thundered onward it lent a feverish bloom to such processes of hers as wholesale buying [of luxuries], like the flush of a fireman's face holding his post before a spreading blaze.

Sometimes Fitzgerald's heroines are candid, even brutal, about class relations. "Let's start right," Judy Jones says to Dexter Green on the first evening they spend alone together. "Who are you?"

"I'm nobody," Dexter tells her, without adding that he had been her father's caddy. "My career is largely a matter of futures."

"Are you poor?"

"No," he says frankly, "I'm probably making more money than any man my age in the Northwest. I know that's an obnoxious remark, but you advised me to start right."

"There was a pause," Fitzgerald adds. "Then she smiled and the corners of her mouth drooped and an almost imperceptible sway brought her closer to him, looking up into his eyes." Money brings them together, but later they are separated by something undefined—a mere whim of Judy's, it would seem, though one comes to suspect that the whim was based on her feeling that she should marry a man of her own caste. Dexter, as he goes East to earn a still larger income, is filled with regret for "the country of illusions, of youth, of the richness of life, where his winter dreams had flourished." It seems likely that Judy Jones, like Josephine Perry in a series of later stories, was a character suggested by a Chicago debutante with whom Fitzgerald was desperately in love during his first years at Princeton; afterward she made a more sensible marriage. As for the general attitude toward the rich that began to be expressed in "Winter Dreams," it is perhaps connected with his experience in 1919, when he was not earning enough to support a wife and Zelda broke off their engagement. Later he said of the time:

> During a long summer of despair I wrote a novel instead of letters, so it came out all right: but it came out all right for a different person. The man with the jingle of money in his pocket who married the girl a year later would always cherish an abiding distrust, an animosity, toward the leisure class—not the conviction of a revolutionist but the smoldering hatred of a peasant.

His mixture of feelings toward the very rich, which included curiosity and admiration as well as distrust, is revealed in his treatment of a basic situation that reappears in many of his stories. Of course he presented other situations that were not directly concerned with the relation between social classes. He wrote about the problem of adjusting oneself to life, which he thought was especially difficult for self-indulgent American women. He wrote about the manners of flappers, slickers, and jelly beans. He wrote engagingly about his own boyhood. He wrote about the patching-up of broken marriages, about the contrast between Northern and Southern life, about Americans going to pieces in Europe, about the self-tortures of gifted alcoholics, and in much of his later work—as notably in *The Last Tycoon*—he was expressing admiration for inspired technicians, such as brain surgeons and movie directors. But a great number of his stories, especially the early ones, start with the basic situation I have mentioned: a rising young man of the middle classes in love with the daughter of a very rich family. (Sometimes the family is Southern, in which case it needn't be so rich, since a high social status could still exist in the South without great wealth.)

From that beginning the story may take any one of several turns. The hero may marry the girl, but only after she loses her fortune or (as in "Presumption" and " 'The Sensible Thing' ") he gains an income greater than hers. He may lose the girl (as in "Winter Dreams") and always remember her with longing for his early aspirations. In "The Bridal Party" he resigns himself to the loss after being forced to recognize the moral superiority of the rich man she has married. In "More Than Just a House" he learns that the girl is empty and selfish and ends by marrying her good sister; in "The Rubber Check" he marries Ellen Mortmain's quiet cousin. There is, however, still another development out of the Fitzgerald situation that comes closer to revealing his ambiguous feelings toward the very rich. To state it simply—too simply—the rising young man wins the rich girl and then is destroyed by her wealth or her relatives.

It is the ballad of young Lochinvar come out of the West, but with a tragic ending—as if fair Ellen's kinsmen, armed and vengeful, had overtaken the pair or as if Ellen herself had betrayed the hero. Fitzgerald used it for the first time in a fantasy. "The Diamond As Big As the Ritz," which he wrote in St. Paul during the winter of 1921–22. In the fashion of many fantasies, it reveals the author's cast of mind more clearly than his realistic stories. It deals with the adventures of a boy named John T. Unger (we might read "Hunger"), who was born in a town on the Mississippi called Hades, though it also might be called St. Paul. He is sent away to St. Midas', which is "the most expensive and most exclusive boys' preparatory school in the world," and there he meets Percy Washington, who invites him to spend the summer at his home in the West. On the train Percy confides to him that his father is the richest man alive and owns a diamond bigger than the Ritz-Carlton Hotel.

The description of the Washington mansion, in its hidden valley that wasn't even shown on maps of the U.S. Geodetic Survey, is fantasy mingled with burlesque, but then the familiar Fitzgerald note appears. John falls in love with Percy's younger sister, Kismine. After an idyllic summer Kismine tells him accidentally—she had meant to keep the secret—that he will very soon be murdered, like all the former guests of the Washingtons. "It was done very nicely," she explains to him. "They were drugged while they were asleep—and their families were always told that they died of scarlet fever in Butte. . . . I shall probably have visitors too—I'll harden up to it. We can't let such an inevitable thing as death stand in the way of enjoying life while we have it. Think how lonesome it would be out here if we never had *any*one. Why, father and mother have sacrificed some of their best friends just as we have."

In *The Great Gatsby*, Tom and Daisy Buchanan would also sacrifice some of their best friends. "They were careless people, Tom and Daisy—they smashed up things and creatures and then retreated back into their money or their vast carelessness, or whatever it was that kept them together, and let other people clean up the mess they had made." "The Diamond As Big As the Ritz" can have a happy ending for the two lovers because it is a fantasy; but the same plot reappears in *The Great Gatsby*, where for the first time it is surrounded by the real world of the 1920s and for the first time is carried through to what Fitzgerald regarded as its logical conclusion.

There is a time in any true author's career when he suddenly becomes capable of doing his best work. He has found a fable that expresses his central truth and everything falls into place around it, so that his whole experience of life is available for use in his fiction. Something like that happened to Fitzgerald when he invented the story of Jimmy Gatz, otherwise known as Jay Gatsby, and it explains the richness and scope of what is in fact a short novel.

To put facts on record, *The Great Gatsby* is a book of about fifty thousand words, a comparatively small structure built of nine chapters like big blocks. The fifth chapter—Gatsby's meeting after many years with Daisy Buchanan—is the center of the narrative, as is proper; the seventh chapter is its climax. Each chapter consists of one or more dramatic scenes, sometimes with intervening passages of narration. The scenic method is one that Fitzgerald possibly learned from Edith Wharton, who had learned it from Henry James; at any rate, the book is technically in the Jamesian tradition (and Daisy Buchanan is named for James's Daisy Miller).

Part of the tradition is the device of having events observed by a "central consciousness," often a character who stands somewhat apart from the action and whose vision frames it for the reader. In this instance the observer plays a special role. Although Nick Carraway does not save or ruin Gatsby, his personality in itself provides an essential comment on all the other characters. Nick stands for the older values that prevailed in the Midwest before the First World War. His family is not tremendously rich like the Buchanans, but it has a long-established and sufficient fortune, so that Nick is the only person in the book who has not been corrupted by seeking or spending money. He is so certain of his own values that he hesitates to criticize others, but when he does pass judgment—on Gatsby, on Jordan Baker, on the Buchanans—he speaks as for ages to come.

All the other characters belong to their own brief era of confused and dissolving standards, but they are affected by the era in different fashions. Each of them represents some particular variety of moral failure; Lionel Trilling says that they are "treated as if they were ideographs," a true observation; but the treatment does not detract from their reality as persons. Tom Buchanan is wealth brutalized by selfishness and arrogance; he looks for a mistress in the valley of ashes and finds an ignorant woman, Myrtle Wilson, whose raw vitality is like his own. Daisy Buchanan is the butterfly soul of wealth and offers a continual promise "that she had done gay, exciting things just a while since and that there were gay, exciting things hovering in the next hour"; but it is a false promise, since at heart she is as self-centered as Tom and even colder. Jordan Baker apparently lives by the old standards, but she uses them only as a subterfuge. Aware of her own cowardice and dishonesty, she feels "safer on a plane where any divergence from a code would be thought impossible."

All these except Myrtle Wilson are East Egg people, that is, they are part of a community where wealth takes the form of solid possessions. Set against them are the West Egg people, whose wealth is fluid income that might cease to flow. The West Egg people, with Gatsby as their tragic hero, have worked furiously to rise in the world, but they will never reach East Egg for all the money they spend; at most they can sit at the water's edge and look across the bay at the green light that shines and promises at the end of the Buchanans' dock. The symbolism of place plays a great part in *Gatsby*, as does that of motorcars. The characters are visibly represented by the cars they drive: Nick has a conservative old Dodge, the Buchanans, too rich for ostentation, have an "easy-going blue coupé," and Gatsby's car is "a rich cream color, bright with nickel, swollen here and there in its monstrous length with triumphant hat-boxes and supper-boxes and tool-boxes, and terraced with a labyrinth of wind-shields that mirrored a dozen suns"—it is West Egg on wheels. When Daisy drives the monster through the valley of ashes, she runs down and kills Myrtle Wilson; then, by concealing her guilt, she causes the death of Gatsby.

The symbols are not synthetic or contrived, as are many of those in more recent novels; they are images that Fitzgerald instinctively found to represent his characters and their destiny. When he says, "Daisy took her face in her hands as if feeling its lovely shape," he is watching her act the charade of her self-love. When he says, "Tom would drift on forever seeking, a little wistfully, for the dramatic turbulence of some irrecoverable football game," he suggests the one appealing side of Tom's nature. The author is so familiar with the characters and their background, so absorbed in their fate, that the book has an admirable unity of texture; we can open it to any page and find another of the details that illuminate the story. We end by feeling that *Gatsby* has a double value: it is the best picture we possess of the age in which it was written, and it also achieves a sort of moral permanence. Fitzgerald's story of the suitor betrayed by the princess and murdered in his innocence is a fable of the 1920s that has survived as a legend for other times.

ROBERT ORNSTEIN

Scott Fitzgerald's Fable of East and West

After a brief revival, the novels of Scott Fitzgerald seem destined again for obscurity, labeled this time, by their most recent critics, as darkly pessismistic studies of America's spiritual and ideological failures. *The Great Gatsby*, we are now told, is not simply a chronicle of the Jazz Age but rather a dramatization of the betrayal of the naive American dream in a corrupt society. I would agree that in *Gatsby* Fitzgerald did create a myth with the imaginative sweep of America's historical adventure across an untamed continent. But his fable of East and West is little concerned with twentieth century materialism and moral anarchy, for its theme is the unending quest of the romantic dream, which is forever betrayed in fact and yet redeemed in men's minds.

From the start, Fitzgerald's personal dreams of romance contained the seeds of their own destruction. In his earliest works, his optimistic sense of the value of experience is overshadowed by a personal intuition of tragedy; his capacity for naive wonder is chastened by satiric and ironic insights which make surrender to the romantic impulse incomplete. Though able to idealize the sensuous excitement of an exclusive party or a lovely face, Fitzgerald could not ignore the speciosity inherent in the romantic stimuli of his social world—in the unhurried gracious poise that money can buy. Invariably he studied what fascinated him so acutely that he could give at times a clinical report on the very rich, whose world seemed

---

From *College English* 2, vol. 18, (November 1956).

to hold the promise of a life devoid of the vulgar and commonplace. A literalist of his own imagination (and therefore incapable of self-deception), he peopled extravagant phantasy with superbly real "denizens of Broadway." The result in the earlier novels is not so much an uncertainty of tone as a curious alternation of satiric and romantic moments—a breathless adoration of flapper heroines whose passionate kisses are tinged with frigidity and whose daring freedom masks an adolescent desire for the reputation rather than the reality of experience.

The haunting tone of *Gatsby* is more than a skilful fusion of Fitzgerald's satiric and romantic contrarieties. Nick Carraway, simultaneously enchanted and repelled by the variety of life, attains Fitzgerald's mature realization that the protective enchantment of the romantic ideal lies in its remoteness from actuality. He knows the fascination of yellow windows high above the city streets even as he looks down from Myrtle Wilson's gaudy, smoke-filled apartment. He still remembers the initial wonder of Gatsby's parties long after he is sickened by familiarity with Gatsby's uninvited guests. In one summer Nick discovers a profoundly melancholy esthetic truth: that romance belongs not to the present but to a past transfigured by imagined memory and to the illusory promise of an unrealizable future. Gatsby, less wise than Nick, destroys himself in an attempt to seize the green light in his own fingers.

At the same time that Fitzgerald perceived the melancholy nature of romantic illusion, his attitude towards the very rich crystalized. In *Gatsby* we see that the charming irresponsibility of the flapper has developed into the criminal amorality of Daisy Buchanan, and that the smug conceit of the Rich Boy has hardened into Tom Buchanan's arrogant cruelty. We know in retrospect that Anthony Patch's tragedy was not his "poverty," but his possession of the weakness and purposelessness of the very rich without their protective armor of wealth.

The thirst for money is a crucial motive in *Gatsby* as in Fitzgerald's other novels, and yet none of his major characters are materialists, for money is never their final goal. The rich are too accustomed to money to covet it. It is simply the badge of their "superiority" and the justification of their consuming snobberies. For those who are not very rich—for the Myrtle Wilsons as well as the Jay Gatsbys—it is the alchemic reagent that transmutes the ordinary worthlessness of life. Money is the demiurgos of Jimmy Gatz's Platonic universe, and the proof, in "Babylon Revisited," of the unreality of reality (". . . the snow of twenty-nine wasn't real snow. If you didn't want it to be snow, you just paid some money"). Even before *Gatsby*, in "The Rich Boy," Fitzgerald had defined the original sin of the very rich: They do not worship material gods, but they "possess and enjoy early, and it does something to them, makes them soft where we are hard, and cynical where we are trustful. . . ." Surrounded from childhood by the artificial security of wealth, accustomed to owning rather than wanting, they lack anxiety or illusion, frustration or fulfillment. Their romantic dreams are rooted in the adolescence from which they never completely escape—in the excitement of the prom or petting party, the reputation of being fast on the college gridiron or the college weekend.

Inevitably, then, Fitzgerald saw his romantic dream threaded by a double irony. Those who possess the necessary means lack the will, motive, or capacity to pursue a dream. Those with the heightened sensitivity to the promises of life have it because they are the disinherited, forever barred from the white palace where "the king's daughter, the golden girl" awaits "safe and proud above the struggles of the poor." Amory Blaine loses his girl writing advertising copy at ninety a month. Anthony Patch loses his mind after an abortive attempt to recoup his fortune peddling bonds. Jay Gatsby loses his life even though he makes his millions because they are not the kind of safe, respectable money that echoes in Daisy's lovely voice. The successful entrepreneurs of Gatsby's age are the panderers to vulgar tastes, the high pressure salesmen, and, of course, the bootleggers. Yet once, Fitzgerald suggests, there had been opportunity commensurate with aspiration, an unexplored and unexploited frontier where great fortunes had been made or at least romantically stolen. And out of the shifting of opportunities from the West to Wall Street, he creates an American fable which redeems as well as explains romantic failure.

But how is one to accept, even in fable, a West characterized by the dull rectitude of Minnesota villages and an East epitomized by the sophisticated dissipation of Long Island society? The answer is perhaps that Fitzgerald's dichotomy of East and West has the poetic truth of James's antithesis of provincial American virtue and refined European sensibility. Like *The Portrait of a Lady* and *The Ambassadors, Gatsby* is a story of "displaced persons" who have journeyed eastward in search of a larger experience of life. To James this reverse migration from the New to the Old World has in itself no special significance. To Fitzgerald, however, the lure of the East represents a profound displacement of the American dream, a turning back upon itself of the historic pilgrimage towards the frontier which had, in fact, created and sustained that dream. In *Gatsby* the once limitless western horizon is circumscribed by the "bored, sprawling, swollen towns beyond the Ohio, with their interminable inquisitions which spared only the children and the very old." The virgin territories of the frontiersman have been appropriated by the immigrant families, the diligent Swedes—the unimaginative, impoverished German farmers like Henry Gatz. Thus after a restless nomadic existence, the Buchanans settle "permanently" on Long Island because Tom would be "a God damned fool to live anywhere else." Thus Nick comes to New York with a dozen volumes on finance which promise "to unfold the shining secrets that only Midas, Morgan and Maecenas knew." Gatsby's green light, of course, shines in only one direction—from the East across the Continent to Minnesota, from the East across the bay to his imitation mansion in West Egg.

Lying in the moonlight on Gatsby's deserted beach, Nick realizes at the close just how lost a pilgrimage Gatsby's had been:

> . . . I became aware of the old island here that had flowered once for Dutch sailors' eyes—a fresh, green breast of the new world. Its vanished trees, the trees that had made way for Gatsby's house, had once pandered in whispers to the last and greatest of all human dreams; for a transitory moment man must have held his breath in the presence of this continent, compelled into an aesthetic contemplation he neither understood nor desired, face to face for the last time in history with something commensurate to his capacity for wonder.

Gatsby is the spiritual descendant of these Dutch sailors. Like them, he set out for gold and stumbled on a dream. But he journeys in the wrong direction in time as well as space. The transitory enchanted moment has come and gone for him and for the others, making the romantic promise of the future an illusory reflection of the past. Nick still carries with him a restlessness born of the war's excitement; Daisy silently mourns the romantic adventure of her "white" girlhood; Tom seeks the thrill of a vanished football game. Gatsby devotes his life to recapturing a love lost five years before. When the present offers nothing commensurate with man's capacity for wonder, the romantic credo is the belief—Gatsby's belief—in the ability to repeat the disembodied past. Each step towards the green light, however, shadows some part of Gatsby's grandiose achievement. With Daisy's disapproval the spectroscopic parties cease. To preserve her reputation Gatsby empties his mansion of lights and servants. And finally only darkness and ghostly memories tenant the deserted house as Gatsby relives his romantic past for Nick after the accident.

Like his romantic dream Jay Gatsby belongs to a vanished past. His career began when he met Dan Cody, a debauched relic of an earlier America who made his millions in the copper strikes. From Cody he received an education in ruthlessness which he applied when the accident of the war brought him to the beautiful house of Daisy Fay. In the tradition of Cody's frontier, he "took what he could get, ravenously and unscrupulously," but in taking Daisy he fell in love with her. "She vanished into her rich house, into her rich full life, leaving Gatsby—nothing. He felt married to her, that was all."

"He felt married to her"—here is the reaction of bourgeois conscience, not of calculating ambition. But then Gatsby is not really Cody's protégé. Jimmy Gatz inherited an attenuated version of the American dream of success, a more moral and genteel dream suited to a nation arriving at the respectability of established wealth and class. Respectability demands that avarice be masked with virtue, that personal aggrandisement pose as self-improvement. Success is no longer to the cutthroat or the ruthless but to the diligent and the industrious, to the boy who scribbles naive resolves on the flyleaf of *Hopalong Cassidy*. Fabricated of pulp fiction clichés (the improverished materials of an extraordinary imagination), Gatsby's dream of self-improvement blossoms into a preposterous tale of ancestral wealth and culture. And his dream is incorruptible because his great enterprise is not side-street "drugstores," or stolen bonds, but himself, his fictional past, his mansion and his gaudy entertainments. Through it all he moves alone and untouched; he is the impressario, the creator, not the enjoyer of a riotous venture dedicated to an impossible goal.

It may seem ironic that Gatsby's dream of self-improvement is realized through partnership with Meyer Wolfshiem, but Wolfshiem is merely the post-war successor to Dan Cody and to the ruthlessness and greed that once exploited a virgin West. He is the fabulous manipulator of bootleg gin rather than of copper, the modern man of legendary accomplishment "who fixed the World's Series back in 1919." The racketeer, Fitzgerald suggests, is the last great folk hero, the Paul Bunyan of an age in which romantic wonder surrounds underworld "gonnegtions" instead of raw courage or physical strength. And actually Gatsby is destroyed not by Wolfshiem, or association with him, but by the provincial squeamishness which makes all the Westerners in the novel unadaptable to life in the East.

Despite her facile cynicism and claim to sophistication, Daisy is still the "nice" girl who grew up in Louisville in a beautiful house with a wicker settee on the porch. She remains "spotless," still immaculately dressed in white and capable of a hundred whimsical, vaporous enthusiasms. She has assimilated the urbane ethic of the East which allows a bored wife a casual discreet affair. But she cannot, like Gatsby's uninvited guests, wink at the illegal and the criminal. When Tom begins to unfold the sordid details of Gatsby's career, she shrinks away; she never intended to leave her husband, but now even an affair is impossible. Tom's provinciality is more boorish than genteel. He has assumed the role of Long Island country gentleman who keeps a mistress in a mid-town apartment. But with Myrtle Wilson by his side he turns the role into a ludicrous travesty. By nature a libertine, by upbringing a prig, Tom shatters Gatsby's façade in order to preserve his "gentleman's" conception of womanly virtue and of the sanctity of his marriage.

Ultimately, however, Gatsby is the victim of his own small-town notions of virtue and chivalry. "He would never so much as look at a friend's wife"—or at least he would never try to steal her in her husband's house. He wants Daisy to say that she never loved Tom because only in this way can the sacrament of Gatsby's "marriage" to her in Louisville—his prior claim—be recognized. Not content merely to repeat the past, he must also eradicate the years in which his dream lost its reality. But the dream, like the vanished frontier which it almost comes to represent, is lost forever "somewhere back in that vast obscurity beyond the city, where the dark field of the republic rolled on under the night."

After Gatsby's death Nick prepares to return to his Minnesota home, a place of warmth and enduring stability, carrying with him a surrealistic night vision of the debauchery of the East. Yet his return is not a positive rediscovery of the well-springs of American life. Instead it seems a melancholy retreat from the ruined promise of the East, from the empty present to the childhood memory of the past. Indeed, it is this childhood memory, not the reality of the West which Nick cherishes. For he still thinks the East, despite its nightmarish aspect, superior to the stultifying small-town dullness from which he fled. And by the close of *Gatsby* it is unmistakably clear that the East does not symbolize contemporary decadence and the West the pristine virtues of an earlier America. Fitzgerald does not contrast Gatsby's criminality with his father's unspoiled rustic strength and dignity. He contrasts rather Henry Gatz's dull, grey, almost insentient existence, "a meaningless extinction up an alley," with Gatsby's pilgrimage Eastward, which, though hopeless and corrupting, was at least a journey of life and hope—an escape from the "vast obscurity" of the West that once spawned and then swallowed the American dream. Into this vast obscurity the Buchanans finally disappear. They are not Westerners any longer, or Easterners, but merely two of the very rich, who in the end represent nothing but themselves. They are careless people, Tom and Daisy, selfish, destructive, capable of anything except human sympathy, and yet not sophisticated enough to be really decadent. Their irresponsibility, Nick realizes, is that of pampered children, who smash up "things and creatures . . . and let other people clean up the mess." They live in the eternal moral adolescence which only wealth can produce and protect.

By ignoring its context one can perhaps make much of Nick's

indictment of the Buchanans. One can even say that in *The Great Gatsby* Fitzgerald adumbrated the coming tragedy of a nation grown decadent without achieving maturity—a nation that possessed and enjoyed early, and in its arrogant assumption of superiority lost sight of the dream that had created it. But is it not absurd to interpret Gatsby as a mythic Spenglerian anti-hero? Gatsby *is* great, because his dream, however naive, gaudy, and unattainable is one of the grand illusions of the race which keep men from becoming too old or too wise or too cynical of their human limitations. Scott Fitzgerald's fable of East and West does not lament the decline of American civilization. It mourns the eternal lateness of the present hour suspended between the past of romantic memory and the future of romantic promise which ever recedes before us.

MICHAEL MILLGATE

Scott Fitzgerald as Social Novelist: Statement and Technique in "The Last Tycoon"

In most of Fitzgerald's novels the theme of 'the-American-as-businessman', so important in American fiction from the time of James's *The American* onwards, is only lightly touched upon, and the operations of business play no greater part than they do in the typical Edith Wharton novel. Business is the invisible seven-eighths of the iceberg, the indispensable basis on which the flimsy structure of the social world is reared, the 'given' quantity to which no reference need be made except in times of personal or general disaster—as it intrudes into *The House of Mirth* only because of the social repercussions of Beaufort's 'failure'. This is true above all of *This Side of Paradise* and, despite Gatsby's background, of *The Great Gatsby. The Beautiful and Damned* is concerned with money-power rather than with business as such—Maxwell Geismar calls it 'a sort of postscript to the *Great American Fortunes*'— while *Tender is the Night*, so far as it is the story of the Warren sisters, is a novel of the businessman's womankind with the businessman himself a shadowy background figure. If, however, Fitzgerald had lived to complete *The Last Tycoon* (1941), we might have had a business novel of considerable comprehensiveness and power.

On September 29, 1939, Fitzgerald wrote to his publisher that his new novel, *The Last Tycoon*, had been set 'safely in a period of five years

From *English Studies* 1, vol. 43 (February 1962).

ago to obtain detachment'. A year later, in September 1940, he told Gerald Murphy that the novel was 'as detached from me as *Gatsby* was, in intent anyhow'. That final qualifying phrase raises doubts which the letterhead reinforces ('Twentieth Century-Fox Film Corporation Studios, Beverley Hills, California'), and in fact the detachment sought isn't, somehow, achieved: *The Last Tycoon* lacks the distanced, curiously 'classical' air of *The Great Gatsby*. What we have is a collection of brilliant and powerful scenes, which yet hardly begin to cohere into a novel—and this not only because the book was unfinished.

It is not at all clear, indeed, that Fitzgerald could have finished *The Last Tycoon* in anything like the form in which he had planned and written it up to that point. The trouble seems almost to have been that Fitzgerald was really trying to write two novels in one: a 'psychological' novel about Monroe Stahr, and a 'social' novel about Hollywood. In his letter to Edmund Wilson of November 25, 1940, the emphasis appears to be on the latter: 'I honestly hoped someone else would write it [the novel] but nobody seems to be going to'. It is fairly clear, however, that the starting-point of this novel had been the genius of Stahr himself, 'the last tycoon', just as the central interest of *The Great Gatsby* had been in Gatsby himself.

It is true that the 'social' interest in *The Great Gatsby* is considerable, but it is there primarily to display and explain the human relationships: it never takes control. In *The Last Tycoon*, as far as it had gone, the 'social' content is also reasonably functional, but Fitzgerald's plans for the continuation and conclusion of the novel indicate a distinct movement away from interest in character in favour of an interest in events—notably the intrigue, corruption and violence of Hollywood—for their own sakes. It seems likely that had Fitzgerald tried to work out the plot of *The Last Tycoon* along the lines he proposed he would have found the 'social' interest taking control and swamping the rest.

Fitzgerald does not seem to have fully realised that in *The Last Tycoon* he faced a problem of construction that was quite different from the one he had so brilliantly solved in *The Great Gatsby*: otherwise he would surely not have tried to cast his new book so completely in the *Gatsby* mould. The frequent references to *The Great Gatsby* in Fitzgerald's notes for *The Last Tycoon* and in his letters at this time make it clear that while he was planning and writing the new book the earlier one was very much in his mind. This would, in any case, have been sufficiently plain from a comparison of the two. Each is the story of a man who, from humble beginnings, has risen to a position of great power. In each we come to know of the man first not in person but by reputation and by the attitude of others towards him. Then we see the man himself in the centre of his world, his position and his greatness defined by the nature of that world which revolves upon him as its axis: Fitzgerald's outline for *The Last Tycoon* says explicitly that the chapters describing Stahr's day are 'equal to guest list and Gatsby's party', that is, to Chapter III and the first two pages of Chapter IV of *The Great Gatsby*. We watch in each the failure of the man in his personal life, in an all-important relationship with a woman; then his violent, senseless death; and finally his funeral, in such strong contrast with his life (in notes for the end of *The Last Tycoon* Cecilia imagines Stahr present at the funeral and saying 'Trash!').

The most important and perhaps the most questionable of *The Last Tycoon's* debts to *The Great Gatsby* is the half-involved first-person narrator. Cecilia is '*of* the movies but not *in* them': a very similar comment could have been made about Nick Carraway's place in the world of *The Great Gatsby*. But Nick, as a piece of structural machinery, is a superb invention: he is on stage almost throughout the novel, and even when he is not it is easy to see where his information comes from. Nick as narrator never strains our credulity; Cecilia as narrator worries us from the start. She is clearly meant to play a Nick Carraway role, but because of her own limited participation in this action she isn't adequate to fulfil Nick's narrative function.

Nick's other major function is to act as a vehicle for moral judgements, and here again Cecilia falls short. The proposed final scene in the sanatorium was intended to invest Cecilia, through her illness, with greater portentousness, but it isn't easy to take her very seriously in the story as we have it. She is too immature to be able to make worthwhile judgements or to help us to judge, and her own emotions are too deeply involved. An emotional involvement in his character and his story may have been to some extent Fitzgerald's own problem. Irving Thalberg had been dead for three years and more, but Stahr isn't just Thalberg, he is partly Fitzgerald himself as well. Stahr's anticipation of an early death, for example, carries strong suggestions that this is Fitzgerald's own anticipation: 'If I live long enough, I'll hear your side of the story', he writes to his daughter in the spring of 1940.

The correspondences between *The Last Tycoon* and *The Great Gatsby* are not accidental, and they may have helped to twist *The Last Tycoon* out of its proper path, whatever that may have been. Gatsby's violent death has ironic appropriateness, but the violent death proposed for Stahr seems unmotivated and relatively without point, except in so far as Fitzgerald was planning a reference back to the airliner episode in Chapter I. The unsatisfactory love-affair forms the core of *The Great*

Gatsby and indeed of Gatsby himself, but, although Fitzgerald told his publisher that he wanted Stahr's affair with Kathleen to be 'the meat of the book', he seems not to have had a completely clear conception of their relationship. Nor does that relationship seem to be a very important part of Fitzgerald's total conception of Stahr. It is certainly Stahr the producer who emerges the more vividly from the chapters we have: Stahr the lover remains a comparatively shadowy figure.

Since Fitzgerald planned *The Last Tycoon* as a short novel, of about 51,000 words, it was natural that he should turn to *The Great Gatsby* for a usable pattern, even though the pattern may not have been altogether appropriate. Whatever its final length, it seems likely that if *The Last Tycoon* had been completed it would have been in important ways a 'weightier' book than any other of Fitzgerald's novels. This is not to say that it would necessarily have been a better book than *The Great Gatsby* nor more ambitious in scope than *Tender is the Night*. The suggestion is simply that the Hollywood setting would have been not merely evoked, as the Long Island setting is so brilliantly evoked in *The Great Gatsby*, but recreated with complete solidity and understanding; while Monroe Stahr, for his part, would have become not only, with the possible exception of Dick Diver, the most fully drawn of Fitzgerald's characters, but one of the outstanding portraits of a businessman in the history of the American novel.

The cinema, because it involves questions of artistic merit, is, as Fitzgerald saw, a rather odd kind of business. But it unquestionably is a business: as Cecilia Brady tells us on the first page, 'My father was in the picture business as another man might be in cotton or steel'. It is largely because of Brady's exclusively business approach to film-making that he and Stahr are such enemies, but Stahr himself, though he must pronounce on matters of taste, is inevitably a businessman as well. When Wylie White challenges Stahr's description of himself as a 'merchant', Stahr sticks to the word and suggests that Charles Francis Adams, when he criticised 'Gould, Vanderbilt, Carnegie, Astor', was 'probably a sourbelly . . . He wanted to be head man himself, but he didn't have the judgment or else the character'.

Stahr, that is to say, seems to align himself with the great American capitalists. But the tone of his answer works together with the admiration of Wylie White to prevent our thinking of him entirely in these terms, and at lunch with the financiers it quickly becomes clear that he is an isolated figure among them. As a young man he had been 'more than now . . . a money man among money men. Then he had been able to figure costs in his head with a speed and accuracy that dazzled them'.

Since then, we are told, Stahr 'had grown away from that particular gift, though it was always there'. Stahr remains a brilliant businessman, but he has become something more. His business ability is included within Fitzgerald's grand conception of him, but it is transcended:

> He spoke and waved back as the people streamed by in the darkness, looking, I suppose, a little like the Emperor and the Old Guard. There is no world so but it has its heroes, and Stahr was the hero. Most of these men had been here a long time—through the beginnings and the great upset, when sound came, and the three years of depression, he had seen that no harm came to them. The old loyalties were trembling now, there were clay feet everywhere; but still he was their man, the last of the princes. And their greeting was a sort of low cheer as they went by.

The kind of representative importance with which Fitzgerald intended to invest Stahr is not wholly clear in the novel as we have it. But it is sufficiently plain that if Stahr is an embodiment of heroic individualism there is, despite his paternalism, his dislike of unions and his fight with Brimmer, nothing of the Fascist about him. Indeed, one of the major themes of *The Last Tycoon* seems to be the partial identification of Stahr with Abraham Lincoln. Arthur Mizener has pointed out the importance of the Lincoln motif in Fitzgerald's presentation of Stahr: he relates it, with the episode at the Hermitage in the opening chapter, to the 'political fable' Fitzgerald seems to have been developing in the book. It may be, however, that the identification of Stahr with Lincoln, though never complete, goes a little further than this, affecting other sides of Stahr's character and other aspects of the book.

Boxley, the English novelist, is irritated by Stahr but, we are told: 'he had been reading Lord Charnwood and he recognized that Stahr like Lincoln was a leader carrying on a long war on many fronts . . . Stahr was an artist only, as Mr. Lincoln was a general, perforce and as a layman'. Going to Lord Charnwood's biography, *Abraham Lincoln*, it is interesting to discover Charnwood quoting contemporary references to Lincoln as 'the Tycoon' and as 'King Abraham I'. The coincidence with Fitzgerald's title is striking, and it is useful to be reminded in this way that Stahr is intended to be a 'tycoon' in the original sense of that word quite as much as in the modern sense. There is a possible hint here, too, of the description of Stahr as 'the last of the princes' and of Kathleen's assurance to Stahr that her real king was not nearly as much like a king as he was himself.

There are other points of similarity between Charnwood's Lincoln and Fitzgerald's Stahr: both are men of humble origins and little education but of great ability and vision; both practise in their relations with subordinates complete accessibility and an unforced personal democracy; both accept without hesitation the full responsibility of their position while disliking many of the duties involved. As Fitzgerald saw, there is an obvious analogy to be drawn between Stahr's position and Lincoln's: Stahr can be seen as the commander-in-chief, receiving reports from the battleline, issuing orders to his generals (the directors), overseeing work which has to be done in detail by others. In a smaller way Lincoln's habit of telling a little story when a reproof had to be administered is not unlike Stahr's method of handling Boxley, while it is surely in terms of the Lincoln analogy that the curious scene with the Negro on the beach at Malibu begins to take on fuller meaning: Stahr like Lincoln, but unlike Wylie White earlier in *The Last Tycoon*, will transform his kingdom for the Negro's sake.

Like Lincoln, above all, Stahr responds supremely to the demands of power. Writers, he tells Brimmer,

> ". . . are not equipped for authority . . . There is no substitute for will. Sometimes you have to fake will when you don't feel it at all."
>
> "I've had that experience."
>
> "You have to say, 'It's got to be like this—no other way' —even if you're not sure. A dozen times a week that happens to me. Situations where there is no real reason for anything. You pretend there is."
>
> "All leaders have felt that," said Brimmer. "Labor leaders, and certainly military leaders."

Stahr is the centre, the keystone of his world: in Fitzgerald's imagery, he is 'the King', 'the helmsman', 'the oracle'. He is himself the 'unity'. When he delivers a judgement: 'The oracle had spoken. There was nothing to question or argue. Stahr must be right always, not most of the time, but always—or the structure would melt down like gradual butter'. If the power of decision is, as many people would say it is, the essence of business success, then Stahr is one of the very few businessmen in fiction in whom we see the process of decision actually at work. His method, hinted at in the exchange with Brimmer, is magnificently expounded in his conversation with the pilot of the aircraft in the opening chapter:

> [Stahr] was looking down at the mountains.
>
> "Suppose you were a railroad man," he said. "You have to send a train through there somewhere. Well, you get your surveyors' reports, and you find there's three or four or half a dozen gaps, and not one is better than the other. You've got to decide—on what basis? You can't test the best way except by doing it. So you just do it."
>
> The pilot thought he had missed something.
>
> "How do you mean?"

"You choose some one way for no reason at all—because that mountain's pink or the blueprint is a better blue. You see?"

The pilot considered that this was very valuable advice. But he doubted if he'd ever be in a position to apply it.

"What I wanted to know," he told me ruefully, "is how he ever got to be Mr. Stahr."

We know from Fitzgerald's notes that he took this passage almost verbatim from an actual conversation, but that scarcely detracts from its impressiveness: it is indeed a tribute to Fitzgerald's shrewdness that he should have recognized, despite the almost absurd simplicity of the remark, its revealing accuracy. Fitzgerald records that, listening to the speaker, he was impressed by 'something more than shrewdness—by the largeness of what he thought'. It is possible to argue that such characterisation of Stahr betrays traces of Fitzgerald's old tendency to uncritical hero-worship; certainly his attempt to invest Stahr with 'largeness' in the last two paragraphs of Chapter I, whatever its rhetorical success, is not altogether substantiated by what we see of Stahr in action in the book as we have it. The very solidity and concreteness of Fitzgerald's presentation of Stahr, the very convincingness of the scenes in what Cecilia calls 'A Producer's Day', work against an acceptance of Stahr as a larger-than-life figure. However impressive his omnicompetence few of Stahr's individual decisions—apart, perhaps, from his insistence on making a picture that will lose money—are especially remarkable. The shadowiness with which Jay Gatsby is presented, that is to say, may raise occasional questions in the reader's mind but it has undoubted artistic advantages.

But it would be wrong to conclude on a note of criticism which, if he had lived, Fitzgerald's completion and revision of the book might well have made irrelevant. There can be no question of the seriousness and thoroughness of Fitzgerald's attempt in this novel to present a detailed portait of a specific industry and of a dominating figure in that industry. His portrayal of Stahr and of Stahr's world is scarcely less deliberate as social documentary than Dreiser's portrayal of Cowperwood. This is made clear by such notes as: '[Brady] is the monopolist at his worst—Stahr, in spite of the inevitable conservatism of the self-made man, is a paternalistic employer'. In his paternalism, indeed, Stahr is rather reminiscent of Amherst in Edith Wharton's *The Fruit of the Tree*, but Fitzgerald has here an advantage over both Edith Wharton and Dreiser, and even over the author of his own earlier books, in the comprehensive knowledge of the world he presents and in his understanding, both as moralist and as novelist of manners, of all sides of his hero's personality.

ROY R. MALE

"Babylon Revisited": A Story of the Exile's Return

F. Scott Fitzgerald's "Babylon Revisited," although widely reprinted, has not produced many commentaries. James Frake and Isadore Traschen give a brief explication in their text on short fiction, Arthur Mizener refers to the story a number of times in his biography, and Seymour Gross has recently offered a full-length analysis. But compared to, say, "Rappaccini's Daughter," or "The Turn of the Screw," or "The Bear," Fitzgerald's story seems to have provoked almost no concern—mainly, I suppose, because its meaning is clear. It has some symbols, but they are not mysterious; some ambiguity, but it is not hidden; considerable irony, but it is readily discernible. It strikes us, in short, as an example of the really excellent story that is widely read and reread, usually with considerable appreciation and understanding. This paper asks, in effect, whether it is possible to write profitably about a story that everybody already understands, or nearly understands.

My basic assumption is not particularly startling, but it does run counter to that of the extreme formalists (now perhaps nearly extinct), who used to maintain that criticism and teaching of a short story should be rigorously limited to an examination of the text. "Stay inside the story," they said, as if one story is of no help in understanding another, as if the time spirit supplies nothing to shape an author's fiction, as if his life tells us nothing about his art. No, I would maintain that we should place a story in as many contexts as possible. I limit myself here to the three just

From *Studies in Short Fiction*, vol. II, (1964–65).

mentioned: generic, historical, and biographical, paying particular attention to the first because it is the least familiar.

What kind of story is "Babylon Revisited"? To this deliberately broad and blunt question the answers, whether from students, English teachers, or writers, would be something short of unanimous. Here are some typical student replies: "It's a good story." "It's realistic." "No, it's impressionistic." "It's a story about life in the twenties." "It's a short story." These students were not stupid; their chaotic response simply reflects the relatively primitive state of the generic critcism of fiction. Having jettisoned the whole idea of genres somewhere in the nineteenth century, we lack descriptive terms to define fictions in any fundamental and illuminating way. The major exceptions to this generalization are terms like picaresque novel, *Bildungsroman*, *Künstlerroman*, and Lionel Trilling's description of the story of the Young Man from the Provinces. These terms define stories either according to the situation of the hero or according to the action imitated; they have the great advantage of being easily recognizable; and I think that their defining principle can be extended. It is not that every story can or should be classified in this way; but if we do find a group of stories imitating the same basic action, we are being critically and pedagogically provincial if we ignore their interrelationship.

From this point of view, "Babylon Revisited" belongs with a number of stories in which the protagonist returns after a prolonged absence, either to his home or to some substitute for it. This category we may call the story of the Exile's Return, and in American fiction it would include (among others) Washington Irving's "Rip Van Winkle," Nathaniel Hawthorne's "Ethan Brand," Hamlin Garland's "The Return of a Private," Henry James's "The Jolly Corner," Ernest Hemingway's "Soldier's Home," Theodore Dreiser's "The Old Neighborhood," Lionel Trilling's *The Middle of the Journey*, and Frederick Buechner's "The Tiger." Behind these American stories, of course, are such prototypes as Ulysses returning to Penelope, Plato's myth of the cave, the Biblical account of the return of the prodigal son, and Dante's return from his vision of hell, purgatory, and paradise.

The advantages of placing stories together in this way are obvious: first, certain conventions and common themes emerge clearly, aiding explication of each individual story; and second, once the similarities are established, differences in execution or technique are more clearly discernible. As Henry James said, in a somewhat different connection, "our aim is to get the correspondences and equivalents that make differences mean something."

Certain themes are inherent in the basic situation of a man returning after a long absence. In fiction as in life, the most obvious and the most poignant is the mutability theme or, more specifically, the sense of permanence and change. Although some aspects of the setting seem unchanged, their apparent permanence simply emphasizes the fundamental law of life, that all things pass. Thus we have in these stories something like the *ubi sunt* formula in poetry. Rip Van Winkle asks, "Where's Nicholas Vedder? Where's Brom Dutcher? Where's Van Bummel, the schoolmaster?" Gone, all of them gone. Even Vedder's wooden tombstone, Rip learns, is "rotten and gone." This, of course, is where Fitzgerald's story begins. "Where's Mr. Campbell?" "And George Hardt?" "And where is the Snow Bird?" "What's become of Claude Fessenden?" All gone, some of them "rotten and gone." In the Babylonian Ritz Bar only the "strident queens" remain; "they go on forever."

The hero may ask about the men, his former friends, but the essential motivation for his return is always a reunion with some form of the feminine principle. She may be a person: the faithful wife as in "The Return of a Private," the daughter as in "Rip Van Winkle" and "Babylon Revisited," the stable and intimate friend Alice Staverton in "The Jolly Corner." Or it may be more abstract and symbolic: the "mother earth" invoked and then rejected by Ethan Brand, the "girls" that bother Krebs in "Soldier's Home," or the alma mater as in "The Tiger." Thomas Wolfe, whose fiction flowed forth from the archetypal pattern of departure and return, described the impulse this way: "By the 'earth again' I mean simply the everlasting earth, a home, a place for the heart to come to, and earthly mortal love, the love of a woman, who, it seems to me, belongs to the earth and is a force opposed to that other great force that makes men wander, that makes them search, that makes them lonely, and that makes them both hate and love their loneliness."

As anyone who has returned home after a long absence will testify, the experience often has a dreamlike quality, a curious mixture of pain and pleasure as one feels his identity dissolving into two selves, past and present, private and public. The threatened loss of identity is explicit in "Rip Van Winkle" when he is confronted by a double, unaware of course, that he is his son:

> Rip looked and beheld a precise counterpart of himself as he went up the mountain: apparently as lazy and certainly as ragged. The poor fellow was now completely dumfounded. He doubted his own identity, and whether he was himself or another man. In the midst of his bewilderment, the man in the cocked hat demanded who he was and what was his name? "God knows," [says Rip] "I'm not myself—I'm somebody else—that's me

> yonder—no—that's somebody else got into my shoes—I was myself last night, but I fell asleep on the mountain and they've changed my gun and everything's changed and I can't tell what's my name or who I am."

As Philip Young remarks in his acute, if somewhat over-elaborate interpretation of "Rip," the character has a universal quality. "If we mock him for whatever he has missed, we do it tenderly—partly because it is something hidden in ourselves we mock. It is all our own lost lives and roles, the lives and roles that once seemed possible and are possible no more." This aspect of the exile's return is central, of course, in "The Jolly Corner," where Spencer Brydon hunts down his alter ego, the self he missed becoming when he left America, " 'the American fate' with which he never has come to terms." And this theme of split identity recurs, as we shall see, in "Babylon Revisited," where the basic question about Charlie is whether he is indeed "the old Wales," as his former friends call him, or the new.

A final theme given in the situation of the returning exile is that of freedom and responsibility. The mere fact that he has been gone suggests the possibility of egotism and escapism. Rip, we recall, was dodging not merely his wife "but all the obligations of maturity: occupation, domestic and financial responsibility, a political position, duty to his country in time of war." This is the major issue in Trilling's short novel, *The Middle of the Journey*. The protagonist, John Laskell, has returned midway in the journey of life from an inferno of pain, a nearly fatal illness. His image on the cover of the Anchor paperback might stand for all the modern exiles, returning not "home"—Laskell's hot bachelor apartment in New York—but to friends in the country. He is "the stranger, the outlander, the foreigner from New York," and in his weakened condition he is overwhelmed by irrational terror when no one meets the train. One is reminded of Randall Jarrell's poem "On the Railway Platform" and its lines: "What we leave we leave forever:/Time has no travellers. And journeys end in/No destinations we meant." That no one met the train, it turns out, was the fault of his friends' handy man, Duck Caldwell. Later, while conversing with his friends, Laskell quickly decides to "drop the whole matter of fault and blame," but this, of course, is precisely what Trilling does not do. The book's complex though somewhat abstract plot, culminating in the death of Caldwell's daughter (who has heart trouble), turns on the question of involvement, responsibility, and guilt. So, too, in "Babylon Revisited," we find Charlie Wales maintaining that he is now a responsible person but denying responsibility for his wife's death. " 'Helen died of heart trouble,' " he says. " 'Yes, heart trouble,' " Marion retorts, "as if the phrase had another meaning for her."

So much for the important themes these stories have in common. They are equally notable, of course, for their differences of technique. In a full-length study one might profitably observe in some detail what we will here summarize in a paragraph: the movement toward dramatization, immediacy, and restricted point of view in the modern stories as contrasted with the pictorialism, detachment, and omniscient point of view in "Rip Van Winkle," "Ethan Brand," and "The Return of a Private"; Fitzgerald's skillful transitions in this story, particularly the way he whisks Charlie out of the Ritz Bar in the first scene, as compared with Dreiser's lumbering shifts of scene in "The Old Neighborhood"; and the way in which Fitzgerald's dialogue is both realistic in tone and radiant with meaning, compared with the gritty, often trivial speech of Garland's story or the rather melodramatic rhetoric of "Ethan Brand."

To grasp some of the reasons why Fitzgerald's story came off so well, we need to see it as a product of his life and times. William Rose Benét, reviewing Fitzgerald's best novel in *The Saturday Review of Literature* (May 9, 1925), wrote, "*The Great Gatsby* reveals thoroughly matured craftsmanship. It has high occasions of felicitous, almost magic phrase. And most of all, it is out of the mirage. For the first time Fitzgerald surveys the Babylonian captivity of this era unblinded by the bright lights." In this review, which Fitzgerald quite probably read, we have important clues to the success of "Babylon Revisited," written five years later. It suggests, in the first place, why he gave the story its title, avoiding the more obvious "Paris Revisited," with its narrowing of connotation. Fitzgerald was writing about the end of an era, not just some changes in a corner of tourist France.

We do not need the description of Charlie Wales—"He was good to look at. The Irish mobility of his face was sobered by a deep wrinkle between his eyes"—to know that he is close to Scott Fitzgerald. In 1930 his wife was not in a grave in Vermont, but she was in a sanitarium; his daughter, though not living with his sister-in-law, was attending school in Paris. But even though the story clearly flows from emotional autobiography, it also has the perspective that Malcolm Cowley summed up in his memorable remark about Fitzgerald's work: "It was as if all of his novels described a big dance to which he had taken . . . the prettiest girl . . . and as if at the same time he stood outside the ballroom, a little Midwestern boy with his nose to the glass, wondering how much the tickets cost and who paid for the music." This double vision of actor and spectator, with the mature spectator no longer a gawky outsider but a judge, informs all of Fitzgerald's best work, and in this story it allows him to view Charlie Wales with both sympathy and ironic detachment.

Benét's remark about Fitzgerald's "almost magic" phrasing also provides a clue to the all-important relation between art, spending, and morality in this story. When Charlie says of the old times, "We were a sort of royalty, almost infallible, with a sort of magic around us," we see the precise appeal of the rich, or at least of the spenders, for Fitzgerald. He not only wrote about how he lived; he also saw life in the high style as allied to, though not identical with, writing. It was a spending of one's resources to gain release from the rigid grip of time, space, and circumstance. "The snow of twenty-nine wasn't real snow. If you didn't want it to be snow, you just paid some money." The spenders juggled time and space as the novelist does, making "months into days," shrinking and magnifying dimensions at will. "In the little hours of the night, every move from place to place was an enormous human jump, an increase of paying for the privilege of slower and slower motion." The squandering of unearned money called forth "effort and ingenuity" and imagination; it permitted or demanded the playing of roles, wearing the old derby rim and carrying the wire cane.

The basic conflict of the story, then, is not just between Charlie and Marion; it is between Charlie Wales (who presumably takes his last name from the prince who was the epitome of the good-time Charlies in the twenties) and "Mr. Charles J. Wales of Prague," sound businessman and moralist, between the regally imaginative but destructive past and the dull, bourgeois but solid present. As Charlie now sees it, the old time spent did bring about transformations, but they were all morally destructive. To "dissipate" was to perform a magic disappearing act, "to make nothing out of something." It was all, he now realizes, on an "utterly childish scale," like the pedalling of Lorraine on a tricycle all over Paris between the small hours and dawn.

With our natural sympathy for the Charlie who at the end sees that he lost everything he wanted in the boom, we are likely to think that he wants only the honorable part of the past, that he would like to disengage himself from the rest of it, that, as he tells Marion, he *has* radically changed. But Fitzgerald, is not at all sentimental on this point; he insists upon the reader's seeing more clearly than Charlie does. For the trouble with Charlie is that he *still* wants both worlds. The harsh fact is that if he had not stopped in the Ritz Bar in the first place, had not tried to get in touch with Duncan Schaefer, he would have won back his daughter. Fitzgerald has him commit this fatal act in the very beginning of the story; it comes back to haunt him inexorably in the "ghosts" of Dunc and Lorraine.

The two sides of Charlie are clearly revealed, of course, in the luncheon scene with Honoria. " 'Now, how about vegetables?' " he asks. " 'Oughtn't you to have some vegetables?' " This is Charlie trying to prove to himself and Honoria that he is the ordinary or garden variety of father. But he gently mocks this role by formally introducing himself as Charles J. Wales of Prague and is delighted when she quickly responds, imaginatively accepting the role of an adult woman. The game is short, however, because it rapidly evokes too many parallels with the destructive aspects of playing at life:

> "Married or single?"
> "No, not married. Single."
> He indicated the doll. "But I see you have a child, madame."
> Unwilling to disinherit it, she took it to her heart and thought quickly.
> "Yes, I've been married, but I'm not married now. My husband is dead."
> He went on quickly, "And the child's name?"
> "Simone. That's after my best friend at school."

It is probably significant that it is Honoria who brings the conversation back to reality with this reference to school, because in this whole scene she is educating her father. She approves his suggestion that they go to the vaudeville but frowns on his approval of unlimited spending at the toy store. She is polite but cool to Lorraine, who makes clear the link between the tarnished magic of the old times and the world of childhood. " 'There,' " she says, " 'That's what I want to do . . . I want to see some clowns and acrobats and jugglers.' "

The acrobats, the imagery of the vaudeville, remind us, finally, that this is a story of suspension between two worlds. Charlie's dream of his wife concludes with this vision: "she was in a swing in a white dress, and swinging faster all the time, so that at the end he could not hear clearly all that she said." Fitzgerald continues this image in the climactic scene when the drunken Lorraine and Dunc invade the Peters' apartment. After they leave, Lincoln is "still swinging Honoria back and forth like a pendulum from side to side." Up to this point Charlie has virtually convinced even Marion that his feet are "planted on the earth now," but actually, as we have seen, he is caught between two worlds. Fitzgerald has arranged their representatives with a symmetry reminiscent of James. On the one hand is the pale blonde, Lorraine, with her escort Duncan Shaeffer; on the other, Marion, clothed in a "black dress that just faintly suggested mourning," with her husband, Lincoln, who appropriately works in a bank. Charlie is indebted to both of the women: to Marion for taking care of Honoria; to Lorraine, as she unpleasantly reminds him, for playing the game. " 'I remember once,' " she says, " 'when you hammered on my door at four A.M. I was enough of a good sport to give you a drink.' "

Fitzgerald does not need to force the association, for the reader, along with Marion, silently balances the equation: Lorraine let him in at four A.M.; he locked his wife out in the snowstorm.

And so here is Charlie at the end, back at the Ritz Bar, the place where his old friend Claude Fessenden had run up a bill of thirty thousand francs, until Paul finally told him he "had to pay." Half-heartedly thinking he will send Honoria some things, lots of things, tomorrow, asking the waiter how much he owes him, Charlie is left with his remembrances of time spent and his determination to "come back some day; they couldn't make him pay forever." But he knows and we know that they can and he will. The prodigal has returned, but his effort to "conciliate something," to redress the balance, has failed, and he remains an exile.

ARTHUR MIZENER

"Tender Is the Night"

F. Scott Fitzgerald was the first of the gifted American novelists of the 1920's to become famous; he had a Byronic, overnight success with his first novel, *This Side of Paradise*, which was published in the first year of the decade. It was a brash, immature novel that Fitzgerald's lifelong friend Edmund Wilson called "one of the most illiterate books of any merit ever published." Later in his life Fitzgerald himself said of it, with the queer impersonality he could always give his considered judgments of himself, "A lot of people thought it was a fake, and perhaps it was, and a lot of others thought it was a lie, which it was not."

The essential quality of Fitzgerald's insight is shown by that comment. Looked at objectively, *This Side of Paradise* was in many ways a fake; it pretended to all sorts of knowledge and experience of the world its author did not in fact have. But it was not a lie; it expressed with accuracy and honesty its author's inner vision of himself and his experience, however false to literal fact that vision might be at certain points. Fitzgerald's reality was always that inner vision, but he had a deep respect for the outer reality of the world because it was the only place where his inward vision could be fulfilled, could be made actual. The tension between his inescapable commitment to the inner reality of his imagination and his necessary respect for the outer reality of the world is what gives his fiction its peculiar charm and is the source of his ability to surround a convincing representation of the actual world with an air of enchantment that makes the most ordinary occasions haunting.

The success of *This Side of Paradise* did not do Fitzgerald any good. It gave him the fame and money to plunge into the gay whirl of New York parties that in postwar America somehow seemed to be a more significant life than the provincial one pre-war America had lived. Fitzgerald and his beautiful wife, Zelda, rode through New York on the tops of taxis, jumped fully clothed into the Pulitzer Fountain in front of the Plaza, and quickly became leaders among the bright spirits of postwar New York. It was all harmless enough in itself, but it left very little time for serious writing, particularly for a man to whom alcohol was very damaging, almost a poison.

Yet all the time Fitzgerald was busy being the handsome hero of the Younger Generation, there was a serious writer inside him struggling to get out. That serious writer got control for a moment when he wrote *The Great Gatsby* (1924). But then the Fitzgeralds fell back into the life of parties—now mostly in Paris and on the Riviera—that gradually became for them a more and more desperate and self-destructive effort to be happy. It ended in 1930, when Zelda became a serious schizophrene and Fitzgerald, pulled up short by this disaster, found himself an alcoholic. He spent the rest of his brief life—he died in 1940, shortly after his forty-fourth birthday—fighting a grim battle to save Zelda, to cure his own alcoholism, and to fulfill his promise as a writer. "I have been a poor caretaker of everything I possessed," he said at this time, "even of my talent." He lost Zelda—she never grew better—and he was only partly successful in his fight against alcoholism. But, sick and discouraged though he was, he managed before he died to write *Tender Is the Night*, published in 1934, and a marvelous fragment of another novel called *The Last Tycoon*.

Tender Is the Night has certain defects traceable to the conditions in which it was written. As Fitzgerald himself said of it with his remarkable honesty, "If a mind is slowed up ever so little, it lives in the individual parts of a book rather than in a book as a whole; memory is dulled. I would give anything if I hadn't had to write Part III of 'Tender Is the Night' entirely on stimulant." Despite these defects, *Tender Is the Night* is the most mature and moving book Fitzgerald ever wrote.

It is not, however, an easy book to understand. Its difficulty is at least partly due to the odd discrepancy in it between the almost frivolous insignificance—by conventional standards anyhow—of the hero's life and the importance Fitzgerald obviously means us to attach to it. This difficulty in *Tender Is the Night* is only a particular instance of the general problem created in American fiction by the subjective novel as distinguished from the objective novel of social history such as Dos Passos wrote.

Fitzgerald and Dos Passos were friends, but it is evident that neither could understand what the other was up to. In 1933, the year before Fitzgerald completed *Tender Is the Night*, he wrote a mutual friend, "Dos was here, & we had a nice evening—we never quite understand each other & perhaps that's the best basis for an enduring friendship." As if to prove how right Fitzgerald was, Dos Passos wrote him, when he published the revealing essays called "The Crack-Up" that describe the personal experience underlying *Tender Is the Night*, "I've been wanting to see you, naturally, to argue about your *Esquire* articles—Christ, man, how do you find time in the middle of the general conflagration to worry about all that stuff? . . . most of the time the course of world events seem so frightful that I feel absolutely paralysed." Clearly, Dos Passos is baffled by Fitzgerald's preoccupation "with all that stuff" about the meaning of his personal experience. Fitzgerald was equally baffled by Dos Passos' obsession with "the course of world events."

There was of course a subjective novelist somewhere in Dos Passos, but Dos Passos relegated this novelist to the Camera Eye passages of *U.S.A.* and he affects the narrative only indirectly. There was also a man with a considerable sense of history in Fitzgerald: as Malcolm Cowley once put it, Fitzgerald lived in a room full of clocks and calendars. But Fitzgerald's knowledge of history, astonishing as his memory for it was, gets into his novels almost entirely as metaphors for the life of his consciousness, for the quality of his private experience. His summary of the year 1927—the year in which the slow decline of Dick Diver, the hero of *Tender Is the Night*, becomes clearly evident—is characteristic:

> By 1927 a wide-spread neurosis began to be evident, faintly signalled, like a nervous beating of the feet, by the popularity of cross-word puzzles. I remember a fellow expatriate opening a letter from a mutual friend of ours, urging him to come home and be revitalized by the hardy, bracing qualities of the native soil. It was a strong letter and it affected us both deeply, until we noticed that it was headed from a nerve sanitarium in Pennsylvania.

Fitzgerald tended to notice only those events that had this kind of meaning for him, that came to life for him as images of his personal feelings. The advantage of knowing the world in this way is that anything you notice at all takes on the vividness of your strongest private emotions. But because Fitzgerald knew the world this way, he had little capacity for sharing the common, public understanding of it. For readers to whom a novel is a dramatic representation of the world as that understanding knows it, Fitzgerald often appears to be treating with ridiculous seriousness characters and situations that "everyone knows" are insignificant.

One can frequently see in Fitzgerald's actual life, where conventional judgments are more important—or at least more difficult to ignore—how little such judgments really counted for him. All his life, for instance, he remembered bitterly his failure to achieve social success as an undergraduate at Princeton. The conventional judgment is that undergraduate social life is trivial, but Fitzgerald's failure at Princeton—whatever common sense may say of its circumstances—involved his deepest private feelings. Princeton was his first independent experience of the world, and he threw himself into realizing his ambitions there exactly as if Princeton had been the great world itself. For him the common judgment of Princeton's unimportance did not count; what counted was what he felt. He came very close to succeeding at Princeton, except that he neglected what was to him the trifling business of passing his courses, which seemed to him a great bore, and just as he was about to come into his kingdom as a big man on campus, he was forced to leave the university.

He tried for the rest of his life to tell himself that society always has this power to enforce its own values and that it was foolish of him to ignore the university's academic requirements simply because they were insignificant to him. But he never could really believe it, and gradually this experience at Princeton became for him—despite the objective insignificance of its occasion—one of his two or three major images for the unjust suffering that is the essence of human defeat.

This typical episode makes it evident that Fitzgerald, subjective novelist though he was, was not the kind of man who could commit himself wholly to the life of inner reality or be content as a novelist "with a very slight embroidery of outward manners, the faintest possible counterfeit of real life." In his life Fitzgerald strove to achieve in the actual world the ideal life he could so vividly imagine, and he was intent as a writer on producing the most lively possible counterfeit of real life.

But if this episode shows us that both in his life and his work he was determined to live in the actual world, as he often did quite dazzlingly, it also shows us that for him the meaning and value of the world were something that was determined by his private feelings, which operated independently of the established, conventional understanding of the world, not because he was consciously defying that understanding—his desire to realize the good life as he conceived it made him struggle to conform—but because the subjective life of his imagination was so intense, so overwhelmingly real for him, that even his efforts to conform to conventional ideas transformed them into something personal and queer.

Fitzgerald's first mature novel, *The Great Gatsby*, for example, is a brilliant picture of Long Island society in the 1920's. But that is only one aspect of it, the image Fitzgerald creates for a feeling too complex to be expressed in any other way. *The Great Gatsby* is a fable, marked at every important point by the folklore qualities of fables and charged with meaning by a style that is, despite the sharpness of its realistic detail, alive with poetic force. At the crisis of the story, the heroine, Daisy Buchanan, unintentionally reveals to her husband by the unguarded tone of her beautifully expressive voice that she loves Gatsby. The narrator says anxiously to Gatsby, "She's got an indiscreet voice. It's full of—" and when he hesitates Gatsby says suddenly, "Her voice is full of money." And the narrator thinks, "That was it. I'd never understood before. It was full of money—that was the inexhaustible charm that rose and fell on it, the jingle of it, the cymbals's song of it . . . High in a white palace the king's daughter, the golden girl. . . ."

This passage is resonant with an irony that echoes back and forth between the gross actual fact of money jingling in the pocket and the romance of beauty adorned, of the golden girl. On the surface Daisy Buchanan is a convincing, historically accurate portrait of the charming and irresponsible upper-class girl of the American twenties. But she is also the princess, high in a white palace, for whom the disregarded younger son longs hopelessly, until the great moment when he astonishes everyone by performing the impossible feat that wins her hand.

One of the things that has certainly helped make *Tender Is the Night* less popular than *The Great Gatsby* of ten years earlier is that the image it uses, its story, is not, as social history, so significant as Gatsby's. Its story describes the life of well-to-do American expatriates on the Riviera during the 1920's, and such people are usually thought to be about as insignificant as Princeton undergraduates. They were especially thought to be so when the novel was published in 1934 at the depth of the Great Depression, and the idea that Fitzgerald was naively impressed by rich people became widely accepted. This is one of those foolish ideas put about by people who cannot read. Fitzgerald was no more a mere worshiper of rich people than Henry James was a snob. He was a man who dreamed of actually living the good life men can imagine. He had, as did Jay Gatsby, "a heightened sensitivity to the promises of life," and he had the elementary common sense to see that in real life the rich have an opportunity to live the good life that the rest of us do not.

One consequence of his seeing they do was that he felt the deepest scorn—what he called "the smouldering hatred of the peasant"—for rich people who did not take full advantage of the opportunity their wealth gave them. About rich people of this kind *Tender Is the Night* is devastating. Another consequence of it was his fascination with the intelligent and sensitive among the rich, like Dick Diver, who could see that opportunity. With his Irish sense of the absurd aspect of what he believed most deeply, Fitzgerald could make fun of this ideal as he had formulated it for himself, what he called "the Goethe-Byron-Shaw idea, with an opulent American touch—a sort of combination of Topham Beauclerk, St. Francis of Assisi, and J. P. Morgan"; and in the end he came to feel that the unimaginative brutality and organized chaos of the life of the rich always defeated men like Dick Diver. In Dick's best moment, *Tender Is the Night* shows us how beautiful the realized ideal life is; but in the end it shows us that people with the sensitivity and imagination to conceive that life cannot survive among the rich.

Tender Is the Night begins with the arrival of a young movie star named Rosemary Hoyt at Cap d'Antibes on the Riviera. When Rosemary goes down to the beach she finds herself between two groups of expatriates. The first is an incoherent mixture. There is "Mama" Abrams, "one of those elderly 'good sports' preserved by an imperviousness to experience and a good digestion into another generation." There is a writer named Albert McKisco who, according to his wife, Violet, is at work on a novel "on the idea of Ulysses. Only instead of taking twenty-four hours [he] takes a hundred years. He takes a decayed old French aristocrat and puts him in contrast with the mechanical age. . . ." There is a waspishly witty young man named Royal Dumphry and his companion, Luis Campion, who keeps admonishing Mr. Dumphry not to "be too ghastly for words." The other group consists of Dick Diver and his wife, Nicole, their friends Abe and Mary North, and a young Frenchman named Tommy Barban.

Rosemary is instinctively attracted to the second group but she is quickly picked up by the first group, who cannot wait to tell her they recognize her from her film. It is not a very happy group. For one thing, it is clearly jealous of the second group. "If you want to enjoy yourself here," Mrs. McKisco says, "the thing is to get to know some real French families. What do these people get out of it? They just stick around with each other in little cliques. Of course we had letters of introduction and met all the best French artists and writers in Paris." For another thing, Mr. McKisco is being difficult, as if, in spite of his extensive collection of secondhand attitudes from the best reviews, he does not quite know who he is or where he is going. When his wife makes a harmless joke, he bursts out irritably, "For God's sake, Violet, drop the subject! Get a new joke, for God's sake!" and when she leans over to Mrs. Abrams and says apologetically, "He's nervous," McKisco barks, "I'm not nervous. It just happens I'm not nervous at all."

It is the poverty of ideas and the mediocrity of imagination in these people, the shapelessness of their natures, that depresses and discomforts Rosemary and makes her dislike them. It is her glimpses of the opposite qualities in the second group that attracts her. What Rosemary sees in Dick Diver is his consideration, his grace, his sensitivity to others, and—behind them all—his intense vitality. No wonder she falls in love with him.

At this point Fitzgerald goes back to trace Dick's history. He is the son of a gentle, impoverished clergyman in Buffalo, from whom he had inherited his old-fashioned, formal manners and what Fitzgerald calls " 'good instincts,' honor, courtesy, courage." He has gone to Yale, been a Rhodes Scholar, and been trained as a psychiatrist at Johns Hopkins, in Vienna, and in Zurich. After the war, he returns to Zurich, where he meets again a young mental patient named Nicole Warren, who has clung to their slight relation all through the war and her slow recovery from an illness that is not congenital but has been brought on by her father's seducing her.

Dick falls in love with Nicole, and in spite of his professional knowledge that she may be a lifelong mental problem, despite the unconscious arrogance with which the Warrens make it clear they are buying a doctor to take care of Nicole, he marries her. This act reveals the defect of uncontrollable generosity in Dick's character. "He wanted," Fitzgerald says, "to be good, he wanted to be kind, he wanted to be brave and wise . . . ; [and] he wanted to be loved, too. . . ." He had an "extraordinary virtuosity with people . . . the power of arousing a fascinated and uncritical love." This power was a kind of imaginative unselfishness; "it was themselves he gave back to [people]," as Fitzgerald says, "blurred by the compromise of how many years." This power he could not resist exercising, not merely to give Nicole back her self but to make everyone he came close to feel once more the self he had been at his best.

Dick knows from the start that in taking up his life with Nicole among the Warrens and their kind he is making the task he has set himself as difficult as possible, but with his youthful vitality intact, that seems to him only to make it more challenging and interesting. For five years he meets that challenge effortlessly. Then, at first imperceptibly, his life begins to slip from his control. Something within him, some essential vitality, is beginning to decline, and he slowly realizes that he has exhausted the source of energy for the superb self-discipline that makes it possible for him to perform for others what he calls his "trick of the heart."

This change occurs very deep in his nature. Fitzgerald is careful to prevent the reader from thinking it is some change controllable by the will, some drift into dissipation or the idleness of the rich. Dick does begin to drift in these ways, but that is only a symptom of his trouble, a desperate search for something to fill the time and stave off boredom after the meaning and purpose have gone out of his life. What destroys Dick is something far more obscure and difficult to grasp, some spiritual malaise that is anterior to any rational cause and is—as has become much plainer since Fitzgerald noticed it—as widespread among sensitive people in our time as was accidie in the middle ages or melancholia, the "Elizabethan malady," in Shakespeare's. Dick Diver is, as Fitzgerald put it in one of his notes for the book, not simply an *homme manqué*, but an *homme épuisé*. He is in a state of terrible spiritual ennui that is without visible cause and yet makes men like him—talented, attractive, successful—feel quite literally that *all* the uses of the world are weary, stale, flat, and unprofitable. "I did not manage, I think in retrospect," Fitzgerald once said of Dick Diver, "to give Dick the cohesion I aimed at. . . . I wonder what the hell the first actor who played Hamlet thought of the part? I can hear him say, 'The guy's a nut, isn't he?' (We can always find great consolation in Shakespeare)."

Perhaps he did not manage to give Dick all the cohesion he might have, but the real difficulty is that the source of Dick's disaster is indescribable. It can be shown and felt, but it can no more be analyzed than Hamlet's disaster can. As a result the main action of *Tender Is the Night* is, for all its haunting emotional appeal, as puzzling and unparaphrasable as is the famous passage from Keats's *Ode to a Nightingale* from which its title comes.

What Fitzgerald can—and does—do is to create for the reader a group of characters who, as dramatic parallels or contrasts with Dick, show what he is. The first of these we learn all about is Abe North, a musician who, after a brilliant start, has done nothing for the last seven years except drink. When Mary North says, "I used to think until you're eighteen nothing matters," he says, "That's right. And afterwards it's the same way." And when Nicole, frightened at what he is doing to himself and irritated by his lack of any visible reasons for doing it, says to him, "I can't see why you've given up on everything," he can only say, "I suppose I got bored; and then it was such a long way to go back in order to get anywhere." Dick has understood from the beginning what has happened to Abe, even though he will not know what it feels like until later. "Smart men," he has said of Abe, "play close to the line because they have to—some of them can't stand it, so they quit." Thus, at the very start of the novel, Abe North has reached the point Dick will reach at its end.

About halfway through the novel, just as Dick is beginning his own desperate battle with the impulse to quit, he hears—in fact, he overhears, as a piece of idle, feelingless gossip—that Abe has been beaten up in a New York speakeasy and crawled to the Racket Club to die—or was it the Harvard Club? The gossips' grumbling quarrel over where it was Abe died fades out around Dick as he tries to face the meaning of Abe's death, a death more shocking—more grubby and humiliating as well as more terrifying to him—than anything he had dreamed of.

There is also Tommy Barban, a sophisticated and worldly barbarian of great charm, who stands for everything Dick Diver most disapproves of. The carefully ordered life that Dick first constructed for Nicole and himself because it was necessary to Nicole's health has, as Nicole's need for it has slowly decreased, been gradually transformed to another purpose, until it has became an alert but elaborate, almost ritualized ordering of the pleasures of a highly cultivated existence. The whole business irritates Tommy, partly because it is all strictly under Dick's control and holds Nicole, with whom Tommy has been in love for years, a prisoner, but partly too because it represents in itself a way of life that offends him deeply. When he is about to leave the Riviera, Rosemary Hoyt asks him if he is going home. "Home?" he says, "I have no home. I am going to a war," and when Rosemary asks him what war, he says, "What war? Any war. I haven't seen a paper lately but I suppose there's a war—there always is." A little shocked by this, Rosemary asks him if he doesn't care at all about what he may find himself fighting for, and he says, "Not at all—so long as I'm well treated. When I'm in a rut I come to see the Divers, because I know that in a few weeks I'll want to go to war."

The novel's central group of characters consists of Dick, Nicole, Rosemary, and these two. It is surrounded by a larger group of minor characters, each of whom shows us an aspect of the world Dick Diver lives in. There is Lady Caroline Sibley-Biers, the latest wild woman from London, petulant and stupid, whose idea of amusement is to dress up as a French sailor and pick up a girl in Antibes. There is Baby Warren, Nicole's sister, "a tall fine-looking woman deeply engaged in being thirty" who "was alien from touch" and for whom "such lingering touches as kisses and embraces slipped directly through the flesh into the forefront of her consciousness." She is supremely confident that the most dehumanized routines of British social life are the ideal existence and that her series of engagements to socially eligible Englishmen, which even she no longer really expects will come to anything, constitutes a full life. There is Albert McKisco, the confused but proud possessor of a host of secondhand ideas that safely insulate him from experience. Such characters define for us the chic grossness, the neurotic orderliness, the lifeless intellectuality of the world Dick Diver lives in. They are not what they are because they are rich, though, being rich, they are able to be what they are with a freedom and completeness that ordinary people cannot. Still, they are not what they are merely because they are rich; they are so because the world is.

In this world Dick Diver's need to reach out to people, to galvanize them into life by reminding them of the selves they originally were, is like a wound, a "lesion of vitality" as Fitzgerald calls it, from which his spiritual energy slowly drips away until there is nothing left. At the beginning of the novel, "one June morning in 1925" when Rosemary meets Dick, the first faint signs of the loss have begun to show. He is still able to produce for people such enchanted moments as the one on the beach that Rosemary has watched with delight, when he holds a whole group of people enthralled, not by what he does—what he does is almost nothing—but by the quality of his performance, the delicate sense of the tone and feeling of occasion and audience by which he can make a small group of people feel they are alone with each other in the dark universe, in some magically protected place where they can be their best selves. He performs this trick of the heart once again for Rosemary when she goes to dinner with the Divers just after she has met them. At the climax of that dinner, the table seemed for a moment "to have risen a little toward the sky like a mechanical dancing platform" and

> the two Divers began suddenly to warm and glow and expand, as if to make up to their guests, already so subtly assured of their importance, so flattered with politeness, for anything they might still miss from that country well left behind. Just for a moment they seemed to speak to every one at the table, singly and together, assuring them of their friendliness, their affection. And for a moment the faces turned up toward them were like the faces of poor children at a Christmas tree.

But now, each such moment is followed for Dick by a spell of deep melancholy in which he looks "back with awe at the carnival of affection he had given, as a general might gaze at a massacre he had ordered to satisfy an impersonal blood lust." Rosemary catches a glimpse of that melancholy, without recognizing it, her very first morning on the beach when, after all the others have gone, Dick stops to tell her she must not get too sunburned and she says with young cheerfulness, "Do you know what time it is?" and Dick says, "It's about half-past one."

They faced the seascape together momentarily.
"It's not a bad time," said Dick Diver. "It's not one of the worst times of the day."

These periods of melancholy are one consequence of his decreasing vitality; another is his inability to maintain the self-discipline he has heretofore exercised almost unconsciously because it is only by not yielding to his momentary impulses that he can fulfill his central need to make the world over for others. The first failure of this discipline—and the major one—is allowing himself to fall in love with Rosemary. Though he cannot control that impulse, he knows that it "marked a turning point in his life—it was out of line with everything that had preceded it—even out of line with what effect he might hope to produce on Rosemary." Then he finds himself drinking just a little too much in a carefully controlled way—"an ounce of gin with twice as much water" at carefully spaced intervals. The book on psychiatry he has been working on for years begins to seem to him stale and unimportant and his work at the clinic tiresome. "Not without desperation he had long felt the ethics of his profession dissolving into a lifeless mass." When Nicole has a third serious breakdown, the long months of "restating the universe for her" leave him exhausted in a way he has never known before.

He goes off alone to try to rest and get himself together and discovers to his horror that he cannot stop yielding to every vagrant impulse of his nature—to charm a pretty girl, to blurt out without regard for his listeners the bitterness in his heart. He sees more clearly than anyone what is happening to him, but since it is happening somewhere below the level of reason, beyond the control of his will, he can only watch helplessly. "He had lost himself—he could not tell the hour when, or the week, the month, or the year. . . . Between the time he found Nicole flowering under a stone on the Zurichsee and the moment of his meeting with Rosemary the spear had been blunted."

The first faint signs of this loss of self had appeared at that first meeting with Rosemary Hoyt on the beach at Antibes. When, five years later, he and Rosemary meet again on the same beach, now crowded with dull, fashionable people, he says to her, "Did you hear I'd gone into a process of deterioration? . . . It's true. The change came a long way back—but at first it didn't show. The manner remains intact after the morale cracks." By a desperate effort he can still force himself at moments to exercise that manner, but these moments come more and more rarely and require him to be drunker and drunker, a condition in which he is as likely to assert the black despair in his heart in some outburst of incoherent violence, as he does when he picks a fight in Rome with a detective and is beaten up and thrown in jail, or when at Antibes he gets into a drunken, confused argument with Lady Caroline Sibley-Biers and even she is able to make him look foolish. These scenes are almost intolerably moving, for Fitzgerald's lifelong habit of giving events the value they have for the person who suffers them rather than their conventional public value makes us feel these trivial misfortunes as what they are, the loose ends of life, as Zelda once said, with which men hang themselves.

Finally Dick accepts the exhaustion of his vitality and its consequences, his inability to control himself to any purpose, his inability to love and be loved by others. He sets himself to cut his losses—his responsibilities for Nicole and the children and his friends—and to bury his dead—himself. The task is made simpler by the fact that Nicole has now recovered completely. Though she still depends on Dick, her dependence is now only old habit, not necessity. As she has recovered she has become more and more the superficially orderly, inwardly anarchic barbarian that has always been her true Warren self. As such, she turns instinctively away from Dick and toward Tommy Barban. Dick therefore sets himself to break her dependence on him and to push her toward Tommy. At the last moment he deliberately provokes a quarrel with her and then watches silently while she struggles to deny him and assert her independence. When she succeeds, "Dick waited until she was out of sight. Then he leaned his head forward on the parapet. The case was finished. Doctor Diver was at liberty."

Dick stays at Antibes just long enough to make sure Nicole is safe in Tommy's hands and then leaves for America, taking with him nothing, least of all himself.

> Nicole kept in touch with Dick after her marriage [to Tommy]. . . . [He] opened an office in Buffalo, but evidently without success. Nicole did not find what the trouble was, but she heard a few months later that he was in a little town named Batavia, New York, practicing general medicine, and later that he was in Lockport, doing the same thing. . . . He was considered to have fine manners and once made a good speech at a public health meeting on the subject of drugs; but he became entangled with a girl who worked in a grocery store, and he was involved in a law suit about some medical question; so he left Lockport. After that he didn't ask for the children to be sent to America and didn't answer when Nicole wrote asking him if he needed money. . . . His latest note was post-marked from Hornell, New York, which is some distance from Geneva and a small town; in any case he is certainly in that section of the country, in one town or another.

JAMES GINDIN

Gods and Fathers in F. Scott Fitzgerald's Novels

Fitzgerald's fiction always, in one form or another, reveals a strong element of moral judgment against which the heroes can be seen. The Fitzgerald hero is charming, intelligent, impressed by the glitter of a sparkling new world, and sensitive, a special person in the sense that the romantic hero is always someone particularly sensitive, intelligent, and vulnerable. But against the romantic hero Fitzgerald places a moral judgment, a stern rebuke, functioning either within the character or from the outside, which inevitably limits the freedom and possibility of the romantic hero. The romantic hero would be God, would dominate through his own individual capacity, but the moral judgment demonstrates that no man, no matter how special in secular terms, can play God. The hero is also, simultaneously, the archetypal contemporary American, the confident and eager representative of his country trying his talents against an older and more universal moral order.

In Fitzgerald's earliest novel, *This Side of Paradise* (1920), the moral framework is not fully developed, and the romantic hero's sin never reaches proportions sufficient to earn inevitable damnation. The next novel, *The Beautiful and Damned* (1922), however, articulates the doom of the special creature, and in *The Great Gatsby* (1925), Fitzgerald echoes the paradox implicit in the doctrine of original sin, the concept of man inevitably trapped by the difference between what he would desperately like to be and what he is. In subsequent novels, *Tender Is the Night*

From *Modern Language Quarterly*, vol. 30, (1969).

(1934) and the unfinished *The Last Tycoon* (1941), the romantic hero is also doomed, but the moral framework, the judgment that makes the usurping hero's damnation inevitable, is more equivocal, more questionable, less confidently a statement about man's destiny. God weakens in Fitzgerald's last two novels, and although the hero, the man who would be God, never achieves his vision of experience, the forces that prevent him are more accidental and capricious, less articulately a moral order. The hero sometimes seems doomed by the lingering residue of firm moral commitment.

Most of *This Side of Paradise* depicts the trivial glitter of Amory Blaine's social conquests and the student-like notebook of his philosophical and literary observations. Yet Amory Blaine is one of Fitzgerald's special creatures, established less by anything he does than by the quality of his introspection and by the assurances the author gives of Amory's special talents and sensitivity. Like many romantic heroes, Fitzgerald's heroes are distinguished within themselves and, until the later novels, need not do anything to prove their special capacity. Although Amory spends most of his time at parties and in random intellectual speculation, he is conscious of the morality of his thought and actions. At times, he is fiercely puritanical, disdaining the juvenile country-club vamps at the very moment he is attracted to them. As he goes through Princeton and the army in World War I, he continues to lament the moral vacuum of his wild weekends and to question the unapologetic materialism of the society he sees around him. Amory is also a patriot, looking for an American literature, an American destiny, a unique and valuable national synthesis of experience.

Apart from the moralism and nationalism, however, Amory is explained most frequently as the Keatsian romantic hero strung between inevitably abstract polarities. Not as profound as the polarity involved in the doctrine of original sin, Amory's polarity is that of the "cynical idealist," a paradox that both the author and Amory himself use frequently to explain the man always aware of two different sides of his own nature. Amory's ideal of nobility and magnanimity is undercut by shallow social snobbery; his interest in rising materially in the world batters his honest sympathy and concern for others; his pride in his exterior charm fights his intellectual self-examination. His language often expresses his doubleness: his charm at parties is "a spiritual tax levied"; he fears his need for money may cause him to "commit moral suicide"; he tells one of his girl friends that "selfish people are in a way terribly capable of great loves." Fitzgerald's point of view parallels Amory's two-sidedness, for the author often switches scenes and interjects comments to inflate, then explode, the romantic bubble. One chapter ends with Amory and a young girl moving together toward a cinematic kiss; the next chapter begins with her "Ouch!" and her continued petulance because his shirt stud had touched her neck. The paradoxes from the nineties, including the epigraph from Oscar Wilde's work, are Fitzgerald's as well as Amory's, the language and structure that give the novel its dated smartness.

Although the doubleness of the "cynical idealist," the paradoxical characterization of the romantic hero, provides the novel with whatever unity it possesses, other elements important for Fitzgerald's later fiction appear. The novel contains many sharp observations on how social barriers operate between people, as well as a careful development of the complexities of combined close friendship and competition in the relationship between Amory and Alec. In addition, Amory acknowledges his sense of morality and connects it to established religion. Although he sometimes doubts and blasphemes, he sharply rebukes an unconventional girl friend who is completely atheistic, invariably centers his self-examination on religious principles, and makes his intellectual confessions to Monsignor Darcy.

Wise and sophisticated, Monsignor Darcy serves as Amory's surrogate father, guiding Amory's reading, debating his ideas, maintaining frequent connection with him through letters and visits. He regards Amory as part of his "family," his spiritual descendant. Since Amory's real father is shadowy and irrelevant (having abrogated all except financial responsibilities toward him) and Amory has been brought up by his eccentric, cosmopolitan, hypochondriacal mother (who keeps losing and regaining her faith in the Roman Catholic church because she enjoys being converted), the turn toward the surrogate is necessary for the transmission of any moral and spiritual ideas. Amory never loses his respect and affection for the older man; when he learns of Monsignor Darcy's death, he recognizes that he must become a man, must perpetuate, in his own terms, the humanity, spirituality, and wisdom of the Monsignor. The transmitted value has some effect. At the end of the novel, when Amory feels that he has finally found himself, Fitzgerald explains:

> His mind turned a corner suddenly and he found himself thinking of the Catholic Church. The idea was strong in him that there was a certain intrinsic lack in those to whom orthodox religion was necessary, and religion to Amory meant the Church of Rome. Quite conceivably it was an empty ritual but it was seemingly the only assimilative, traditionary bulwark against the decay of morals. Until the great mobs could be educated into a moral sense some one must cry: "Thou shalt not!" Yet

> any acceptance was, for the present, impossible. . . . He wanted to keep the tree without ornaments, realize fully the direction and momentum of this new start.

Like Amory, Fitzgerald is keeping his moralism in reserve, just barely below the surface.

As a central force in Fitzgerald's fiction, the moralism emerged soon thereafter. One of the most brilliant early stories, "May Day" (published in *Tales of the Jazz Age* in 1922), chronicles the waste and emptiness of selfish party-going and dissipation, contrasting this with the humane concern for all the inequities and injustices in American society. *The Beautiful and Damned* is also, in many ways, a moral parable. At the beginning of the novel, the author inserts a Faustian dialogue between "Beauty" and "The Voice," in which "The Voice" promises "Beauty" fifteen years of triumph as "a ragtime kid, a flapper, a jazz-baby, and a baby vamp" in the new and opulent America, in return for which "Beauty" will inevitably be spoiled and tarnished by vulgarity. The dialogue serves as the model for the novel: Anthony and Gloria Patch, the special people, the beautiful couple of the new and exciting America, spoil and squander themselves, are damned as finally as if they had sold their souls to the devil. In part, they tarnish their own beauty. Gloria is selfish and extravagant, afraid to spoil her figure by having a child, reckless, imperious, and narcissistic. Anthony, externally gracious and intelligent, superficially the perfect product of upper-class America, is centrally weak. He drifts, never works despite his many resolutions, and can exert his will only when he is drunk, making petulant scenes in public.

Fitzgerald's judgment of Anthony and Gloria springs from a puritanical perspective: indolence breeds decay, and hard work would save a man; behaving badly in public, the loss of public composure no matter what the circumstances, is the surest sign of hollowness and dissolution. In addition, Fitzgerald views his characters as originally "clean," spiritually antiseptic, not the "clean like polished pans," but the "blowy clean" connected with "streams and wind." As the novel progresses, as indolence, parties, and selfishness take their inevitable toll, the characters, particularly Gloria, become sullied and unclean, the beauty is tarnished. This is not caused by any particular act—Gloria is never unfaithful to Anthony—but there remains an aura, a judgment that indicates both the decay of Gloria's freshness and beauty and the puritanical severity of Fitzgerald's perspective. The antiseptic sense of virtue seems to require a spiritual virginity. Once the woman is no longer the idol, remote and virginal, she introduces sin into the world. Had Anthony remained single, he might have been able to save himself, to redeem his transgressions by hard work and abstinence. But married—he first met Gloria at a time when he was feeling despondent about himself and then substituted living through sexual attraction for working through despondency—Anthony has no chance for salvation; he is tied to the devil's agent.

Anthony's moral hollowness is also caused by the fact that he has no father, no law-giver, no agent to transmit a usable moral framework. His father, an ineffectual dandy of the nineties, had died when Anthony was very young, and the boy had been raised by his grandfather. In *The Beautiful and Damned*, the father-surrogate is too distant and too unconcerned to provide an acceptable substitute for a real father. Adam Patch, Anthony's grandfather, is a rigorous and strong old puritan who amasses a fortune and then decides to "consecrate the remainder of his life to the moral regeneration of the world." He educates Anthony carefully and expensively, but then expects him to engage in useful, ennobling work and to support puritanical causes like prohibition. In the climactic scene of the novel, the staged drama that marks the inevitability of Anthony's doom, his grandfather visits him unannounced to discover a particularly wild and dissolute party in progress. The judgment against Anthony, like his grandfather's withdrawal of financial support, is final and unyielding. Although severe and bitter from Anthony's point of view, his grandfather is highly respected by others, especially by those who see him only from a remote and public distance, like Bloeckman, the alien within the society, who calls old Adam Patch "a fine example of an American." The example, removed and hardened by an extra generation, cannot help Anthony.

Other surrogates in the novel are no more successful. Like Amory Blaine, Anthony is both cynic and idealist. But in this novel the possibilities are extrapolated into polar characters, Anthony's friends, the idealist Dick Caramel and the cynic Maury Noble (the names themselves are ironic tags), who function as surrogates, constantly providing instructions and propounding their solutions to the dilemmas that face Anthony. The surrogates provide no help, for the cynic and the idealist cannot be reconciled. Each polar extreme goes in its own direction: Dick Caramel becomes foolish, soft-headed, unconsciously corrupt; Maury Noble becomes embittered and completely materialistic. When Anthony tries to combine the two, he does nothing; finally, cut off from any father figure, any morality, he lapses into madness.

As they live out their doom, without morality, Anthony and Gloria are forced to feed more completely on each other, to exist only in terms of the relationship that is an inadequate substitute for a sense of human purpose. Their concentration on their relationship is the initial symptom of their decline; but Fitzgerald also probes the relationship itself with insight: the strong sexual attraction, the disastrous mixture of her nervous recklessness and his cowardice, the complete lack of self-knowledge at the beginning, the spoiled childishness of both, yet the moments of fierce loyalty to the marriage. The relationship develops with an ironic reversal of the initial balance. At the beginning of the marriage, Gloria is willing to abandon people or relationships the moment she no longer feels attracted to them, just as she has no interest in antiques or traditions, whereas Anthony says he is more committed to his choice and marriage, just as he is more sentimental about history and period furniture. Yet, finally, it is Anthony who is unfaithful and petulant, while Gloria tries to keep the marriage together just because it is a marriage. Gloria, the spoiled beauty who had married for "safety," needs to assume the dominant role and is capable of staking everything on their staying together. Anthony, having always evaded the hollowness at his center, increasingly lacks the capacity to deal with any relationship and is driven to literal madness when his wartime mistress later demands that her love be returned. A woman, if not governed by the dictates of a moral framework, is invariably the agent of destruction.

Fitzgerald's interest in character itself, however, keeps obtruding into the structure of using character to illustrate the parable of doom. Another example is Bloeckman, the Jew, the character who represents what in America is alien to the central moral tradition. Originally uncouth, naïve, commercial, and too desperate in his attempt to get every social custom right, Bloeckman develops dignity as the novel progresses; he is also the only person willing to help Anthony when all his supposed friends have turned against him. In view of Anthony's anti-Semitism, the use of Bloeckman demonstrates the hollowness of Anthony, who would hold rigidly to superficial social standards while at the same time ignoring moral standards completely; but for Fitzgerald the rise of Bloeckman is also, in part, a story of character, of humanity, apart from any moral framework. Yet Bloeckman is not at the center of the novel, nor, despite all its fascination, is the alternating humanity in the relationship between Anthony and Gloria; rather, the center is the moral parable, the dissolution of the potentially special couple.

The fact that Gloria and Anthony spend so much time within their relationship, within themselves, reflects their hollowness and eventual doom. But the complexity with which the relationship is presented, besides enriching the texture of the novel, adds another dimension to the parable. In contrast to all the other simple illustrations in the parable, Anthony is complex. Unable or unwilling to adopt a single pose, to live by a single attitude like that of the "idealist" or the "cynic," he is damned. His choice of Gloria, of marriage, is sinful, but it is also more complex, more fully human, than the choices of his simplified celibate friends. Anthony and Gloria are the only fully human characters in the novel, the only people who do not hypocritically limit themselves to the singularity that survives. Contemporary America, as Fitzgerald depicts it, rewards hypocrisy, simplification, the person who restricts his humanity to the salvageable single pose and rules out any humanely contradictory impulses. Anthony and Gloria are "beautiful" because they do not simplify, and they are spoiled because they represent something exceptional to the people around them; but their inability or unwillingness to simplify, to restrict themselves, insures their damnation in contemporary America.

The novel's flaw lies in Fitzgerald's failure to work out convincingly the balance between the couple's inability and unwillingness, or to develop any coherent relationship between their responsibility for their doom and an indictment of the American society that dooms its "beautiful." Responsive, directionless, impulsive, capable at times of love for each other, as no other characters in the novel are capable of love, Anthony and Gloria try to sustain their status as special people. Even toward the end, Anthony defends his own feelings of aristocracy: "Aristocracy's only an admission that certain traits which we call fine—courage and honor and beauty and all that sort of thing—can best be developed in a favorable environment, where you don't have the warpings of ignorance and necessity." In the novel, however, contemporary America, despite all its opulence, is a land of "ignorance and necessity," a land that requires hard simplification, callous dishonesty, or rigorous moral restriction from those who are determined to survive. The "beautiful," the flexible and evanescent, are "damned." Because of the depiction of America, the relentless environment that promises so much and punishes so fiercely, Anthony and Gloria gain sympathy well beyond that usually accorded to illustrations in a moral parable. Hollow as they finally are, and harshly as Fitzgerald judges them, Anthony and Gloria are still preferable to all the self-seeking simplifications around them. Although Fitzgerald never makes the relevance of the moral judgment clear, never allows the judgment to stand as a final statement about the principal characters, he never modifies the stringency of the judgment itself.

The moral structure of *The Great Gatsby* is far more coherent. The narrator of the novel, Nick Carraway, more honest than anyone else, serves as "a guide, a pathfinder, an original settler." Frequently obtruding with judgments on characters and general observations on society, Nick provides the perspective through which the issues of the novel are apparent. He speaks for the author when he cries across the lawn to the defeated, deluded, hopelessly naïve Gatsby, "You're worth the whole damn bunch put together." Appropriately, Nick is close to his real father, whom he quotes at the very beginning of the novel and returns to at the end. A solid, sane, highly moral Midwesterner, Nick's father provides the secure basis from which his son can see and judge the chaotic modern world morally and effectively.

Jay Gatsby, the subject of the novel, is the embodiment of the American Dream: the mystery of its origins, its impossible romanticism, its belief in its capacity to recapture a past that may never have existed (as Gatsby believes he can re-create his past with Daisy), its faith in an unknown future, its ultimate futility. He attempts to create a new Eden, derived from the past, through money, silk shirts, and an Oxford accent. Gatsby is also the Horatio Alger hero in his dedication to "dumbbell exercise," the study of "needed inventions," and the pure vision of the future that involves making a lot of money. Like the Horatio Alger hero, Gatsby abandons his own ineffectual and undistinguished father (a man only too willing to relinquish his son to the demands of commercial manifest destiny) and attaches himself to a surrogate, the millionaire miner, Dan Cody. The romantic American myth, predicated on the democratic unpredictability of the origins of the specially virtuous and sensitive man, requires a surrogate father, a willful and deliberate attachment. But, in Fitzgerald's terms, the failure of Gatsby is further demonstration that the myth is false, for the moral guide can only be transmitted by a real father, a true God. The vertical line of virtue must be direct and close, from father to son, and only the vertical line can preserve the sensitive son from the chaos of the modern world.

Gatsby's vision might have been a more plausible version of experience in an earlier, simpler America which had not yet become increasingly materialistic and increasingly distant from the morality of true fathers. His aspirations, then, might not have necessarily involved him, as they do now, with the criminal, the callous, and the corrupt.

> And as I sat there brooding on the old, unknown world, I thought of Gatsby's wonder when he first picked out the green light at the end of Daisy's dock. He had come a long way to this blue lawn, and his dream must have seemed so close that he could hardly fail to grasp it. He did not know that it was already behind him, somewhere back in that vast obscurity beyond the city, where the dark fields of the republic rolled on under the night.

Yet in another sense, as Nick clearly sees at the end of the novel, the dream Gatsby represents was always flawed, always impossible to achieve, the promise of the glittering new land which could never be fulfilled no matter how dedicated the aspirant:

> And as the moon rose higher the inessential houses began to melt away until gradually I become aware of the old island here that flowered once for Dutch sailors' eyes—a fresh, green breast of the new world. Its vanished trees, the trees that had made way for Gatsby's house, had once pandered in whispers to the last and greatest of all human dreams; for a transitory enchanted moment man must have held his breath in the presence of this continent, compelled into an aesthetic contemplation he neither understood nor desired, face to face for the last time in history with something commensurate to his capacity for wonder.

The difference between promise and achievement, between vision and reality, is the story of America, but it also suggests, in Fitzgerald's terms, the story of man, the aspiring creature limited by himself and the world around him, the worthwhile human creature who invariably wants to have more than he has, to be more than he is. Man's two sidedness, the difference between his vision and his inevitable destiny, has developed in range and meaning, far from Amory Blaine's superficial "cynical idealism." In *The Great Gatsby*, Fitzgerald's tightest novel both artistically and theologically, both sides of man are locked, the romantic hero's aspiration and defeat are equally necessary. Man's destiny, the sin of the attractive romantic hero, is immutable in Fitzgerald's moral and religious perspective.

The continuity of the human paradox is also applied specifically to America, for all the characters are products of history, are intrinsically related to the past. Tom Buchanan, the stupid and corrupt aspect of the American past, triumphs over Gatsby, the idealized and romanticized version of the past, to win Daisy, the prize in the present which has been spoiled, corrupted, and victimized by the past. What Gatsby's vision represents has, in America, both past and present, never been articulated or imagined in concrete terms, has always been attenuated by Tom's kind of callous, brutal, stupid materialism. Another paradox implicit in Fitzgerald's version of American history is apparent in the incompatibility of two American myths: the democratic myth of the importance of the common man and the myth of the opportunity for the special creature, the exceptionally visionary, resolute, and dedicated. The common man, Wilson, in revenge for the death of his common wife, kills the specially visionary and idealistic Gatsby rather than the specially corrupt and culpable Tom and Daisy. The common man cannot tell one special man from another and finally destroys the American Dream that theoretically provides the symbol for his own aspiration. All these paradoxes, all these, for Fitzgerald, necessary destructions of the ideal or of the transcendence of human possibility, make the novel a moral fable. But Fitzgerald's morality in *The Great Gatsby* is not the simple morality of single-minded judgment, of excoriating the unrighteous. Rather, as articulated through the wise and temperate Nick, the morality is the inflexible necessity of the harsh dilemma of human experience, the invariable human defeat involved in the difference between vision and reality. Because he understands and accepts this, Nick is able to survive and look back on the events of the novel through distance and time.

Dick Diver, the hero of *Tender Is the Night*, is characterized as an American moral agent in the amoral world of Europe after World War I. Initially puritanical in respect to women and to his work, Dick is depicted as a superior representative of America, powerful, intelligent, charming and not aware of his charm, full of fresh ideas and naïve illusions: "the illusions of eternal strength and health, and of the essential goodness of people: illusions of a nation, the lies of generations of frontier mothers who had to croon falsely, that there were no wolves outside the cabin door." Dick recognizes that the American is not perfect, that he needs to be less strident, to cultivate a "repose" that traditional culture brings easily to the European. At the same time, he attempts to exert an American moral force within European society, a force expressed in terms of personal relationships, of consideration for others, of humanity. And he does, at least early in his career, build the small, humane moral society around the small Riviera beach he discovers, then molds and carefully rakes. Fitzgerald consistently points out the moral center of Dick's charm, the exquisite consideration, the recognition of the value of everything around him, the capacity to extract the full humanity from his associates in the way that the priest, ideally, both guides and understands his parishioners. Dick's psychiatry, too, is moral, attempting to "cure" homosexuality and to "save" his patients from themselves. Even Abe North, the most self-destructive of the American characters, acknowledges that everyone must have a moral code; ironically and bitterly, he claims that his is an opposition to burning witches. For Fitzgerald, such a flippantly limited moral implies certain destruction.

Dick fails, like Jay Gatsby, partly because his innocent and moral ideals no longer apply to contemporary experience. Increasingly throughout the novel, Dick's public moralism is inappropriate in a new, more private world that he cannot understand. Although he is much less the smugly dense American than McKisco is, he never appreciates Tommy Barban's private justifications for wandering service as a mercenary soldier. Dick never understands the world of Mary North's Levantine second husband, or the cosmopolitan skepticism of the newer rebels like Lady

Caroline Sibly-Biers, or, finally, the female nature of his wife, the new and revitalized Nicole, who successfully poses her "unscrupulousness against his moralities." Despite all his external charm, Dick is too committed to the past, to an old American morality, ever to recognize fully the private, separate particles of contemporary European life. At one point, Dick sees a party of middle-aged American women who impress him as forming a cohesive unit, and he discovers that they are a group of goldstar mothers who have come to Europe to visit their sons' graves:

> Over his wine Dick looked at them again; in their happy faces, the dignity that surrounded and pervaded the party, he perceived all the maturity of an older America. For a while the sobered women who had come to mourn for their dead, for something they could not repair, made the room beautiful. Momentarily, he sat again on his father's knee, riding with Moseby while the old loyalties and devotions fought on around him. Almost with an effort he turned back to his two women at the table and faced the whole new world in which he believed.

Dick may believe in two worlds, the moral one of the old America and the new one of his women, but he cannot live in both. And as he fails, his own morality, his own center, begins to dissolve. He works less and less, becomes more dependent on Nicole's money, and is increasingly drunken, careless, and inconsiderate. When Rosemary Hoyt, who had once idolized him, tells him that he still seems the man he was, he replies, "The manner remains intact for some time after the morale cracks" —almost as if he is Dorian Gray with a deeply imbedded sense of sin just under the easy façade. Dick's "manner" eventually cracks, too, for he becomes violent and petulant, picks fights, indulges in self-pity, and is pointlessly vulgar in talking with Nicole. All these are symptoms of an advanced stage of dissolution: for Fitzgerald, not behaving well, not observing superficial amenities and conventions, always indicates the hero's irreversible defeat.

The doom is not as elemental and universal as that of *The Great Gatsby*, for *Tender Is the Night* is a more complicated novel. For example, the father figures proliferate, suggesting a more equivocal morality than that of *The Great Gatsby*. Dick's real father is an American clergyman who had taught Dick all he knew of "manners" and "matters of behavior," a man halfway between Nick Carraway's wise and sophisticated father and Gatsby's humble simpleton. Though honest and direct, he lacks the intellect, the range, and the insight to be transportable to the new and more complicated world of postwar Europe. Despite the distance in space and time between Dick and his father, Dick often "referred judgments to what his father would probably have thought or done." Yet he recognizes that, in choosing Europe, he has abandoned his father. He temporarily returns to America to attend his father's funeral: "These dead, he knew them all, their weather-beaten faces with blue flashing eyes, the spare violent bodies, the souls made of new earth in the forest-heavy darkness of the seventeenth century. 'Good-by, my father—good-by, all my fathers.' " Dick attaches himself to a surrogate father, Dr. Dohmler, the psychiatrist in charge of the clinic where Dick initially works. Dr. Dohmler is fiercely moral, an instructor, a guide, and Dick is strongly influenced by his precepts and judgments. Yet in marrying Nicole, in confusing the separate relationships between husband and wife and between doctor and patient, Dick disobeys one of Dr. Dohmler's strongest injunctions. The real father is not necessarily preferable to the surrogate, for either might have served to transmit his morality to Dick. But Dick abandons one and disobeys the other; left alone, he cannot sustain himself. The father also has responsibilities toward his child: Nicole's father, in forcing incest upon her, actually converts his daughter into his mistress and so violates the relationship between father and child in the most disastrous way possible.

In this complicated novel, Dick Diver is a multiple father as well as a multiply errant son. Having rejected the gods offered him, Dick establishes himself as a series of gods, playing a different kind of father in each of his varying relationships. Although certain moral judgments still obtain in *Tender Is the Night* (e.g., the prescription against incest), the plurality of gods makes the moral issues more equivocal and perplexing than those of *The Great Gatsby*. As a real father to his two children, Dick finds his only lasting success. To Lanier and Topsy, he is warm and firm, able to mean something even after he has ceased to mean anything to anyone else. Dick is less successful as a surrogate father to Rosemary, the starlet who gains recognition in *Daddy's Girl*. For her, Dick is the cosmopolitan father, introducing her to Europe, to history, to the world of sensitivity. When first attracted to her, he regards her as too much the child to make love to her, but Rosemary, who has always sensed the ambivalence between the father and the lover, eventually grows beyond the need of a surrogate and recognizes the hollowness within Dick. Even so, in the scene in which they recognize that their whole relationship has been superficial, that they have only been playing parts like the actors they are, that neither is really capable of loving the other, Rosemary says, "I feel as if I'd quarrelled with Mother."

More importantly, Dick is a surrogate father for Nicole, replacing the father who had violated her. First as psychiatrist and then as husband, Dick still plays the father, sheltering Nicole from the world, guiding her, and giving her the time and understanding necessary for her restoration to psychic health. But the roles of father and of husband are incompatible: Nicole, once restored, must reject Dick because, as a grown-up woman, she no longer needs a father; Dick, in marrying the woman he needed to guide, had really committed a kind of symbolic incest. In the multiplicity of his fatherhood, Dick tries to be a universal father, the controller and guide for all the relationships around him, the lord and creator of the beach. Images like the "deposed ruler," or the "spoiled priest," applied to Dick after his decline is evident, underline the universal nature of his fatherhood.

In general terms, Dick's doom is unambiguous, the folly and presumption of playing God, of attempting, while still a human being, to guide and control all the lives around him. Yet the specific moral framework of the novel is far more ambiguous. The reader wonders which God, if any, might have been the true one: Dr. Dohmler? Dick's father? Dick as psychiatrist? Dick as the charming and responsive master of the civilized world? The novel charts Dick's doom, but part of his doom is the confusion and ambiguity of whatever moral order specifically destroys him. When, in his final defeat, Dick makes the sign of the cross over the populous beach he had once created from the debris between shore and sea, his action is neither an ironically unrecognized truth nor a presumptuous falsehood, but, rather, a pathetic and irrelevant gesture of his failure.

In the moral ambiguity of *Tender Is the Night*, much of Fitzgerald's attention shifts from the vertical relationship, the transmission of truth or moral values from parent to child, to the lateral relationship, the equivalent relationship between man and woman, the mutual recognition of humanity. The focus often changes from fathers to women, to the representatives of an amoral principle of accepting what is and holding "things together." For Fitzgerald, the father is more characteristically, although not entirely, connected with America, a continent that is a "nursery." In contrast, the new world of postwar Europe neglects the transmission of moral values, the father, and concentrates on the woman. Early in the novel, after Dick has been presented at the apex of his talent and control, there is a shooting at the railway station, an unforeseen and unexpected event. Both Rosemary and Nicole wait in vain for "Dick to make a moral comment on the matter and not leave it to them." From that moment on, as a kind of counterpoint to the theme of Dick's dissolution, Fitzgerald develops an interest in the two women's attempt to discover themselves. Both Rosemary and Nicole begin to understand the world around them without Dick's guiding judgment.

Because she has had more to overcome and has been more completely involved with Dick, Nicole's is the more interesting consciousness, and, appropriately, Fitzgerald devotes more time to her gradual breaking away from dependence on Dick and developing an independent self-awareness. Like Gloria in *The Beautiful and Damned*, Nicole has a kind of reckless courage. Originally dependent, she is able to become wiser, more competent, more self-assured as the man she regarded as her master dissolves. To some extent both novels show the roles of the partners reversing within the marriage. But Fitzgerald's attitude changed. In *The Beautiful and Damned*, as the wife became more human and competent, less the porcelain trophy, she was inevitably soiled, unclean; in *Tender Is the Night*, the loss of spiritual virginity indicates the capacity for human relationship, and no moral judgment, no antisepsis, is involved. When Nicole realizes that Dick, the father, cannot also be a husband, she turns, in her new self-confidence, toward Tommy Barban:

> Her ego began blooming like a great rich rose as she scrambled back along the labyrinths in which she had wandered for years. She hated the beach, resented the places where she had played planet to Dick's sun.
>
> "Why, I'm almost complete," she thought. "I'm practically standing alone, without him. And like a happy child, wanting the completion as soon as possible, and knowing vaguely that Dick had planned for her to have it, she lay on her bed as soon as she got home and wrote Tommy Barban in Nice a short provocative letter.

After she and Tommy Barban make love, Nicole almost expects an explanation or interpretation of the experience, such as Dick would have given. But Tommy provides none, and Nicole is content and a "child" no longer. Fitzgerald indicates his final approval of Nicole, or at least his refusal to pass judgment against her, by portraying her as neither bitter nor petulant when she decides to leave Dick; indeed, she can recognize that in her need she had contributed to his indolence and unwittingly encouraged his decline. She can be gracious, always the sign of a kind of virtue in Fitzgerald's terms. Most of the events in the last third of the novel are seen from Nicole's point of view. And, using her point of view, Fitzgerald shows that he is as interested in dissecting an incompatible relationship—the strain between a woman who needed a surrogate father before she was ready for a husband and a man who was too much of a father to change himself into a husband—as he is in chronicling the destruction of the romantic ego.

Despite the use of Nicole's point of view, the structure of the novel does not justify reading the emphasis on Nicole as equal to the emphasis on Dick's decline. A consideration of the structure, of the movement from one episode to another, focuses attention on Dick and his failure. Yet Fitzgerald himself was uneasy and dissatisifed with the shape of the novel.

As originally published and as usually read today, the novel begins with Rosemary's point of view toward Dick on the beach, Rosemary naïvely worshiping the Dick who is then at the height of his power and charm. Then, following Dick, with flashbacks into the past and the meeting between Dick and Nicole, the novel traces Dick's decline. In some editions the first ten chapters of Book II have been placed before Book I, a change that Fitzgerald later advocated and one that would make the novel read chronologically. Like the original version, however, the chronological version emphasizes the rise and fall of the hero, the only real difference being that the chronological version places greater emphasis on psychological causes, on Nicole's illness, Dick's work, and Dick's disobedience of Dr. Dohmler's injunction. Since Fitzgerald's explicit treatment of psychological issues (in contrast with his implicit treatment of character in a way that could be explained in psychological terms) is so heavily moralistic and simplistically unconvincing to contemporary readers, the chronological organization seems even less satisfactory than does the original. The counterpoint to the theme of Dick's dissolution—the growth of Nicole's capacity to understand experience and the partial shift to the amoral female perspective—is not represented in either structure or given coherently meaningful shape. A conversation about Abe North between Nicole and Dick illustrates something of the problem:

> Nicole shook her head right and left, disclaiming responsibility for the matter: "So many smart men go to pieces nowadays."
>
> "And when haven't they?" Dick asked. "Smart men play close to the line because they have to—some of them can't stand it, so they quit."
>
> "It must lie deeper than that." Nicole clung to her conversation; also she was irritated that Dick should contradict her before Rosemary. "Artists like—well, like Fernand don't seem to have to wallow in alcohol. Why is it just Americans who dissipate?"
>
> There were so many answers to this question that Dick decided to leave it in the air, to buzz victoriously in Nicole's ears.

Nicole is right, for the novel shows that it does "lie deeper than that." But whatever is "deeper," like whatever version of God dooms Dick, is never made fully coherent, never brought finally into focus. The structural reliance on only the theme of Dick's decline almost seems a substitute for the failure to control fully the ultimate skepticism about God and the issues of lateral relationship in the novel. Yet, despite this failure and the lack of a universal order as tight as that of *The Great Gatsby*, a sense of richness, density, and disordered humanity emerges from *Tender Is the Night.*

No fathers exist in *The Last Tycoon*. The protagonist, Monroe Stahr, is the man of enormous talent who has achieved his dominance over others, his special stature, by his own brilliance, energy, and hard work. No moral code or dedication to manners or principle infuses his background. In a scene with Kathleen, he explains:

> "When I was young I wanted to be a chief clerk—the one who knew where everything was. . . . I'm still a chief clerk. . . . That's my gift, if I have one. Only when I got to be it, I found out that no one knew where anything was. And I found out that you had to know why it was where it was, and whether it should be left there."

Stahr has sympathy as well as talent, the capacity to understand people around him, the willingness to soothe the narcissistic actor and to help the cameraman ruined by rumor. Yet all his talents and humanity are solely individual, not part of any country or code or truth. A humane employer, he is still not willing to side with labor in a struggle against capital in the principal issue of his time (this aspect was never fully worked out in the portion of the novel finished; Fitzgerald's notes indicate that he planned to develop the labor agitation further, but arguing further from notes and guesses would not be very rewarding); a capitalistic movie-maker, he is far from a defender or a representative of the system. When in power, Stahr relies only on himself, even if he is not always sure just what that self is. While flying in a plane, Stahr goes up to the cockpit to talk with the pilot:

> He was looking down at the mountains.
>
> "Suppose you were a railroad man," he said. "You have to send a train through there somewhere. Well, you get your surveyors' reports, and you find there's three or four or half a dozen gaps, and not one is better than the other. You've got to decide—on what basis? You can't test the best way—except by doing it. So you just do it."
>
> The pilot thought he had missed something.
>
> "How do you mean?"
>
> "You choose some one way for no reason at all—because that mountain's pink or the blueprint is a better blue. You see?"

In addition, Stahr is a Jew, an alien in America, a force without locus and a talent without background. The novel revolves around a man and his relationship rather than around an inherited principle and its application to the modern world.

In *The Last Tycoon*, the American past is false or irrelevant in the Hollywood that manufactures dreams for contemporary society. Abraham Lincoln eats the forty-cent dinner, including dessert, in the studio cafeteria, and the Danish visitor who notices him feels that Lincoln now makes more sense than he ever had before; a telephone call to Stahr, supposedly from the President, turns out to be a joke to get Stahr to talk with an ape; a trip to the Hermitage, Andrew Jackson's home, taken because the plane is delayed by bad weather, holds no message for the characters and provides only the setting for a suicide. Comically, absurdly, the men of Hollywood make their myths, legends just as true and just as false as the ones enshrined by history. Stahr's dream woman, Kathleen, attractive to him because she resembles his dead wife, is also not American. An English girl who has been to "all the places that Stahr made movies of," Kathleen is first seen riding on the head of a Hindu goddess, a stage prop for a movie, through a flood in the studio.

Throughout the novel, fortunes change rapidly, people appear and disappear unexpectedly, and those concerned with the movies are apt to be powerful and arrogant one minute and jobless and desolate the next. No one is secure and no one is sure of himself. Kathleen tells Stahr that he is three or four people, a comment echoed by Cecilia Brady, the narrator of part of the novel, who claims that all writers are several people; a genuine Russian prince refuses to play the part of a Russian prince because he has turned Communist; in looking for Kathleen, after he has seen her once, Stahr gets the wrong woman first. In fact, the wrong woman is named Smith, a name Stahr also uses for anonymity when he flies across the country. And the man Kathleen marries, as a result of both mistiming and misunderstanding between herself and Stahr, is also named Smith. As the multiple Smiths, some true and some false, indicate, the principal concern of the novel is identity, discovering who or what one is, rather than any form of moral judgment or evaluation.

At the same time, Stahr is another of Fitzgerald's doomed romantic heroes whose attempt to play God must inevitably be defeated. His role as the "last" tycoon amidst the changes of social history, the verdict from the doctor that gives him only a few months to live, and prophetically introduced observations from other characters demonstrate, even in the completed portion of the novel, that Stahr's dissolution and defeat were to be inescapable. Yet, as in *Tender Is the Night*, the cause of the doom, the triumphant morality or the true God, is never manifest. Playing God, for Fitzgerald, is a sin no matter how attractive, and it is a sin even in a chaotic universe with no moral framework or principle that can define or label what sin is. The guilt, the sense of sin, lingers even after the intellect and understanding can no longer accept the system that assigned the sin.

Like all Fitzgerald's romantic heroes, Stahr tries to relieve the barren dedication of his quest with an interest in women. But, unlike the earlier heroes, Stahr changes, learns from his relationship with a woman. Kathleen, Stahr's mistress, is formless, can play mother, "trollop," temporary wife, anything Stahr might momentarily need. Kathleen's previous relationship, too, had been defined by the man, and, in the course of the novel, she marries Smith because he happens, decisively, to arrive unexpectedly at the moment when she and Stahr are between definitions. The other woman who loves Stahr, Cecilia Brady, also makes the point that women exist to understand men, to be defined by them and attach themselves to them. Significantly, Cecilia is "in" but not "of" the movies, and Kathleen refuses to let Stahr show her around the studio: both women are less interested in the thing itself, the life outside the man, than in the definition the man creates of his own "thing." This, to Fitzgerald, makes them genuine women in contrast to the starlets who gain their only identity through being "of" the movies, created by the glittering and fabricated dreams.

That Kathleen can marry Smith because of her uncertainty about Stahr indicates that Stahr himself, despite his success as a talented producer, is far from certain about his own identity or about the definitions he wants to impose upon experience. Until too late, he does not know what he feels about Kathleen, what his personal identity is. At one point, Kathleen gives him a note, then later asks that it be returned, but neither can find it in the car. After he has taken her home, Stahr finds the note and brings it back to his house:

> He was proud of resisting his first impulse to open the letter. It seemed to prove that he was not "losing his head." He had never lost his head about Minna [his dead wife], even in the beginning—it had been the most appropriate and regal match imaginable. She had loved him always and just before she died, all unwilling and surprised, his tenderness had burst and surged forward and he had been in love with her. In love with Minna and death together—with the world in which she looked so alone that he wanted to go with her there.
>
> But "falling for dames" had never been an obsession—his brother had gone to pieces over a dame, or rather dame after dame after dame. But Stahr, in his younger days, had them once and never more than once—like one drink. He had quite another sort of adventure reserved for his mind—something better than a series of emotional sprees. Like many brilliant men, he had grown up dead cold. . . . And so he had learned tolerance, kindness, forbearance, and even affection like lessons.

Stahr's belated growth refers to public issues as well as personal ones. Only during the course of the novel does he, the capitalistic entrepreneur of dreams, begin to realize how unfairly he has always used labor. Although he is still fascinated by the power one man can hold, by playing God, he begins to question himself and his aims more closely. He becomes more concerned with others, with politics, with art, as well as with women. Yet, for all his richer sense of humanity, Stahr is still doomed, and, if Fitzgerald's notes for the rest of the novel can be credited, he might have been finished off melodramatically because the sense of doom has no logical corollary in terms of the novel.

The point of view of *The Last Tycoon* is never developed sufficiently to order all the elements. The novel's action is ostensibly seen through Cecilia Brady, the daughter of Stahr's partner. Cecilia is a Bennington girl, a "new" woman, honest, flippant, and direct. She is not even disillusioned when she accidentally surprises her father making love to his secretary in his office, for she has seen that before and has already shifted from a childish reliance on fathers and moralities to an interest in the humane development of the self. In this sense, she is a satisfactory narrator for the novel. But the subject of the novel is Stahr, and Cecilia tells more than she could possibly know. Fitzgerald has her collecting information from others, piecing together stories of Stahr's life in the studio from several sources, and acting like a zoomar-lens consciousness when she enters Stahr's mind as he approaches Kathleen, Cecilia standing a hundred yards away. The device of Cecilia's narration breaks down entirely in its irrelevance to the central and private love scenes between Stahr and Kathleen. The gossip and the quick cutting from one scene to another, which disrupt Cecilia's narrative, are justified, even effective, as a mirror of Hollywood. Cecilia can also see the ironic pathos in Stahr's decline. But as a device to record Stahr himself and what defeats him, to present his growing humanity, and to suggest the order in terms of which he sins, Fitzgerald's use of Cecilia as narrator is inadequate. She is even further from the God who may not exist than is Stahr himself. And, in secular as well as religious terms, no structurally coherent device, at least none apparent in the unfinished novel, manages to articulate all that is there.

In his last two novels, Fitzgerald's compassion grew. His concern for his characters increased, as did his sympathy for their human struggles and relationships, for all the questions they could never answer. Correspondingly, the element of morality or judgment diminished, and God or truth disappeared; the romantic hero, although still doomed, seemed doomed less by a moral order or original sin than by accident. Still unable to control his own destiny as he so powerfully wanted to, the romantic hero turned his attention to the very human relationships that contributed to his doom, sometimes even, as in the instance of Monroe Stahr, ironically learning from them. Yet despite the interest in the strictly secular relationship and the lack of an implicit moral order, Fitzgerald's form was always that of the parable, no less in *Tender Is the Night* than in *The Beautiful and Damned.* In the last two novels, the parable form was less appropriate, less able to summarize and direct the issues of the novel, and Fitzgerald never found a form to express coherently the greater human dimensions and complexity of his later fiction. The form broke, particularly in *Tender Is the Night*, in which the energy and perception of the novel leap out from the inadequate structure and the ultimately superficial point of view. Yet in the very breaking of the form, the very collapse of the parable as an explanation that can support the weight of contemporary experience, the sense of Fitzgerald's achieved compassion inheres. Compassion seldom is tidy or neatly measurable in a formal equation, and Fitzgerald's last two novels explode from the tidiness of judgment and evaluation of the "American experience" into deeper questions, as well as richer and less systematic understandings about the perplexities of man.

MARY E. BURTON

The Counter-Transference of Dr. Diver

During his last, most artistically productive years F. Scott Fitzgerald was reading Marx and Spengler, and his absorption of their theories plus his own hard bought experience in the world of the very rich resulted in the critique of the American bourgeois capitalistic system that underlies his two greatest works, *The Great Gatsby* and *Tender Is The Night*. But Fitzgerald is no economist or sociologist; he is above all the artist, and perhaps the greatest American romantic idealist of them all, and, characteristically, his critique is not directed specifically or scientifically on the economy but on what the economy produced—The Great American Dream, through which the very rich pre-depression American sleptwalked or nightmared out his life.

Of what is this dream composed? It is, first of all, an amorous dream—a love dance of American idealism with money: more specifically, of the American male, embodying a composite of ideals ranging from New England Humanism to Midwestern Egalitarianism to Southern Gentility with the elusive, seductive American Aphrodite, foam-born from the American capitalistic society. This Aphrodite (she is Daisy Buchanan, Nicole Diver and many others) has no lineage of familial values, no code of morals; she is always new minted, rich, fresh, beautiful, childish, and morally devastating. The love dance of the American male and female is conducted on the homeland, as in *The Great Gatsby*, or on nostalgic memories of the homeland, as in *Tender Is The Night*—"a fresh, green

From *English Literary History* 3, vol. 38, (September 1971).

breast of the new world" which anonymously has suckled and nurtured the daughters of dollars. And in this dance, almost anthropomorphically—or Jungianly (Fitzgerald was also reading Jung at the time he was composing *Tender Is The Night*)—though his own experience could have taught him the same thing, the male is always destroyed, and the female always goes on.

For the two last and greatest completed works, *The Great Gatsby* and *Tender Is The Night*, and also in his uncompleted *The Last Tycoon*, Fitzgerald chose protagonists who were, above all, exemplars and purveyors of the American dream: the bootlegger, the psychiatrist, and the movie producer. To state that a psychiatrist might be a dealer in dreams may seem dubious, in that supposedly a psychiatrist seeks to free his patients from their dream-lives (neuroses) and return them to reality. But the fact is that after many changes and modifications in his concept of a hero for *Tender Is The Night*, Fitzgerald did indeed choose to make a hero such a doctor, and made him fail, not only in his profession but in his life. It would appear that in Fitzgerald's mind, no American male, however sage, scientific, and detached, could ever free himself from the American dream-neurosis, and by making his hero not only an American romantic but a psychiatrist he could best illustrate the nature of the neurosis of his society and the tragedies it inevitably produces. The ironies and double ironies compound; the analyst, healer, corrector of "dream worlds" becomes victimized by the dream world itself: it is inevitable, in the Fitzgeraldian vision, that Dr. Diver will effect a counter-transference and become morally infected with the dream he sought to break and cure.

II

Dr. Richard Diver is from the start "Lucky Dick." He sails brilliantly through New Haven, a Rhodes Scholarship at Oxford, studies in Zurich (the Jungian fortress) but manages to get to Vienna "under the impression that, if he did not make haste, the great Freud would eventually succumb to an airplane bomb. Even then Vienna was old with death, but Dick managed to get enough coal and oil to sit in his room in the Damenstiff Strasse and write the pamphlets that he later destroyed, but that, rewritten, were the backbone of the book he published in Zurich in 1920." In simple words, Dick has studied Jung, but basically he is a Freudian. As such he must be cognizant of the original neurosis Freud had treated—female hysteria caused by either real or fantasied rape of the patients by their fathers—and also of two of Freud's chief theoretical discoveries:

those of transference and counter-transference. Ripe with this knowledge he comes back to Dr. Gregorovious' clinic, meets, falls in love with, and marries the adorably pretty neurotic Nicole, victim of just such a father-seduction, and through his love for her is, inevitably, destroyed. The heart of the matter is, then, why does Lucky Dick, analytic Dick, forewarned and forearmed Dick, make this disastrous choice of mate, and how and why is the counter-transference which destroys him effected?

In Freudian theory of treatment of neurosis, transference as a part of therapy is essential and necessary. The psychiatrist allows and encourages the patient to play out or talk out before him the problems, dreams, anxieties most distressing to him, while himself remaining a neutral non-reacting "blank face," permitting all, anonymous and discreet. Gradually the patient begins to focus on the persons or person (usually a parent) who is most troublesome to him and begins to behave to the doctor as if the doctor were that parent. But the doctor refuses to "play back," insisting that the patient work through and analyse his own problems, correcting the patient when he goes astray from the central theme, guiding him by example, support and encouragement to rid himself of the neurosis and begin to lead a life more consistent with reality. If transference is completed, the cure is hopeful.

Counter-transference, on the other hand, is a very dangerous situation, both for doctor and patient. Here the psychiatrist, instead of being the uninvolved blank face begins to involve himself with the patient's neurotic situation: for example, a young girl patient whose problem is her hidden desire for her father plays this role out in front of the psychiatrist who, through weaknesses of his own, actually starts behaving like the desired forbidden parent. (The incidence of psychiatrists who fall in love with their patients is not statistically recorded, but is fairly well known to anyone who has frequented therapeutic circles.)

And so, knowing all this, a brilliant young medical comer, Lucky Dick, arrives face to face with the lovely young waif of Gregorovious' clinic with whom he has been corresponding—the correspondence seemingly innocent, the product originally of Dr. Gregorovious' effort to make Nicole take an interest in something outside herself and answered by Dick with perfect professional probity. Yet just before the second, climactic, meeting of Dick and Nicole, Dr. Gregorovious lets fall a few highly dubious remarks which will echo later when he suggests using Nicole's money to build a clinic for himself and Dick to run. Of the letters between Dick and Nicole: " 'Naturally I saw all the first letters,' he said in his official basso. 'When the change [in Nicole] began, delicacy prevented me from opening any more. Really it had become your case.' " And later:

" 'It was the best thing that could have happened to her,' said Franz dramatically, 'a transference of the most fortuitous kind.' " Whatever these remarks reveal of the cupidity of Dr. Gregorovious, once again Dick has been warned: Nicole has effected a transference onto him. And yet Lucky Dick, clever Dick, Dick the psychiatrist who should know better, ignores the fact that he is now, to all intents and purposes, her doctor; instead he falls in love with her in the most seemingly fatuous and incredible way. "The impression of her youth and beauty grew on Dick until it welled up inside him in a compact paroxysm of emotion. She smiled, a moving childish smile that was like all the lost youth in the world." And again, "there was that excitement about her that seemed to reflect all the excitement of the world." For Dick is, in spite of his scientific training, above all the romantic idealist, and slowly the love dance of the American romantic idealist and the American Cyprian commences. At the moment of their first dance, "They were in America now."

But why the love-marriage? Consciously Dick knows that Nicole is possibly incurably sick: " 'She's a schizzoid—a permanent eccentric,' " he tells Baby Warren. He is consciously both amused and revolted by Baby's obvious attempt to buy Nicole a keeper: "a burst of hilarity surged up in Dick, the Warrens were going to buy Nicole a doctor"; he attempts scrupulously, later in their marriage, to keep his honor unsullied by paying his way and not using Nicole's money for personal benefit. Yet unmistakably, unstated yet present in every scene, every nuance of their relationship, it is Nicole's money which reveals and actuates Nicole's glamor, before which magic Dick, the analyst, the scientist, the man of reason is helpless. Numberless small scenes and descriptions build up this picture: the enormous villa the Divers occupy, the practically royal state in which they travel, the way Nicole, astonishing Rosemary who has plenty of money of her own but who has earned it and knows its value, spends money shopping; perhaps the most perfect image is Nicole herself when we first see her on the beach—"Nicole Diver, her brown back hanging from her pearls . . . looking through a recipe book for chicken Maryland." Who but the Aphrodite-Americana could sit on a French beach, clad in bathing suit and pearls, searching for a simple recipe? Dick might never have fallen for a conventional rich debutante, but to the combination of the beautiful hurt child and the American dream girl, Dick, incurably a doctor, and also incurably an American romantic, succumbs.

The basic reason for Dick's fascination with Nicole, finally his absorption into her very being—"a wild submergence of soul, a dipping of all colors into an obscuring dye"—is exposed in a highly significant early meditation of Dick's. Back in his Vienna days Dick muses to himself,

" 'And Lucky Dick can't be one of these clever men' [he has been doubting the quality of his own mind *vis-a-vis* Freud, Adler, Jung]; 'he must be less intact, even faintly destroyed. If life won't do it for him it's not a substitute to get a disease, or a broken heart, or an inferiority complex, though it'd be nice to build out some broken side till it was better than the original structure.' " The metaphor of the broken side has an appalling reality. Dick is at least preconsciously aware that he has already been "broken" by the American dream, that his "broken side" (Adam's rib) is that side of him from which the American Aphrodite has been born—she who is, henceforth, his chosen mate and destiny. His decision not to cure his "broken side," setting it, hardening himself, strapping himself into a purely analytical detached stiffness, but rather "building it out" is a fantastically daring and romantic psychic gesture. He will not renounce the dream or fully recognize the neurosis which pervades him; he will not bring himself to compromise with reality—for compromise seems to every romantic a reduction. Instead, he will dare to "fly with the light-winged Dryad," "mid-May's eldest child" of Keats's poem, through "charm'd magic casements, opening on the foam"; he will take his dream to heart and create of it a work of art. Pygmalion-like, he will bring Nicole to life, and in doing so, transcend the American neurosis into a beatific vision of the romantic dream. The psychiatrist will become artist—is it too daring to speculate, in connection with the extraordinary amount of free-floating Christian symbolism—will become God?

III

The outcome of the marriage we know. Riches, indolence, the necessity of providing for Nicole's every need, the pressure of too much money, the need constantly to create and be loved (God must be loved) in one sense cause Dr. Diver's failure. But in another and more organic sense the failure has already been set up for us, in Fitzgerald's analysis of Dick's passion for the Dream. Watch his decline. As Nicole becomes older, as that very blond hair which dazzled Dick turns to the chow-color of her late twenties, Dick is drawn into a new romance with another dazzling blond girl-child, Rosemary Hoyt.

How cleverly Dick, like all neurotics, conceals his neurosis from himself. He thinks, and is encouraged by Rosemary's mother to think, that Rosemary is totally different from Nicole—cool, sane, self-sufficient, impervious to the pain of romantic love—and thus fair game for what Dick first imagines will be just an *amour*. (Mrs. Speers has told her daughter, " 'You were brought up to work—not especially to marry. . . . Wound yourself or him—whatever happens it can't spoil you because economically you're a boy, not a girl.' " From the first moment of his confession of love to Rosemary to the consummation five years later this is the protective illusion that sustains him in his long longing for her. But in reality Rosemary is simply the American Aphrodite of a new decade, new-minted once again; it is the freshness, beauty, glamor of the face "with eternal moonlight in it"; it is "Daddy's Girl" whom Dick finds irresistible and toward whom he flings his whole being. Witness his frantic jealousy when Collis Clay tells him of Rosemary's possible indiscretions with the boy Bill Hillis on a train ride: over and over his mind repeats the imaginary words "Do you mind if I pull down the curtain?—Please do. It's too light in here" and again later his almost prurient curiosity about Rosemary's love-life during the years they have been apart—curiosity which Rosemary never directly answers. Here again it is Rosemary's similarity to Nicole which fascinates Dick; both girls partake of the special quality of the Dream—they are violated yet virgin (Nicole sexually violated yet virgin to love, Rosemary ambivalently virgin but spiritually taken by the thousands who have lusted after her cinematographic image as "Daddy's Girl")—the American Aphrodite who can never be entirely chaste, yet never wooed and won.

Returning from the burial of his father in Virginia (" 'Good-bye, my father—good-bye, all my fathers,' " he has murmured over the grave), Dick experiences an almost classical Freudian reaction to the death of the Oedipal father-figure; he is suddenly freed from all those values so carefully inculcated by his father who has raised him, as he himself had been raised, "to believe that nothing could be superior to 'good instincts,' honor, courtesy, and courage." These values have been during the previous years somewhat eroded by Dick's experience in the clinic he and Gregorovious have run together—bitterly Dick reminisces, " 'I've wasted eight years teaching the rich the ABC's of human decency,' " but they have kept Dick true to his original choice of life and life-mate, ill-chosen to be sure, but still loyally adhered to. Now these values suddenly desert him.

Even before his father's death he has had a prevision of the anarchy of spirit which is to come: on a train he casually glances at a peasant girl and suddenly feels, "He would take her in his hands and snatch her across the border. . . . But there he deserted her—he must press on toward the Isles of Greece, the cloudy waters of unfamiliar ports, the lost girl on shore, the moon of popular songs." The barriers are down, and when he meets Rosemary again in Rome "what had begun with a childish infatuation on a beach was accomplished at last."

But why is this perhaps mutual seduction so disastrous to Dick? Other men have and do become bored with a wife of years, seduce any number of lovely little girls and yet maintain their marriages and seemingly their self-respect. The answer can only lie in Dick's comprehension of exactly, precisely and minutely, what he has done. "Part of Dick's mind was made up of the tawdry souvenirs of his boyhood. Yet in that somewhat littered Five-and-Ten, he had managed to keep alive the low painful fire of intelligence." His love affair with Rosemary, always "Daddy's Girl" and always at the same time the elusive nymph (" 'I've got to go to Livorno with the company tomorrow. Oh, why did this have to happen?' There was a new flood of tears. . . . 'Why did you come here?' " forces Dick to recognize what he has always been, and what he has done, and what is indeed his compulsive neurosis. In marrying Nicole he could for a time evade the truth of his illusion; after making love with Rosemary it is slammed home to him with ferocious finality. Morally, he has stepped into Devereaux Warren's shoes; he has slept with Daddy's girl. There is no evasion possible; he has finally, by free will, been "had" by the American Dream. Henceforth his disgust with himself is so great that nothing but humiliation, degradation, self-inflicted torment is possible for him.

Rising from Rosemary's bed, in a passion of self-aggrandizement, he says, " 'I guess I'm the Black Death. . . . I don't seem to bring people happiness anymore.' " In rage and self-disgust he immediately sets out to get into a drunken brawl with the carabinieri in which he is badly beaten up. While Dick waits to be released from jail by Baby Warren, luckily for Dick visiting Rome at the same time, Fitzgerald gives us a highly charged passage of what is going on in Dick's mind: "Dick's rage had retreated into him a little and he felt a vast criminal irresponsibility. What had happened to him was so awful that nothing could make any difference, unless he could choke it to death, and, as this was unlikely, he was hopeless. He would be a different person henceforward, and in his raw state he had bizarre feelings of what the new self would be. The matter had about it the impersonal quality of an act of God. No mature Aryan is able to profit by a humiliation; when he forgives it has become a part of his life, he has identified himself with the thing which has humiliated him—an upshot that in this case was impossible."

If this is not a clear enough account of the counter-transference through which Dick has psychically become Devereaux Warren—the pathetic and criminal American rich man who has committed incest with his daughter of dollars—the following scene reinforces the picture. Coming out of the courtroom Dick is booed and jeered at by a crowd; it is immediately explained that the crowd has mistaken him for a native of Frascati who "had raped and slain a five-year-old child and was to be brought in that morning. . . . 'I want to make a speech,' Dick cried. 'I want to explain to these people that I raped a five-year-old girl. Maybe I did—.' "

Book II ends a few paragraphs later while "Baby waited with him until a woman could arrive from the English nursing home [to look after Dick's wounds]. It had been a hard night but she had the satisfaction of feeling that, whatever Dick's previous record was, they now possessed a moral superiority over him for as long as he proved of any use." And Dick knows too, as of this minute, that he is as ruined as he himself acknowledges later in Fitzgerald's words toward the end of Book III: "The case was finished. Doctor Diver was at liberty."

Dr. Diver's "liberty" is a crushing irony. It is not existential liberty, it is not egalitarian liberty, it is not *eleutheria* nor Anglo-Saxon fréodóm. It is simply the void. Diver has come through his counter-transference and recognized his experience, but it is too late for him; he is helpless beyond it. In the future lie only a random series of tawdry events: "practicing general medicine, . . . he bicycled a lot, was much admired by the ladies, . . . once made a good speech at a public health meeting on the subject of drugs; but he became entangled with a girl who worked in a grocery store, and he was also involved in a lawsuit about some medical question; so he left Lockport. . . . His latest note was post-marked from Hornell, New York, which is some distance from Geneva and a very small town; in any case he is almost certainly in that section of the country, in one town or another."

IV

Fitzgerald's feelings about *Tender Is The Night* were passionately personal and at the same time artistically highly ambivalent. Chief among the problems confronting a modern reader is Fitzgerald's final request that the book be rearranged in chronological sequence, and that what was originally Book I (commonly called "Rosemary's book") be transposed with Book II (the Divers' love affair and marriage).

Fitzgerald's uncertainty about the arrangement of sections surely reflects his unease about his presentation of the hero and the hero's downfall, and indeed there is something to be said for a scheme which would chronologically depict Dick's decline. But artistically, thematically, were not Fitzgerald's original intuitions better? The Now–Then–Now structure of the original perfectly embodies the psychotherapeutic situation, in which the present is first explored, then the past exposed, finally the present again analyzed; in a novel about a psychiatrist, a novel which purports to "analyse" the American neurosis this would seem to be almost a "given" form.

Furthermore, Book II is thematically the crux of the novel; here Nicole's peculiar crippledness is explained, here Dick's more subtle neurosis is laid open, here the two diseases are crossed and married in Dick's counter-transference. Indeed here in Book II the counter-transference is raised into a vision of the transcendent moral illness of Fitzgerald's age, generation and society. Books I and III as originally arranged build up to and away from this crux. They are the flying buttresses; they have beautifully juxtaposed "parallel" scenes, which, by evoking the same kinds of atmospheres and the same characters are illustrative of the continuum of Dick's life—Book I showing the beginning of Dick's terminal illness and Book III the spiritual death itself.

Dick's "bad party" in Book I, for example, seen through Rosemary's naive adoring eyes as the apotheosis of elegance and sophistication and ending in a duel between McKisco and Tommy Barban, has a counterpart in Mary North Menghetti's houseparty in Book III, where the "badness" lies not in the ignorance or vulgarity of the outsiders to the Diver entourage, but between the Divers themselves, and particularly in Dick's losing control of the situation. The wild happy ride through Les Halles in Book I (again seen through Rosemary's ecstatic eyes) has a kind of counterpart in the visit to the Goldings' yacht and Dick's subsequent attempt to perform aquaplaning stunts; here again Dick the magician, the happiness-maker, the genius of human relations of Book I is contrasted with Dick the drunk, the inept, the failure of Book III. More important, though undeniably more ambiguous in meaning, is the juxtaposition of the scene in Book I in which Dick protects both Rosemary and Nicole from the horror of the murder of the Negro in the hotel against the scene in Book III where he is unable to cope with the Mary Menghetti-Lady Caroline Sibley-Biers fracas—so minor compared to the first real, mysterious tragedy, yet a situation which the "old" Dick could easily have managed and the "new" Dick cannot. And again, there are two parallel scenes in Books I and III which unmistakably enforce the picture of young Dick's self-delusion—repression of neurosis—with his later—much-too-late-now—recognition of reality. In Book I, visiting a World War I battlefield ("the tragic hill of Thiepval") Dick mourns, " 'Why, this was a love battle—there was a century of middle class love spent here. This was the last love battle. . . . All my beautiful lovely safe world blew itself up here in a great gust of high-explosive love. . . . Isn't that true, Rosemary?' " In Book III Dick has finally recognized the reality of the meaning of World War I for his class and society. After leaving, significantly, the Café des Allies Dick drunkenly but with bitter accuracy assaults Lady Caroline: " 'It's all right for you English, you're doing a dance of death. . . . Sepoys in the ruined fort, I mean Sepoys at the gate and gaiety at the fort and all that. The green hat, the crushed hat, no future.' "

V

As Dick declines, morally, mentally, and particularly in the psychic energy on which Nicole has fed during all the years of their marriage, Nicole first begins to resent him, "everything he did annoyed her now," then to hate him—" 'Either you think [she muses] or else others have to think for you and take power from you, pervert and discipline your natural tastes, civilize and sterilize you,' " eventually to pity him, and finally, armed with the borrowed strength of Tommy Barban, she breaks with him. "Suddenly, in the space of two minutes she achieved her victory and justified herself to herself without lie or subterfuge, cut the cord forever." She feels "her ego . . . blooming like a great rich rose"; she feels in the classic jargon of those who have been through therapy herself only more so. " 'I've gone back to my true self. . . . My grandfather was a crook and so I'm a crook by heritage.' "

Indeed she has reverted to her primal self, rapacious, amoral, pitiless, using men's strength but herself never used—Aphrodite reborn. And therein lies the essence of Nicole's tragedy. Thinking herself free she has in fact only played out the second act of the female counter-transference as Freud so astutely analyzed it. In layman's terms she is not cured, has not worked out the original neurosis, but simply switched doctors, under the pretext that the new man is a more forceful father-lover figure than the man she has used up.

Fitzgerald makes this very plain, first in her silent final battle with Dick when he specifically says, "Again she struggled with it, fighting him with her small fine eyes, with the plush arrogance of a top dog, with her nascent transference to another man. . . ." The word "transference" is used accurately and specifically. Nicole is not in love in a healthy or normal sense; she has simply found a new protector. When she has a last-minute scruple she says to Tommy, as she sees Dick for the last time on the terrace over-looking the beach on which she and Tommy are lying,

" 'I'm going to him.' Nicole got to her knees. 'No, you're not,' said Tommy, pulling her down firmly." And this is where she wants to be, secure under force, dominance, guidance, this that she craves and always will crave, take and use for her own purpose, and who knows but if the Aphrodite-Nicole, born anew, may in time find Tommy an even more appetizing victim than Dick Diver? We may be sure that for Fitzgerald, Nicole will always go on.

Dick's situation is far more complex and tragic. He has actually been released from the counter-transference, both by the forced removal of his love object and by his own devastating realization that the best, most potentially productive years of his life have been spent in a subtly eroding neurosis which has left him psychically drained. He has not really lived, but rather dreamt out the better part of his life, fled with Keats's "light-winged Dryad" from reality where youth indeed "grows pale and spectre-thin and dies . . . / Where Beauty cannot keep her lustrous eyes / Or new Love pine at them beyond tomorrow." His "mid-May's eldest child," the cheating poetry of his life, romantic love, the Nightingale who "was not born for death" has left him:

> Forlorn! the very word is like a bell
> To toll me back from thee to my sole self!
> Adieu! the fancy cannot cheat so well
> As she is fam'd to, deceiving elf.
> Adieu! adieu! thy plaintive anthem fades
> Past the near meadows, over the still stream,
> Up the hill-side; and now 'tis buried deep
> In this next valley glades;
> Was it a vision, or a waking dream?
> Fled is that music:—Do I wake or sleep?

From his high terrace Dick, released forever into the liberty of the lost, and the loneliness of the self-knowing, the knowledge that life is too little left for living, at last "raised his right hand and with a papal cross he blessed the beach."

DAVID PARKER

"The Great Gatsby": Two Versions of the Hero

Together with many other works of fiction, *The Great Gatsby* is often interpreted as a parable of disenchantment with 'the American Dream'. Such it may be, but the experience of strong idealism, boundless optimism, and a sense of destiny, all terminated by the failure of actuality to measure up to hope, is not an experience peculiar to citizens of the U.S.A. *The Great Gatsby* is a masterpiece not by American standards alone.

I propose to examine the novel against the background of English literature. It makes sense to see Fitzgerald, a student of English at Princeton, as an Anglo-Saxon rather than purely American writer, and it seems to me that the notable position of the novel in the history of Western sensibility is best brought out by studying it against the older tradition. Such a method, incidentally, helps define 'The American Dream' more exactly.

There are in English literature two chief versions of the hero. Often they share characteristics, and sometimes a hero is a blend of the two, but there is a tendency for polarisation in one direction or the other, towards distinct patterns of behaviour and character. The first kind of hero is the one whose prototype we find in mediaeval romance and ancient epic: an idealist, loyal to some transcending object, and relentless in his quest for it. He seeks honour, love, or the Sangreal, and he affects the reader with all the potency of myth. The second kind, though

From *English Studies* 1, vol. 54, (February 1973).

doubtless developed from the first, is in sharp contrast. If he has a quest, it is essentially an inward one. Circumstances compel him to explore his own being, to discover, and perhaps to modify, his own identity. He is typified by the hero of the novel of sentimental education.

Versions of the hero roughly corresponding to these two are to be found in American literature. Philip Rahv, in his witty essay on 'Paleface and Redskin' in American literature, asks the reader to consider 'the immense contrast between the drawing-room fictions of Henry James and the open-air poems of Walt Whitman'. The dichotomy suggested by this contrast is a serious one, he declares, 'a dichotomy between experience and consciousness—a dissociation between energy and sensibility, between conduct and theories of conduct, between life conceived as an opportunity and life conceived as a discipline'. Paleface writers tend naturally to write about paleface heroes, redskin writers about redskin heroes. 'The typical American writer', says Rahv, 'has so far shown himself incapable of escaping the blight of one-sidedness: of achieving that mature control which permits the balance of impulse with sensitiveness, of natural power with philosophical depth'.

The achievement of *The Great Gatsby*, it seems to me, is in the profoundly satisfying way Fitzgerald manages to include both versions of the hero in one vision, balancing each against the other, and avoiding 'the blight of one-sidedness'. Nor, it seems to me, does Fitzgerald thus merely correct a flaw in American letters. His achievement is greater than that. He dramatizes the dilemma of Western twentieth-century man, wavering between energy and sensibility. These terms are embarrassingly wide and vague, perhaps, yet such is the significance of the novel, one hesitates to use narrower, more finical terms. The text, however, unlike the slipshod terms we may use to describe it, does not embarrass in the least.

It has often been observed that Gatsby is in the line of the heroes of romance. 'He had committed himself to the following of a grail', Nick Carraway tells us. It is more profitable, I think, to compare Gatsby, not with the heroes of mediaeval romance, but with a more recent version of the same figure, so that we can detect the tradition modifying itself on a smaller time-scale. Fitzgerald's treatment of Gatsby seems to me to invite comparison with Browning's treatment of his hero in 'Childe Roland to the Dark Tower Came'. Here we see one advantage of studying *The Great Gatsby* against the background of English literature. The knight errant, as such, was still a potent figure for the nineteenth-century English writer and his audience, whereas for their American counterparts, as we see from the writings of Twain for instance, he was a figure of fun. Gatsby is preposterous, but there is something admirable in his chivalrous idealism as well. Fitzgerald manages to generate for Gatsby a kind of wondering respect.

Both Gatsby and Childe Roland pursue their quests in an atmosphere of lies, suspicion, and ambiguity. Gatsby's absurdity inclines the reader to doubt his promise of 'God's own truth', and by chapter six, like Nick, he has 'reached the point of believing everything and nothing' about Gatsby, Gatsby's family, Gatsby's career, and Gatsby's affairs. 'Childe Roland' opens with uncertainty:

> My first thought was, he lied in every word,
> That hoary cripple, with malicious eye
> Askance to watch the workings of his lie
> On mine, and mouth scarce able to afford
> Suppression of the glee that pursed and scored
> Its edge at one more victim gained thereby.

The cripple turns out to have told the truth, though, and so in many instances does Gatsby.

The great difference is that Fitzgerald's hero is himself suspect, whereas Browning's only moves in a world where suspicion is necessary. This difference marks the changing rôle of the romantic hero. In the eighteen-fifties it was possible to believe that a heroic quest might bear fruit. The world seemed hostile and malicious, the goal enigmatic—the Dark Tower is ugly and inscrutable—but nevertheless, the hero might retain his integrity and confront his destiny. Fitzgerald writes for a different era, one which suspects the very possibility of such a quest. Gatsby can neither maintain his integrity unscathed, nor find an ideal 'commensurate to his capacity for wonder'. He has to be content with Daisy, careless, fallible, and treacherous.

Neither Childe Roland nor Gatsby are deterred by delay or the prospect of failure. Finding himself at last within reach of the Dark Tower, Childe Roland meditates:

> For, what with my whole world-wide wandering,
> What with my search drawn out thro' years, my hope
> Dwindling into a ghost not fit to cope
> With that obstreperous joy success would bring,
> I hardly tried now to rebuke the spring
> My heart made, finding failure in its scope.
>
> (st. iv)

Gatsby is no less tenacious, loving Daisy unswervingly for five years, despite their separation and her marriage. When the prospect of reunion is near, his demand is that she should say to her husband, 'I never loved you', no less. But once again there is a difference. Childe Roland admits the possibility of failure, but Browning cuts his poem off short before the contest is decided. It is enough that his hero should confront his destiny undeterred: 'Dauntless the slug-horn to my lips I set / And blew. "*Childe Roland to the Dark Tower came*" '. Gatsby too is dauntless, but absurdly so. He cannot conceive failure, and in a sense fails less than the image he chose to embody his dreams. Even this, however, he does not recognize, keeping a 'sacred' vigil outside Daisy's house after she has revealed herself all too humanly weak. To Browning's generation heroism appeared difficult; to Fitzgerald's it appears absurd.

Both Childe Roland and Gatsby cross symbolic waste lands in their quests. Much of the poem is taken up with descriptions of this sort:

> So on I went. I think I never saw
> Such starved ignoble nature; nothing throve:
> For flowers—as well expect a cedar grove!
> But cockle, spurge, according to their law
> Might propagate their kind, with none to awe,
> You'd think: a burr had been a treasure-trove.
>
> No! penury, inertness, and grimace,
> In some strange sort, were the land's portion. 'See
> Or shut your eyes'—said Nature peevishly—
> 'It nothing skills: I cannot help my case:
> The Judgment's fire alone can cure this place,
> Calcine its clods and set my prisoners free.'
>
> (sts. x–xi)

Fitzgerald's waste land is just as barren:

> About half-way between West Egg and New York the motor road hastily joins the railroad and runs beside it for a quarter of a mile, so as to shrink away from a certain desolate area of land. This is a valley of ashes—a fantastic farm where ashes grow like wheat into ridges and hills and grotesque gardens; where ashes take the forms of houses and chimneys and rising smoke and, finally, with a transcendent effort, of ash-grey men, who move dimly and already crumbling through the powdery air. Occasionally a line of grey cars crawls along an invisible track, gives out a ghastly creak, and comes to a rest, and immediately the ash-grey men swarm up with leaden spades and stir up an impenetrable cloud, which screens their obscure operations from your sight.
>
> But above the grey land and the spasms of bleak dust which drift endlessly over it, you perceive, after a moment, the eyes of Doctor T.J. Eckleburg. The eyes of Doctor T.J. Eckleburg are blue and gigantic—their retinas are one yard high. They look out of no face, but instead,

> from a pair of enormous yellow spectacles which pass over a non-existent nose. Evidently some wild wag of an oculist set them there to fatten his practice in the borough of Queens, and then sank down himself into eternal blindness, or forgot them and moved away. But his eyes, dimmed a little by many paintless days, under sun and rain, brood on over the solemn dumping ground.
>
> (ch. ii)

The image of the waste land was as much a possession of the Victorian sensibility as it is of the modern. For both it performs a complex symbolic function, as we see in these examples. It reminds us of the squalor and destructiveness of industrial civilization. Fitzgerald's 'line of grey cars' has the same effect on the reader as the terrible machine of Browning's poem:

> What bad use was that engine for, that wheel,
> Or brake, not wheel—that harrow fit to reel
> Men's bodies out like silk?
>
> (st. xxiv)

The waste land suggests a withdrawal of value and significance from the world of human affairs. Nature herself, in Browning's poem, explains the predicament: providence is external, remote; only the Last Judgment will set things right. In the novel, all that remains is a ghastly parody of providence. Looking at the faceless eyes of Doctor T.J. Eckleburg, the demented Wilson mutters, 'You may fool me, but you can't fool God!' His surprised neighbour has to tell him, 'That's an advertisement'.

The waste land dramatizes for us the way in which society dwarfs and obscures the efforts of individuals, giving them the appearance of perversion. The inhabitants of Browning's 'grey plain' are evident only in the traces of their struggles:

> What made those holes and rents
> In the dock's harsh swarth leaves—bruised as to baulk
> All hope of greenness?
>
> (st. xxii)

> Who were the strugglers, what war did they wage
> Whose savage trample thus could pad the dank
> Soil to a plash?
>
> (st. xxii)

Similarly, 'the ash-grey men' of Fitzgerald's 'grey land' raise 'an impenetrable cloud, which screens their obscure operations from your sight'. Cruelty, suffering and violent death are the real business of the waste land, we learn. The 'stiff blind horse' Childe Roland encounters 'must be wicked to deserve such pain'. Fording a stream, the Childe fears to set his foot 'upon a dead man's cheek'. The Wilsons mentally torture each other on Fitzgerald's waste land, and it is there that Myrtle Wilson is killed by the 'death car'. All these things point towards the malignity of the contemporary environment; others towards its sterility. Weeds scarcely grow on Browning's waste land, and the ashes on Fitzgerald's mock the beholder by mimicking in ashen shapes wheat, gardens and human habitations.

The Childe and Gatsby both move in worlds in which corruption is the norm. Childe Roland laments the failure of 'the Band', all those who sought the Dark Tower; laments Cuthbert, fallen through 'one night's disgrace', and Giles, 'the soul of honour', at last hanged, 'Poor traitor, spit upon and cursed'. As he confronts his destiny before the Dark Tower, the Childe sees all around him the shapes of his lost and fallen peers, 'met / To view the last' of him. In Gatsby's world it is less the fall from honour that is striking than the failure to attain honour. Gatsby's guests slander him; his colleagues are typified by Mr. Wolfsheim who fixed the world series in 1919; and he is despised by the despicable Tom Buchanan. Childe Roland's end is celebrated with some ceremony by the shades of his disgraced companions. At Gatsby's funeral, however, his former companions are conspicuously absent. For Browning even failure and disgrace have some dignity, but Gatsby's shabby acquaintances are to the end cowardly and ungenerous.

The Childe and Gatsby are finally alike in sharing the courage to believe in the value of the objects of their quests. Childe Roland is prepared for the Tower's unimpressiveness:

> The round squat turret, blind as the fool's heart,
> Built of brown stone, without a counterpart
> In the whole world.
>
> (st. xxxi)

But he and other members of 'The Band' know its value, know its uniqueness. Gatsby's courage is similar, but of a different order. He recognizes the danger of making Daisy the embodiment of his dreams:

> The quiet lights in the houses were humming out into the darkness and there was a stir and bustle among the stars. Out of the corner of his eye Gatsby saw that the blocks of the sidewalks really formed a ladder and mounted to a secret place above the trees—he could climb to it, if he climbed alone, and once there he could suck on the pap of life, gulp down the incomparable milk of wonder.

'. . . if he climbed alone': Gatsby could revel with impunity as a solitary dreamer, but courageously he projects his dream onto actuality:

> His heart beat faster and faster as Daisy's white face came up to his own. He knew that when he kissed this girl, and forever wed his unutterable

> visions to her perishable breath, his mind would never romp again like the mind of God. So he waited, listening for a moment longer to the tuning-fork that had been struck upon a star. Then he kissed her. At her lips' touch she blossomed for him like a flower and the incarnation was complete.
>
> (ch. vi)

Value really does reside in the object of the Childe's quest, proportional to his expectations. The tower is ugly, but unique. Disaster is threatened only by its magnitude and mystery, by the Childe's not being adequate to its challenge. Disaster comes to Gatsby because Daisy is not adequate to his dreams. Once more we notice the changing rôle of the romantic hero. Browning's generation were willing to accept the proposition that he could discover value, albeit with difficulty, in the external world. Fitzgerald's felt that value, more often than not, had to be created by the individual, as best he could.

Nick Carraway, the narrator, is the other sort of hero in *The Great Gatsby*, the sort whose sentimental education is advanced. Though detailed comparison is unnecessary in this case, it is worth remarking that Nick in many respects resembles Lockwood, the narrator of *Wuthering Heights*. Both have obvious deficiencies, as men and as tellers of the particular story, but both, through contemplating the astonishing actions and strange passions of others, learn enough at least to begin the correction of those deficiencies. Both come to contemplate with sympathy that which before they could not, or would not, understand.

As he tells us himself, Nick is slow-thinking. He does not learn immediately from his experiences with Gatsby, but slowly, reluctantly, and in retrospect. At the beginning of the novel he tells us, 'When I came back from the East last autumn [after Gatsby's death] I felt that I wanted the world to be in uniform and at a sort of moral attention forever; I wanted no more riotous excursions with privileged glimpses into the human heart'. Nick's slowness in learning gives an added touch of plausibility to his narration, and makes it very much more dramatic for the reader, who sees him, in the course of the novel, gradually coming to a realization of what his experiences may teach him. This initial response he describes betrays the very deficiency in his character he learns to correct: Nick wants the world and the people in it to be cleaner and simpler than they really are. He values honesty, self-sufficiency, and sticking to the rules—all good things to value, but not in themselves enough. Nick at first is cold-hearted and reluctant to recognize the complexity of human beings.

His narration starts like this:

> In my younger and more vulnerable years my father gave me some advice that I've been turning over in my mind ever since.
>
> 'Whenever you feel like criticizing anyone', he told me, 'just remember that all the people in this world haven't had the advantages that you've had'.

Sound enough advice. It is reflections of this sort that help Nick eventually to appreciate Gatsby. But it is advice that provides a rational as much for cold-heartedness as it does for sympathy. 'Reserving judgments', says Nick, 'is a matter of infinite hope' (ch. i), but it is a niggling sort of hope, compared with Gatsby's 'extraordinary gift for hope' (ch. i). One of the stories Nick tells in *The Great Gatsby* is the story of how he was able to reach his final judgment on Gatsby:

> No—Gatsby turned out all right at the end; it is what preyed on Gatsby, what foul dust floated in the wake of his dreams that temporarily closed out my interest in the abortive sorrows and short-winded elations of men.
>
> (ch.i)

Nick at first is reluctant to come to terms with the 'foul dust'.

Like his father's advice, Nick's family background as a whole, well-established, well-to-do, Middle Western, is both an advantage and a disadvantage in his sentimental education. It gives him a secure sense of identity and a moral standpoint, but also a moral retreat to which he may withdraw from the unfamiliar. In the first chapter Nick is ironical at the expense of 'the secret griefs of wild, unknown men', and takes comfort in his father's maxim that 'a sense of the fundamental decencies is parcelled out unequally at birth'. It is not until the last that he reflects how easy it is to be 'a little complacent from growing up in the Carraway house in a city where dwellings are still called through decades by a family's name'. Admittedly, Nick has always made himself accessible to the 'wild, unknown men', but more out of habit and the respect he has for his self-image than anything else. 'Frequently', he tells us, 'I have feigned sleep, preoccupation, or a hostile levity when I realized by some unmistakable sign that an intimate revelation was quivering on the horizon' (ch. i). Nick wisely does not return to the West until he has sustained the shocks the East gives to his complacency. Only then is he able knowingly to embrace the West's values.

Nick's Western background, perhaps, contributes to the exaggerated value he puts on self-sufficiency. 'Life is much more successfully looked at from a single window, after all', he says. But it is a statement imbued with the irony Nick adopts when reviewing ideas he has discarded. Gatsby tries looking at life through a single window, with lamentable results. Tom Buchanan, Daisy's husband, seeks to interpret life like a football game, and Tom is not admirable. The success that arises from looking at life through a single window is of the sort that confers on the individual a pleasing style, but no readiness to judge and sympathize with the unfamiliar and unexpected. Until he learns otherwise, Nick admires Jordan Baker, 'this clean hard limited person, who dealt in universal scepticism'. 'Almost any exhibition of complete self-sufficiency', he admits, 'draws a stunned tribute from me' (ch. i).

Until he learns otherwise, Nick shares with Jordan Baker more moral inclinations than he cares to admit. Like her, though less pronouncedly, he tends to feel safer 'on a plane where any divergence from a code would be thought impossible' (ch. iii). He is in fact something of a prig. Many men who fought in the world wars returned to civilian life nostalgic for the moral simplicity of army life, and Nick is one of them. He reveals his priggish impulses in the account he gives of his first visit to the Buchanans' house. When he learns that it is Tom's mistress on the telephone, Nick's response is characteristic: 'To a certain temperament the situation might have seemed intriguing—my own instinct was to telephone immediately for the police'. Nick is without sympathy for the way the Buchanans cope with their marital problems: 'I was confused and a little disgusted as I drove away. It seemed to me that the thing for Daisy to do was to rush out of the house, child in arms—but apparently there were no such intentions in her head'. These statements are not free from Nick's self-mocking irony. That is what redeems them. But they do indicate a certain unfeigned inflexibility of sympathy.

Nick prides himself on his honesty: 'Every one suspects himself of at least one of the cardinal virtues, and this is mine: I am one of the few honest people that I have ever known' (ch. iii). He is indeed candid, and refrains from telling lies: in that rests the value of his narration. But Nick's honesty seems almost insignificant compared with Gatsby's peculiar dishonesty. Like any virtue, honesty can be used negatively, to narrow and limit sympathy. Gatsby was dishonest with himself and others; his personality was merely 'an unbroken series of successful gestures', and yet 'there was something gorgeous about him, some heightened sensitivity to the promises of life' (ch. i). The limitations of Nick's honesty are exposed in his reactions to his discovery that Jordan Baker is 'incurably dishonest'. 'It made no difference to me', says Nick. 'Dishonesty in a woman is a thing you never blame deeply—I was casually sorry, and then I forgot' (ch. iii). Nick wears his honesty for adornment, and to simplify things (it enables him to disapprove of Gatsby for instance). It is not something he values absolutely.

He boasts of his honesty in the conduct of his love affairs. Three of Nick's girls are mentioned in the novel. One is the girl to whom, so Tom and Daisy have heard, Nick is engaged. He denies this: 'The fact that gossip had published the banns was one of the reasons I had come East. You can't stop going with an old friend on account of rumours, and on the other hand I had no intention of being rumoured into marriage' (ch. i). When he begins to think himself in love with Jordan, Nick remembers the girl at home:

> I am slow-thinking and full of interior rules that act as brakes on my desires, and I knew that first I had to get myself definitely out of that tangle back home. I'd been writing letters once a week and signing them: 'Love, Nick', and all I could think of was how, when that certain girl played tennis, a faint moustache of perspiration appeared on her upper lip. Nevertheless there was a vague understanding that had to be tactfully broken off before I was free.
>
> (ch. iii)

Nick is indeed full of interior rules; it is a condition of his honesty. But it is also a condition of his coldness. He is so reserved, such a careful scrutineer of persons, their dispositions and their motives, that he is near incapable of achieving any close relationship. Nick's account of his affair with a girl in New York confirms this. He treats her in much the same way, and for the same reasons, as the girl at home: 'I even had a short affair with a girl who lived in Jersey City and worked in the accounting department, but her brother began throwing mean looks in my direction, so when she went on her vacation in July I let it blow quietly away' (ch. iii). In both cases, Nick abandons the relationship in order that his intentions may not be misinterpreted by third persons. He is more anxious that his honesty be publicly recognized, than he is to achieve any genuine intimate relationship.

It is fitting that Nick should toy with the idea of loving Jordan, whom he admires for her self-sufficiency. As Gatsby projects his romantic heroic dreams onto Daisy, so Nick projects his sceptical anti-heroic vision onto Jordan. Both girls become symbolic of their admirers' fantasies; both seem to promise the state of being each eagerly seeks. But where Daisy fails Gatsby by not measuring up to his vision, Jordan educates Nick by showing him the inadequacy of his.

Nick's rupture with Jordan shows him that honesty is not a simple value, that cleanness and simplicity are not enough in the conduct of personal relations. It marks, moreover, the beginning of Nick's maturity.

The initial break occurs during a telephone conversation, shortly after Myrtle Wilson's death. 'We talked like that for a while', says Nick, 'and then abruptly we weren't talking any longer. I don't know which of us hung up with a sharp click, but I know I didn't care' (ch. viii). Nick is puzzled by this departure from his own normal routine, and seeks to tidy things up in a final meeting: 'I wanted to leave things in order and not just trust that obliging and indifferent sea to sweep my refuse away' (ch. ix). But this final meeting forces Nick to recognize the complexity of human beings and their relations. Jordan rebukes him for his attitude: 'I thought you were rather an honest and straightforward person. I thought it was your secret price'. Nick however is no longer so assured about the nature of honesty. 'I'm thirty', he says, 'I'm five years too old to lie to myself and call it honour'. Nick has in fact discovered human complexity within himself: 'She didn't answer. Angry, and half in love with her, and tremendously sorry, I turned away' (ch. ix).

On reflection, Nick learns, not merely to assess experience honestly, but to accept the paradoxes of human conduct and personality, with sympathy as well as understanding. He learns to look at life through a variety of windows, from more than one point of view, and to accept the sobering wisdom this achievement brings. As he says on a more trivial occasion, 'It is invariably saddening to look through new eyes at things upon which you have expended your own powers of adjustment' (ch. vi).

The different ways in which Gatsby and Nick contrast sharpen the difference between the two sorts of hero, and this is nowhere more evident than in their attitudes to time. To the hero of romance, time is insignificant. In the Arthurian romances characters exist in a timeless world; no one ages or dies of natural causes; questing after the Sangreal, the hero seeks a timeless truth. The great age of the Round Table, in the *Morte d'Arthur*, passes away not naturally, but through treachery and catastrophe. 'Childe Roland to the Dark Tower Came' is a poem intensely aware of its era, of the mid-nineteenth century, its peculiar problems and anxieties; but it is a poem, nevertheless, in the romance tradition. Despite 'the woe of years', the Childe is able to confront his timeless destiny. The normal processes of time even seem to be waived so that he may recognize the Tower:

> Not see? because of night perhaps?—Why, day
> Came back again for that! before it left,
> The dying sunset kindled through a cleft.
> (st. xxxii)

The hero of the novel of sentimental education, on the other hand, exists very much in time, and changes with time. David Copperfield and

Clarissa discover truth only in time, and are altered through and by time. The consciousness of each is shaped by time.

The Great Gatsby is a novel deeply concerned with time. It contains repeated allusions to hours, days and seasons suggestive of change. At the beginning of the novel, Nick has 'that familiar conviction that life was beginning again with summer'. In chapter five he speaks of the end of the afternoon, 'the hour of profound human change'; in chapter six of 'a cool night with that mysterious excitement in it which comes at the two changes of the year'. Jordan says, in chapter seven, 'Life starts all over again when it gets crisp in the fall'; and Nick meditates on his age: 'I was thirty. Before me stretched the portentous, menacing road of a new decade'. On the morning after Mrs. Wilson's death, Nick notices 'an autumn flavour in the air', and at the end of the novel he says, 'when the blue smoke of brittle leaves was in the air and the wind blew the wet laundry stiff on the line I decided to come back home'.

Most of these observations on time and change are made by Nick in his rôle as narrator. He has learned to respect time. But during the course of the events he describes in the novel, he was tempted to forget it:

> Thirty—the promise of a decade of loneliness, a thinning list of single men to know, a thinning brief-case of enthusiasm, thinning hair. But there was Jordan beside me, who, unlike Daisy, was too wise ever to carry well-forgotten dreams from age to age. As we passed over the dark bridge her wan face fell lazily against my coat's shoulder and the formidable stroke of thirty died away with the reassuring pressure of her hand.
>
> (ch. vii)

Gatsby, on the other hand, as befits a hero of romance, never once deigns to recognize time. He is prepared to wait years for Daisy, and to unlearn those intervening years when he thinks at last he has her. Nick warns him that Daisy might not be capable of this:

> 'I wouldn't ask too much of her', I ventured. 'You can't repeat the past'.
>
> 'Can't repeat the past?' he cried incredulously. 'Why of course you can!'
>
> He looked around him wildly, as if the past were lurking here in the shadow of his house, just out of reach of his hand.
>
> 'I'm going to fix everything just the way it was before', he said, nodding determinedly. She'll see'.
>
> (ch. vi)

But Gatsby fails to abolish the past for Daisy. She is unable to say she never loved Tom.

Nick, however, learns the importance of time, the way time modifies value. He learns that human experience must be understood in the context of time, human affairs adjusted to a recognition of time. He learns ultimately the generosity that follows when we see each other moving through time towards death:

> Gatsby believed in the green light, the orgastic future that year by year recedes before us. It eluded us then, but that's no matter—to-morrow we will run faster, stretch out our arms still further . . . And one fine morning—
>
> So we beat on, boats against the current, borne back ceaselessly into the past.
>
> (ch. ix)

Another difference between the two sorts of hero is in what they recognize as real. Nick and Gatsby see different realities. Gatsby's is naturally that of the hero of romance. The everyday is unreal for him; reality is what he has discovered through his dreams. The hero of the novel of sentimental education lives in a world where reality is elusive: he thinks he possesses it, but finally discovers it only when his education is completed. The hero of romance, on the other hand, is from the beginning acquainted with reality, though he may have to wait to possess it, as Childe Roland has to wait for the Dark Tower. Heredity makes Gatsby a dreamer. His father, whom we meet only after the son's death, like Gatsby prefers the image to the object. He sets more value on an old and cherished photograph of Gatsby's mansion than on the mansion itself. 'He had shown it so often', remarks Nick, 'that I think it was more real to him now than the house itself' (ch. ix). There is irony in Gatsby's dying at the hand of just such another dreamer, Wilson who projects a dream of divine providence onto the massive eyes of Doctor T.J. Eckleburg watching over the valley of ashes.

Gatsby's apprehension of reality is explained in a much quoted passage:

> The truth was that Jay Gatsby of West Egg, Long Island, sprang from his Platonic conception of himself. He was a son of God—a phrase which, if it means anything, means just that—and he must be about His Father's business, the service of a vast, vulgar, and meretricious beauty. So he invented just the sort of Jay Gatsby that a seventeen-year-old boy would be likely to invent, and to this conception he was faithful to the end.
>
> (ch. vi)

Gatsby touches all his surroundings with this gaudy idealism, in an effort to persuade himself of the 'unreality of reality'. Owl-eyes, the sympathetic drunk inexplicably adrift in Gatsby's world, marvels that the books in his library are real—not 'nice durable cardboard'—and compares Gatsby to

Belasco, the producer noted for his insistence on authentic properties. Like Belasco, Gatsby is more of a showman than an artist, but he puts his heart into the show. Daisy could not but fall short of Gatsby's dream, Nick points out: 'It had gone beyond her, beyond everything. He had thrown himself into it with creative passion, adding to it all the time, decking it out with every bright feather that drifted his way. No amount of fire or freshness can challenge what a man can store up in his ghostly heart' (ch. v).

Nick imagines Gatsby's disenchantment with Daisy and with his dream before he is murdered by Wilson:

> He must have looked up at an unfamiliar sky through frightening leaves and shivered as he found what a grotesque thing a rose is and how raw the sunlight was upon the scarcely created grass. A new world, material without being real, where poor ghosts, breathing dreams like air, drifted fortuitously about . . . like that ashen, fantastic figure gliding towards him through the amorphous trees.
>
> (ch. viii)

Whether Gatsby at last abandoned his dream of reality or not, is less important than 'the colossal vitality of his illusion', at its height. Even more important is what Nick learns about reality from contemplating Gatsby's illusion.

From the beginning of the events described in the novel, Nick observes his surroundings with candour and with imagination, but there is something lacking. His imagination is capable only of aesthetic excursions. Getting drunk in Tom and Myrtle's lofty love-seat, he thinks how the windows of the apartment must appear to watchers in the streets:

> Yet high over the city our line of yellow windows must have contributed their share of human secrecy to the casual watcher in the dark streets, and I saw him too, looking up and wondering. I was within and without, simultaneously enchanted and repelled by the inexhaustible variety of life.
>
> (ch. ii)

Nick's sensitivity to the complexities and subtleties of aesthetic apprehension contrasts with the insensitivity of Mr. McKee, the photographer, whose portfolio contains studies with titles like 'Beauty and the Beast . . . Loneliness . . . Old Grocery House . . . Brook'n Bridge . . .' (ch. ii). It is this sensitivity that Nick shows in his response to Gatsby, Gatsby's parties, Gatsby's possessions; he refrains from oversimplifying, neither sparing the absurdity, nor ignoring the glamour.

But it takes time for Nick to reach the point where he can extend this sensitivity from aesthetic into moral judgment. He does not believe all the scandal about Gatsby, but he disapproves of him, and for the greater part of the novel keeps him at a distance, as it were, by treating him purely as an aesthetic phenomenon. Gatsby's extraordinary account of his life provokes only delighted irony from Nick: 'Then it was all true. I saw the skins of tigers flaming in his palace on the Grand Canal: I saw him opening chests of rubies to ease, with their crimson-lighted depths, the gnawings of his broken heart' (ch. iv). Only slowly, and in spite of himself, does Nick come to appreciate the human and moral reality of Gatsby, to appreciate that 'the inexhaustible variety of life' is operative at the moral as well as at the aesthetic level.

Towards the end of the novel, Nick finds himself able, despite his moral training, to appreciate Gatsby as a man, to compliment him, 'who represented everything for which I have an unaffected scorn', and to recognize his superiority to the Buchanans' set:

> 'They're a rotten crowd', I shouted across the lawn. 'You're worth the whole damn bunch put together'.
>
> I've always been glad I said that. It was the only compliment I ever gave him, because I disapproved of him from beginning to end.
>
> (ch. viii)

After Gatsby's death Nick realises that he has entered—if only posthumously—into a substantial relationship with Gatsby: 'it grew on me that I was responsible, because no one else was interested—interested, I mean, with that intense personal interest to which everyone has some vague right at the end'. 'We were close friends', he tells Gatsby's father. Nick will go back West, at first wanting no more 'privileged glimpses into the human heart', but ready on reflection to accept the enlargement of his sympathies his experiences have produced.

The greatness of *The Great Gatsby*, it seems to me, lies primarily in the way it manages to catch the moment of change, in the development of the Western sensibility, when new attitudes to the heroic were taking shape. Nick is the hero with whom the reader, despite reservations, substantially identifies himself. Gatsby is too absurd, too astonishing. Yet Nick's sentimental education is overshadowed by Gatsby's dazzling career. We may identify with Nick, but our interest is focussed on Gatsby. This off-centre focus, it seems to me, dramatically represents the new configuration of attitudes towards the heroic. Before 1914, let us say, writers were able, either to believe in the possibilities of romantic heroism, like Browning, or to burlesque it, like Jane Austen, pointing to the more appropriate heroism of self-discovery. But even for Jane Austen, heroic action in the world at large is possible. Young officers can win fame, fortune and honour at sea.

What is new about *The Great Gatsby* is that, at the same time, it points to the necessity for heroic effort in self-discovery, burlesques romantic heroism, and laments its passing. This is perhaps where the novel is truly American. It is peculiarly the American experience to witness the disappearance of opportunities for heroic action in the world at large. But it is the experience of all Western nations too. Americans have only felt it more vividly. Philip Rahv complains of 'the dissociation of mind from experience' in American literature, as if it were the fault of American writers, but this dissociation, surely, is a result of the events of modern history, the conditions of modern social life in all developed nations.

The Great Gatsby, then, is a novel about this very dissociation, and a pre-eminently successful one because it evokes the experience of dissociation in vividly human terms. Nick, busy with self-discovery, is nevertheless fascinated by the spectacle of Gatsby attempting heroic action and heroic devotion old-style, and his sentimental education is incomplete until he is able to recognize and accept the thwarted and perverted impulses on which Gatsby's efforts are based, until he is able to feel the loss so eloquently expressed in his threnody for experiences of the sort enjoyed by the discoverers of Long Island:

> . . . gradually I became aware of the old island here that flowered once for Dutch sailors' eyes—a fresh, green breast of the new world. Its vanished trees, the trees that had made way for Gatsby's house, had once pandered in whispers to the last and greatest of all human dreams; for a transitory enchanted moment man must have held his breath in the presence of this continent, compelled into an aesthetic contemplation he neither understood nor desired, face to face for the last time in history with something commensurate to his capacity for wonder.
>
> (ch. ix)

ROBERT ROULSTON

Whistling "Dixie" in Encino: "The Last Tycoon" and F. Scott Fitzgerald's Two Souths

Had he lived to complete *The Last Tycoon*, F. Scott Fitzgerald, with his penchant for extensive revising, might have eliminated from the novel any given passage. Yet even if he had discarded the entire first chapter, the material there would be of interest if only because it offers his last reflections on a region that had preoccupied him from childhood, the South. What makes these opening pages especially noteworthy, however, is that in them he seems to be setting up the old South as a paradigm for the patterns of disintegration which he would later depict as operating upon the newer community where most of the book's action will transpire, Hollywood. This section, furthermore, may even provide clues about the nature of the ending he never lived to write.

Fitzgerald's entrancement with the South is hardly astonishing. His father, after all, was the scion of a pro-Confederate Maryland family, and his wife, Zelda, was a native of Alabama. From early 1932 to the middle of 1937, moreover, he spent most of his time in either Maryland or North Carolina. This lifelong involvement with the land below the Mason-Dixon line is amply reflected in his fiction. Not only do two of his earliest juvenile works and many of his mature short stories deal with the South; all five of his novels contain southern characters and scenes set in the region.

From *South Atlantic Quarterly* 4, vol. 79, (Autumn 1980).

Throughout these writings Fitzgerald expresses two distinct but easily reconcilable attitudes toward the South. Often it epitomizes for him glamour and romance, as it does for the narrator of "The Last of the Belles," who asserts: "I suppose poetry is a Northern man's dream of the South." But it often also represents sloth, inertia, failure—a place where once-grand houses are "yielding to poverty, rot and rain" and where shops seem "only yawning their doors and blinking their windows before retiring into a state of utter coma." As we shall see, both attitudes find their way into chapter 1 of *The Last Tycoon*. Paradoxically, though, the view of the South there is both darker and brighter than it generally is in Fitzgerald's earlier works.

Perhaps the prevailingly bleak picture he offers of Nashville and its environs reflects a new-found hostility to the entire South resulting from his painful experiences in Maryland and North Carolina during the early and middle 1930's. These experiences, we must recall, led to the emotional collapse he had disclosed in "The Crack-Up." Be that as it may, in these tentative opening pages of his last novel he also presents the South as a repository of positive values to a more striking degree than in his previous writings. He began writing *The Last Tycoon* in 1939, when he was living in Encino, and continued working on it after moving in May 1940 to Laurel Avenue in Hollywood. Whatever his other motives might have been, the chances are that, in seeking a symbol of the past to set against that most modern of places, Hollywood, he turned instinctively to the section of the country which then would have seemed to almost any American the most evocative of irrecoverable former glories. How especially evocative of times vanished must the region have been for that resident of Encino with his southern ancestral roots and with his myriad personal memories of the South!

In *The Last Tycoon* Fitzgerald wastes little time in connecting the South with the past when, in the fifth paragraph, he has Cecilia Brady, the narrator, observe that on transcontinental flights she is usually kept awake by memories of her dead sister until the airplane has passed beyond "those lonely little airports in Tennessee." Despite the interest in psychotherapy he had developed after his wife's breakdown, Fitzgerald refrains from providing a textbook-derived rationale for Cecilia's inclination to identify her deceased sister with Tennessee. Instead he soon makes it clear that the South represents not her own past but all America's—the only explanation needed in Fitzgerald's fictional world, where, perhaps because of the author's belief in what Richard D. Lehan has called a "one-to-one relationship between personal and historical tragedy," narrator and protagonist often seem miniature models of their society.

The linkage between the South and the past is expanded a few pages later when weather conditions force Cecilia's plane to land in Nashville. Almost as soon as she touches ground, Wylie White, a Tennessee-born screenwriter, whisks her off in a taxi to the nearby home of Andrew Jackson, the Hermitage. Throughout the predawn ride he reminisces ironically about his youth in the surrounding area. As the vehicle wends its way through the countryside, a Negro driving cattle conjures up for Cecilia an image of the old pastoral South that soon becomes symbolized by "the great grey hulk of the Andrew Jackson house" with its grand steps and wide pillars. Redolent of antebellum days, the building becomes a "raw shrine" before which another of her companions, a failed Hollywood entrepreneur named Manny Schwartz, in search of "something to lay himself beside" will later shoot himself.

All this may seem to suggest that Fitzgerald is preparing to contrast the romantic decay of an old society with the crass vigor of a new one. Indeed, as far back as 1920 he had made exactly such a contrast between the South and his own native northern plains in "The Ice Palace." But, as *The Last Tycoon* unfolds, Southern California emerges not as a new Minnesota but as a bizarre reincarnation of Dixie. Although hardly an ancient society, it comes to seem a place that has seen its grandest days. Cecilia, daughter of a producer, recalls Rudolph Valentino's appearance at her fifth birthday party with that blend of matter-of-factness and nostalgia with which a Georgia belle in 1870 might have remembered a ball in her family's pre-Civil War mansion. And, as Stahr escorts from a dance Kathleen Moore, the woman who is soon to become his lover, he comments on how John Barrymore and Pola Negri used to live in nearby bungalows and notes that the studios have all moved to new locations. When he adds wistfully that he has "had a good time around here, though," he sounds not unlike the narrator of "The Last of the Belles" returning to the scene of youthful memories only to discover the site changed beyond recognition. In fact the elegiac titles of two songs a drunk plays at the Nashville airport on a juke box—"Lost" and "Gone"—seem no less applicable to Southern California than to the old South.

Now, it may be argued that these titles could be applied aptly to most of Fitzgerald's settings because his nearly omnipresent theme of the disillusioned dreamer necessitates either a changing milieu or an altering perception of that milieu—and in his fiction places and people are both generally transformed. But, if for Fitzgerald all communities are subject to the ravages of time, all do not alter at the same pace or in the same manner. Thus, whereas in "Winter Dreams" new families are displacing more refined older ones in Minnesota, or in *The Great Gatsby* New York is becoming more crass, neither place seems threatened by the loss of vitality Fitzgerald saw as afflicting the South. In *The Last Tycoon,* however, he indicates that in this as in other respects Hollywood is to go the way of Dixie.

Fitzgerald sometimes describes Southern California, in fact, as if it were one of Joseph Conrad's tropical backwaters corroding the vitality and corrupting the morals of its exiles from more temperate zones. Thus at one point he has Cecilia contend: "There was lassitude in plenty—California was filling up with desperadoes. And there were tense young men and women who lived back East in spirit while they carried on a losing battle with the climate. But it was everyone's secret that sustained effort was difficult here." And later she asserts: "One doesn't mix motives in Hollywood—it's confusing . . . and the climate wears you down."

Here we should note that for this native of Minnesota, warm climates frequently seemed simultaneously an enticement and a menace. In his first novel, *This Side of Paradise*, he has Amory Blaine exclaim, "There were so many places where one might deteriorate pleasantly: Port Said, Shanghai, parts of Turkestan, Constantinople, the South Seas." The episode in that novel in which Amory cavorts by a pool with the mad enchantress, Eleanor Savage, in rural Maryland and "shuts his mind to all thoughts except of soap-bubble lands where the sun splattered through wind-drunk trees" suggests that he should have added Fitzgerald's father's native state to the list. In *The Beautiful and Damned*, Anthony Patch, while stationed in the South during the war, makes the region sound downright miasmic when he notes that it seems "more of Algiers than of Italy, with failed aspirations pointing back over numerous generations to some primitive Nirvana, without hope or care."

Although in *The Last Tycoon* when he writes of the South he does not ladle on the decadence with such generous globs, Fitzgerald does hint at it impressionistically. During the drive to the Hermitage when Cecilia's taxi passes over "an old rattly iron bridge with planks," Wylie White jests about having been born nearby as "the son of impoverished Southern paupers" with the "family mansion now used as an outhouse." Cecilia senses through the darkness the lushness of the terrain. Finally, at the Hermitage there are resonances of Edgar Allan Poe and his panoply of horrors when a bird flying about the house perches "on the chimney like a raven."

Perhaps because the heroine is based upon the English-born Sheilah Graham rather than upon Zelda and because the design of the book required Cecilia, the only other important woman in the book, to be a native of Hollywood, *The Last Tycoon* contains no Southern Circe such as

Eleanor Savage, Dorothy Ryecroft, or Daisy Buchanan to ensnare the Yankee hero. Nevertheless, the moral corruption we later encounter in Hollywood—especially in the person of the lecherous and ruthless Pat Brady—is foreshadowed in Nashville when Wylie White, standing before the Hermitage, identifies Andrew Jackson as "the inventor of the spoils system." And, indeed, if he had adhered to his last outline, Fitzgerald would have depicted Hollywood as turning into the moral quagmire he described it in a letter in 1940 as having become—a place where everything "is either corruption or indifference" and where, consequently, "heroes are either great corruptionists or supremely indifferent."

Thus Hollywood, the last of Fitzgerald's failed dreamlands, probably would have gone the tarnished way of Princeton in *This Side of Paradise*, New York in *The Beautiful and Damned* and *The Great Gatsby*, and the Riviera in *Tender Is the Night*. No locale, however, more perfectly represented the betrayal of romantic possibilities than the South. Once he had been able to call it "a languid paradise of dreamy skies." But although he seems never to have lost his affection for his father's native Maryland, his devastating experiences there and in North Carolina appear to have destroyed his inclination to view the South as a genteel if somewhat tainted Eden. Surely some of the hostility Wylie White, the alcoholic screenwriter, voices toward all things connected with his birthplace reflects, at least in part, Fitzgerald's attitude toward the region where he reached the spiritual and professional nadir that prompted him to write "The Crack-Up" in a shabby hotel room in Hendersonville, North Carolina.

But, whatever his personal feelings, the contrast Fitzgerald poses between the myth of southern grandeur symbolized by the Hermitage and Wylie White's embittering experiences in Tennessee makes the South in the first chapter illustrative of the way reality besmirches romance. When Cecilia's plane goes "down, down, down, like Alice in the rabbit hole" as it lands in Nashville, the promise is one of glamour and fantasy. But her experiences there provide little of either—only Wylie White's sour reminiscences, a visit to the Hermitage that disappoints her because the building looks merely like a "nice big white box" and because her party is unable to gain entry. The entire episode concludes squalidly when the pilot at the airport refuses to allow a drunk to board the plane and becomes sinister in retrospect because of Manny Schwartz's suicide.

The contrast Cecilia at one point makes between the "real" cows she sees in the "real" countryside outside Nashville and a pastoral scene she saw as a child on the back lot of the Laemmle studio seems to indicate that Fitzgerald is preparing to counterpose an old failed land of romance with a newer place where romantic possibilities still exist. But if that was ever his intention, he abandoned it when he shifted the action to Hollywood. Even in chapter 1 he offers scattered warnings to the reader to expect the worst from what he calls "a mining town in lotus land." Is the South slack? So is Hollywood, where "you can't flunk out unless you're a dope or a drunk." White has even found that the South's notorious xenophobia has a parallel in the capital of the cinema, for he maintains when he went there nobody spoke to him, the explanation being, "We don't go for strangers in Hollywood unless they wear a sign saying that their axe has been thoroughly ground elsewhere."

White makes an appropriate chorus for pointing out the defects of both the South and Hollywood because he embodies the failings of both places. A degraded character who in Fitzgerald's notes is even more contemptible than he is in the portions of the novel published in 1941, he betrays all that is best in the faded tradition of the South as well as whatever promise for the future may linger in Hollywood. Had Fitzgerald adhered to his plans for the unwritten portion of the book, White would have gone on to betray his fellow writers by helping Brady set up a company union and would have betrayed the man who represents the motion picture's last best hope—Monroe Stahr.

Not the least of the many ironies in *The Last Tycoon* is that whereas the southern "gentleman," White, is a cad, a Jew from the Bronx personifies southern patrician values. By assigning his hero the name of the fifth president, Fitzgerald links Monroe Stahr with the upper reaches of the Chesapeake Bay area aristocracy from which Fitzgerald himself was descended. Then, too, he explicitly identifies Stahr with the era in which that aristocracy was at its zenith—the late eighteenth century. In so doing he may have been using Stahr, as John F. Callahan avers, to illustrate the failings of the Enlightenment. But the passage that connects Stahr with the age of Washington and Jefferson does something no less important when it suggests the power of human imagination to provide a standard for present and future conduct: "[Stahr] had just managed to climb out of a thousand years of Jewry into the late eighteenth century. He could not bear to see it melt away—he had the parvenu's passionate loyalty to an imaginary past."

To discover the nature of the "imaginary past" to which Stahr has given his fealty, we must study his behavior, because Fitzgerald never got around to providing either Stahr or Cecilia with explicit statements on the subject. But one thing, at least, seems certain. If through Stahr Fitzgerald is offering a critique of the Englightenment, as Callahan contends, he is presenting a far more devastating one of the twentieth century. Into Fitzgerald's Hollywood flow most modern currents. Effete English novelists collaborate with decadent southerners, driven Jews, temperamental Latins, and ailing Greeks. Money men from the East lurk like predators, and into Stahr's studio comes Prince Agge, an "early Fascist," to remind the reader of horrors in Europe where "Jews were dead miserably beyond the sea." In this motley throng, Stahr, the anachronism, is by far the most admirable person, perhaps the only admirable one. White, as we have seen, is contemptible. Brady is even worse. George Boxley is a pompous ass. And the directors, financiers, actors, and cameramen who weave in and out of the novel are venal, incompetent, or undependable. As for Cecilia and Kathleen, they are too vaguely delineated to fit any precise definition.

Stahr, on the other hand, possesses what has become passé amid the vulgarity, opportunism, lethargy, and treachery that surround him—character, the quality that Charlie Wales in "Babylon Revisited" wanted to trust in again after the 1929 Crash "as the eternally valuable element." Fitzgerald himself, in fact, sometimes seemed to regard character as the best attainable substitute in this fallen century for the "reticences and obligations that go under the poor old shattered word 'breeding' "—a quality he once attributed in a letter to the Maryland side of his family. In the same letter he confessed that, contaminated as he had been by baser influences, he would "still be a parvenu" even if he were "elected King of Scotland tomorrow after graduating from Eton." But in *The Last Tycoon* he makes his fictional parvenu, Monroe Stahr, heroically will himself into embodying the patrician virtues Fitzgerald identified with his own Maryland forebears. Thus Stahr has "developed" a fatherly smile, just as he has "learned tolerance, kindness, forbearance, and even affection like lessons." Character more than talent has made him an artist. Comparing him with another self-made American, Lincoln, Boxley concludes: "Stahr like Lincoln was carrying on a war on many fronts: almost single-handed he had moved motion pictures sharply forward through a decade to a point where the content of the 'A productions' was wider and richer than that of the stage. Stahr was an artist, as Mr. Lincoln was a general, perforce and as a layman."

Here we land in a briar patch of paradoxes. Stahr, avatar of the eighteenth-century gentry and a benign autocrat who runs his studio much as Thomas Jefferson might have run Monticello, is also a latter-day Lincoln, the man who more than any other caused the demise of the old South. The ironies are compounded by the fact that the historical figure whose house in chapter 1 symbolizes the vanished glories of Dixie was no less an upstart than Lincoln or Stahr.

The paradoxes become resolved when we recall that Stahr represents the real South no more than he represents the real eighteenth century. His values, after all, derive from an "imaginary past" which incorporates the two chimeras that entice most of Fitzgerald's heroes—spectacular achievement and patrician grandeur. Both find their concrete embodiment in *The Last Tycoon* in the Hermitage, the mansion built by a frontiersman who became a wealthy planter, a victorious general, and a president of the United States. Here Mount Vernon, in effect merges with the Alger myth. The result is a relic which, while principally southern in its evocations, connotes glories of pre-Civil War America which are northern as well as southern. It also conjures up the failings of antebellum America, because Jackson was a slaveholder and, as Wylie White reminds Cecilia, the inventor of the spoils system. Then, too, the southern setting, with its resonances of decline and the tacky contemporaneity of the Nashville airport along with the cynicism of White, prefigures the forces that will beset Stahr on the West Coast.

It is, alas, impossible to be certain how Fitzgerald would have concluded *The Last Tycoon*. In the "original plans" Edmund Wilson appended to the published version of the novel, Fitzgerald wrote: "Unlike *Tender Is the Night*, it is not a story of deterioration—it is not depressing and not morbid despite the tragic ending." Yet the material Fitzgerald was able to finish before his death suggests that his view of Stahr's fall darkened as the writing progressed. In the last outline Stahr's studio is to come under the control of the unprincipled Fleishaker. And among Fitzgerald's jottings are such chilling items as "Stahr is miserable and embittered toward the end" and "Before death, thoughts from *Crack-Up*."

Perhaps, though, Fitzgerald would have mitigated the horror of his projected climax and denouement by returning in his last pages to one of the themes of his opening chapter. There, despite White's jibes and despite the squalid scene at the airport, the Hermitage looms as the repository of something precious. Both symbol and artifact, it represents the power of a departed glory, transfigured by time and tradition, to become an exemplar and a consolation. White may scoff, but he is the one who wants to go to Jackson's house. And the anguished Manny Schwartz may know nothing about the long-dead president, but he senses that "if people had preserved his house Andrew Jackson must have been someone who was large and merciful, able to understand." For Schwartz the place thus becomes a "shrine . . . to lay himself beside when no one wanted him further."

The material Fitzgerald was able to commit to paper before his death indicates that Stahr, like Jackson, would have left behind a heroic legend to sustain men in unheroic times. Even without the Nashville episode such a conclusion would be a logical extension of what Fitzgerald reveals about a Hollywood already losing its luster and about that community's "hero . . . the last of the princes." With that opening episode such a conclusion seems almost inevitable. The equivalent, however, of Jackson's Hermitage would not be Stahr's house or his studio, both of which presumably would have fallen into other hands, but his films. Just as Jackson's mansion evokes for Cecilia and her companions the flaws as well as the grandeur of Jackson and the South, so inevitably Stahr's films must not only have perpetuated the power of his vision but also have reminded his survivors of the compromises he had sometimes been forced to make by censors, financiers, and a philistine mass audience. Yet, if in his final paragraphs Fitzgerald had imposed upon his new South—Southern California—the patterns he had previously imposed upon the old South, he could still have fulfilled the promise of his earliest outline to produce a novel "not depressing and not morbid," no matter how grimly he had chosen to describe Stahr's destruction and its aftermath. Let us not forget that the acerbic comments of Wylie White, the tackiness of the Nashville airport, and the suicide of Manny Schwartz could not negate the glory represented by the Hermitage. Would not Stahr, therefore, have lived up to his name by brightening even in death the fading firmament of Hollywood?

RONALD J. GERVAIS

The Socialist and the Silk Stockings: Fitzgerald's Double Allegiance

In major works written during the "Red Scare" just after World War I and during the "Red Decade" of the 1930s, F. Scott Fitzgerald cast his responses to Marxism into the form of ambivalent literary debates in which the opponents express as much attraction for the other side as they do attachment to their own. His biography and correspondence during these periods also reveal his two-mindedness toward leftist ideology. For on this subject, too, Fitzgerald cultivated his famed double vision, his ability, as he describes it, "to hold two opposed ideas in the mind, at the same time, and still retain the ability to function." Fitzgerald uses Marxism as an outlet for his ideals and frustrations; his qualified sympathy for it represents his most extreme protest against the excesses and failings of the *haute bourgeois* class which he describes so charmingly and judges so scathingly, and to which he felt his loyalty pledged—even if it seemed to him that the class was historically doomed. He shared what he called a "double allegiance to the class I am part of, and to the Great Change I believe in." Unable to reconcile these two loyalties, he developed in his work an attitude toward Marxism that was neither embrace nor rejection.

Since Marxism tends to polarize virtually everyone who comes into contact with it, such a stance might be rejected as inconsistent, suspicious or even intolerable. But Daniel Aaron sensed its significance and value when he used Fitzgerald's *Note-Book* entry, "Forbearance—good word," as one of the epigraphs to his *Writers on the Left*. Aaron describes the way in

From *Mosaic: A Journal for the Interdisciplinary Study of Literature* 2, vol. 15, (June 1982).

which many writers between the wars impoverished themselves not because they were disgusted with capitalism nor because they damned social inequality, but because they were unable or forbidden to enter into this "double-vision." Similarly, Edmund Wilson asks if it might be possible to hold Marxist political views and yet "not depict our middle class republic as a place where no birds sing, no flowers bloom and where the very air is almost unbreathable." Fitzgerald accomplishes something very close to this. He depicts lovingly the charm and grace of capitalism's upper classes, yet consistently states his conviction, born of personal resentment and a sense of historical necessity, that they are doomed. Not entirely enthusiastic about this prospect, and with "no faith in the future of my kind in the supposedly classless society," Fitzgerald creates in his art a strategy of literary debate that permits him to deal with his ambivalence.

Fitzgerald's Marxist tendencies are more expressive of capitalist culture's disillusion with itself than of hopes for a new communist order. The appeal of Marxism for him comes not from any vision of a new social order, different from and beyond bourgeois society, but from a "socialism" that embodies the highest ideals of bourgeois society. This nostalgically bourgeois origin of Fitzgerald's socialistic strain is indicated by his response to a book that became a favorite text of his for teaching Marxism to the women in his life, *New Russia's Primer* (1931) by M. Ilin. The book is the story of Russia's Five-Year Plan, for school-children in their early teens, and it explains the difference between what it calls America's planless economy for profit and the Soviet's planned production for use. The *Primer* was bed-time reading for Fitzgerald's ten-year old daughter Scotty, was recommended by Fitzgerald to a high-class prostitute in Ashville, and was finally used in the "college of one" he set up for Sheila Graham. In the fly-leaf, he wrote to her: "A beautiful, pathetic, trusting book—old and young, rather haunting and inspiring like the things read and believed in youth. A sort of dawn comes up over the book all through—too often it illuminates old shapes that our cynicism has corrupted into nonsense. But if our totem poles can become their girders, so be it."

This idealist reading of Marxism remained consistent with Fitzgerald over his career. In a letter of 1920, he listed Marx, along with Rousseau and Tolstoi, as a man of thought, an impractical man, an "idealist" who has done "more to decide the food you eat and the things you think than all the millions of Roosevelts and Rockefellers that strut for 20 years." And in a late letter to his daughter from Hollywood, he writes that "poetry is either something that lives inside you—like music to the musician or Marxism to the Communist—or else it is nothing, an empty, formalized bore." However materialistic were the ends of Marxism, its origins, as Fitzgerald saw it, were ideal, and not unrelated to bourgeois idealism.

But underlying Fitzgerald's bourgeois idealism was the all-important idea of the primacy of the individual, and when his half-way Marxism threatened that idea, he pulled back. This was not always so: in *The Beautiful and Damned* (1922), Anthony Patch reads in his Harvard Alumni Bulletin of "a man named Daly who had been suspended from the faculty of a righteous university for preaching Marxian doctrines in the classroom," and Patch places him among "the emerging authentic personalities of his time." By 1933, however, Fitzgerald saw Marxism as at least a damper on personal intellectual freedom, and regarded his friend Edmund Wilson's conversion as "rather gloomy. A decision to adopt Communism definitely, no matter how good for the soul, must of necessity be a saddening process for anyone who has tasted the intellectual pleasures of the world we live in." That world, of course, was bourgeois individualism, with its tolerance for a multiplicity of ideas, any one of which might lead the individual to new heights of awareness and accomplishment. But against this, in Communism's being "good for the soul," is the old dream of an idealism beyond romantic egotism. Finally, Fitzgerald could suspend his ambivalences in 1935 only by saying that even though he had been "a Marxist socialist since [he] started thinking," his "writer's instinct" held him back from going all the way.

The separateness of that "writer's instinct" from ideological commitment is made clear in "The Crack-Up" (1936), in which Fitzgerald feels that someone should have helped him to keep his shop open, though "it wasn't Lenin and it wasn't God." And lest any ideologist try to explain too quickly the immolation Fitzgerald sees around him in men of honor and industry, he cautions: "I heard you, but that's too easy—there were Marxians among those men." Fitzgerald decides in the essay to give up his old dream of becoming a Bourgeois Superman, "a sort of combination of J.P. Morgan, Topham Beauclerk and St. Francis of Assisi," and to become "a writer only." Such a concept of the writer as complete individualist and as reduced from total man to the writing function only, immediately drew the fire of John Dos Passos, who in a letter of October 1936 remonstrated with Fitzgerald in the vein of the committed author: "Christ, man, how do you find time in the middle of the general conflagration to worry about all that stuff. . . . We're living in one of the damnedest tragic moments in history—if you want to go to pieces I think it's absolutely o.k." If cracking up is in question, to the Marxist sympathizer Dos Passos it is the cracking up of a whole world that matters, not of an individual self. Dos Passos could not see that the artist was fulfilling his role by proceeding in

Fitzgerald's manner—that is, by looking inward, by exploring his own inner consciousness.

For Fitzgerald, despite his recognition of forces at work in society and the world, it was his own deepest feeling of self and his hero-worship of other exceptional selves—both legacies from bourgeois individualism—that gave him whatever sense of orientation he had as a writer. What finally mattered to him was not the just society but the exalted individual, though he tried to manage both. "That's the trouble with you radicals," he burst out in 1935; "You know all about communism . . . the Five-Year Plan . . . and the coming revolution, but you don't know a God-damned thing about football." And he went on to tell the story of Ted Coy, the great athlete who was the model for Basil's god-like football hero in "The Freshest Boy." Though more sympathetic to an Emersonian Great Man concept of causality than to Marx's theory of the inexorable forces of history, Fitzgerald could still try to combine both, as in his *Count of Darkness* series (1934, '35, '41), in which he has his tenth-century hero participate in the founding of feudalism, but all "in view of . . . the new Marxian interpretation." Similarly, he praised John Reed, the American radical and author of *Ten Days that Shook the World*, not as a keen observer of social revolution but as a talented and rebellious young man of action, such as Fitzgerald himself yearned to be. Despite whatever radical leanings he professed, Fitzgerald was ultimately less interested in investigating social problems than in illuminating his own experience and feeling.

Yet part of Fitzgerald did seek a social viewpoint founded on a practical observation of the facts. He told Malcolm Cowley in 1932, for example, that his "peasant" mother, Molly McQuillan, was "as realistic as Karl Marx," because she kept telling him, "All this family is a lot of shit. You have to know where the money is coming from." But he then proceeds to tell Cowley how he is descended from Francis Scott Key, to whom there is a statue in Baltimore. Fitzgerald wonders, at first jokingly, if they would put up a statue to him, "because [he] died for communism." But then, more soberly, he imagines a statue to "the author of *The Great Gatsby*!" This mixture of detached social observation and starry-eyed personal aspiration is Fitzgerald's special gift. It is, Cowley observed, as if he were describing a big dance to which he had taken the prettiest girl, and at the same time was wondering how much the tickets cost and who payed for the music. Fitzgerald knew as well as any Marxist "where the milk is watered and the sugar sanded, the rhinestone passed for diamond and the stucco for stone," but was nevertheless committed to the possibilities of romantic wonder offered by his time and place and social class.

In the early works, *This Side of Paradise* and "May Day," both of

1920, the debates make clear how attached Fitzgerald is to the romantic individualism and glittering affluence of the American upper classes, and yet how at odds he is with their debased materialism and exclusiveness. At the end of *Paradise*, Amory Blaine meets "The Big Man with Goggles," a figure—hardly a character—who may be said to represent Capitalism. Riding with him in his magnificent car is his toady, a little man who has suffered the extinction of personality that the system seems to demand of anyone other than the few "big men." The capitalist is presented as strong, confident and commanding. He and Amory seem to strike up an understanding on the basis of shared egotism and ambition. At the end of their debate, they part as friends, wishing bad luck only to each other's theories.

Amory has never argued Socialism before, but he does so here as part of his "gesture of indefinite revolt" against "a system where the richest man gets the most beautiful girl if he wants her." As he has made clear earlier, Amory does not really object to "the glittering caste system. I like having a bunch of hot cats on top, but gosh . . . I've got to be one of them." Against the romantic egotism that would make him a capitalist "hot cat," he is drawn toward a socialist idealism represented by Burne Holiday—a character based on Fitzgerald's classmate, Henry Strater, whose anti-club movement at Princeton and whose socialist pacifism in response to the war suggested to Fitzgerald a new conception of superiority.

Throughout the novel, the students joke about the conflict between capitalism and socialism. They try to get out of restaurant bills by claiming they are "Marxian socialists" and they humorously speculate about which side they will be on in the impending show-down between capitalist machine-guns and Bolshevist bombs. That Amory himself does not even half seriously believe in a socialist revolution is clear. For all of the rebelliousness and iconoclasm he expresses toward capitalism, Amory's chief goal is not to change the system but to fulfill his own uniqueness. He does not sympathize with the overworked and underpaid "bunch of dubs" who submit to capitalism. Rather, he aspires to be a "natural radical," a "spiritually unmarried man" who "continually seeks for new systems." Whatever pull he feels toward a system in which people "work for something besides themselves" is balanced by his need for individual eminence. His proposal for government ownership of industries is based on a plan to attract exceptional individuals to government by offering "blue ribbons" of honor. Amory is willing to go only half-way: his "socialism" is a rebellion against an unequal and unfair society that, by design, prevents him from fulfilling himself, but it is not a program for the good of mankind in general.

This same pattern of friendly rivalry, of jousting between equal opponents who understand and admire each other but find themselves on opposite sides of history, is the pattern of all the debates. The opponents share the same qualities of self-confidence and imaginative vision. They see the attractions in the system that the other represents. In "May Day" they are even brother and sister.

Edith Bradin, who sees herself as "the world's worst social butterfly," yet who has "a streak in her of that . . . adolescent idealism that had turned her brother socialist and pacifist," leaves a Yale fraternity dance at Delmonico's to pay him a surprise midnight visit at the office where he works, pouring "the latest cures for incurable evils into the columns of a radical weekly newspaper." She finds him working under a solitary light at the far end of a long room, at the other end of which works a man who resembles a midwestern farmer on a Sunday afternoon. Fitzgerald's source for this part of the story, the attack on the socialist *New York Call* by a mob of servicemen during a daytime reception for several hundred people, has been changed to emphasize the isolated and alienated minority of Americans that socialists represent. And Fitzgerald's version is more satirical of the servicemen's general ignorance and confused motives than it is serious about any socialist threat. As he wrote later in "Echoes of the Jazz Age" (1931), "the events of 1919 left us cynical rather than revolutionary."

Edith tries to provoke her brother into the disapproval she is sure he must feel toward her, but he expresses annoyance at this and insists that she is behaving only as she was brought up to do. She reflects on their deadly enmity beneath the pleasant surface: "I began thinking how absolutely different the party I'm on is from—from all your purposes. It seems sort of—of incongruous, doesn't it?—me being at a party like that, and you over here working for a thing that'll make that sort of party impossible ever anymore, if your ideas work." But he suddenly interrupts her and says, "You're wearing beautiful stockings. What on earth are they?" She holds up her slim calves and joins him in admiration. "They're embroidered. Aren't they cunning?" Since the opening of the story had emphasized the flood-tide of consumer goods in the new peace-time economy—the trinkets and purses and slippers, the bridal suites that secretaries window-shop for on their lunch-hours—this episode seems to suggest a fatal attraction that the material beauties of capitalism have for even the most idealistic and ascetic of socialists. Henry Bradin's eyes are always described as far away and dreamy, not able to focus on the very proletariat that storms his office. He speaks literally and figuratively over their heads. But he focuses on the embroidered silk stockings and is delighted with them. The golden girl and the reformer are brother and sister under a very thin skin.

On a larger scale, *Tender is the Night* (1934) shows the same pattern. But Dick Diver's debate is more within himself. His idealism is bought out by the sick and dying yet still beautiful and captivating capitalist class that he had hoped to save. The "General Plan" of 1932 for the novel calls Dick "in fact a communist—liberal—idealist, a moralist in revolt." The tension between such commitments and Diver's compulsive tenderness for the psychoses of the leisure class suggests the conflicts that must have moved Fitzgerald while writing this novel.

Dick Diver's "communist" sympathies express themselves practically only in a suggestion, left out of the final version, that he would send his son to the Soviet Union to educate him, "thus having accomplished both his burgeoise [*sic*] sentimental ideals in the case of his wife and his ideals in the case of his son." Another vestige of the plan may also be seen in the fierce anti-communism of Dick's rival for Nicole, Tommy Barban. Tommy has fought the Soviets under Korniloff, the White Russian general, and leaves two young Red Guards dead at the border in helping an old Tsarist aristocrat to escape. But Fitzgerald's mixed intentions are indicated by his making the fatuous *arriviste* Albert McKisco the only avowed socialist in the novel. "Why do you want to fight the Soviets?" McKisco argues with Tommy Barban before their duel. "The greatest experiment ever made by humanity?"

But the book's general failure to follow the plan of 1932 and make Dick Diver a communist fits the changes in Fitzgerald's attitudes during the early 1930s. In 1931, while living in Baltimore, he became full of curiosity about the communists who were beginning to appear on all sides, and for a while his home was full of party members. He later recalled that he had been "on the verge of joining up." But his *Ledger* for 1932 speaks of "political worries that were almost neurosis" and in 1934 he announces that he has "given up politics," because he has "gone half haywire trying to reconcile my double allegiance to the class I am part of, and the Great Change I believe in." Thus, his intention to have Dick Diver be a communist was dropped, he explained in 1935, in order to make him "a living romantic idealist," "an individual," rather than "a type." Dick is finally even described in the novel as being "poor material for a socialist," because his personal ambition to do rare work cuts him off from sympathy with the masses—"God, am I like the rest after all?"

Fitzgerald's love for the romantic possibilities of individualism, against any concept of collectivism, puts him ambivalently on the side of the most individualistic of all socio-economic systems, even when he sees that its freedom has become ruinous. His description of Nicole's shopping trip in *Tender is the Night* is both an indictment of the moneyed aristocracy and a wonder-song to the glittering life-style open to them. Nicole buys from a great list and buys the things in the windows besides; everything she could not possibly use herself, she buys as a present: beach cushions, love birds, rubber alligator, chamois leather jackets and much more. Then Fitzgerald offers his poetic version of Marxist social analysis, penetrating the veil of appearances to discover the sub-stratum of crude human relations and degradations that private property masks.

> Nicole was the product of much ingenuity and toil. For her sake trains began their run at Chicago and traversed the round belly of the continent to California; chicle factories fumed and link belts grew link by link in factories; men mixed toothpaste in vats and drew mouthwash out of copper hogsheads; girls canned tomatoes quickly in August or worked rudely at the Five-and-Tens on Christmas Eve; half-breed Indians toiled on Brazilian coffee plantations and dreamers were muscled out of patent rights in new tractors—these were some of the people who gave a tithe to Nicole, and as the whole system swayed and thundered onward it lent a feverish bloom to such processes of hers as wholesale buying, like the flush of a fireman's face holding his post before a spreading blaze. She illustrated very simple principles, containing in herself her own doom, but illustrated them so accurately that there was grace in the procedure.

Despite its impending doom, the way of life open to the rich is infinitely charming. Its "feverish bloom" and "grace" are insidiously beguiling even to Dick Diver, whose ascetic ideology of the old Protestant work ethic never quite finds an extension in outright radicalism against the spending and gratification of consumer capitalism. Whatever animosity he feels is like Fitzgerald's own, as he describes it in "The Crack-Up" (1936), "not the conviction of a revolutionary but the smouldering resentment of a peasant." And for Diver, to whom "the fine quiet of the scholar is the nearest of all things to heavenly peace," any possible solidarity with girls canning tomatoes or with half-breed Indians toiling on coffee plantations would, again, be as problematic as it was with Fitzgerald himself, who noted with a sigh in "My Lost City" (1932) that Bunny Wilson had left his "cloister in a carnival" and "gone over to Communism," to fret about "the wrongs of southern mill workers and western farmers whose voices, fifteen years ago, would not have penetrated his study walls." Rejecting, then, the more drastic purge of revolution, Dick Diver tries to cure the sick system of which Nicole is the symbol, because he cannot bring himself to abandon it. But he gradually accepts the society on its own terms, becomes master of its revels, and can finally reject it only with his own life.

The debate in *The Last Tycoon* (1941) takes place between Monroe Stahr, the last prince of individualistic capitalism, and Arthur Brimmer, a sympathetically portrayed Communist labor union organizer. Once again, despite their admiration for each other, the opponents "square off" when they meet and carry on a now hidden, now open fight. Brimmer goes so far as to admit to Stahr that the writers he is trying to organize are "unstable," agrees with him that there is no substitute, whether one is a labor leader or studio chief, for the authoritarian and sometimes arbitrary will of leadership, and finally tells Stahr how impressed he is with him and what a privilege it would be to watch him work. "I like your friend," Stahr tells Cecilia Brady, the narrator; "He's crazy, but I like him." But when it comes to the question of the survival of the system under which Stahr works so hard and efficiently, the "little pricking strokes" begin between the men and build to the foreordained battle. "You think to yourself," says Brimmer, " 'He's right,' but you think the system will last out your time."

The fist fight that Stahr later drunkenly insists on having with Brimmer may have been suggested to Fitzgerald by the sparring matches he himself used to have in Baltimore with a lean intellectual who came out to discuss Marxism. The two men squared off in front of La Paix and, as Andrew Turnbull describes it, though "the gallant Marxist did not press his physical advantage, at least he had a busy time defending himself." The similarly ineffectual flurries of Stahr in his ideological show-down with Brimmer suggest Fitzgerald's reluctant belief that a desperate individualism was fighting its last futile battle against collectivism.

But Fitzgerald's ambivalence is revealed by an earlier manuscript version in which the debate and first fight take place not between Stahr and Brimmer but between Stahr and Wylie White, a writer who is sympathetic to the leftist Screen Writers Guild and who tries to tell Stahr that times have changed. In this version, the angry and sober Stahr smashes the drunken Communist writer, who then begins sobbing as they both lapse into the annoyed affection they feel for each other. A significant difference here is that Stahr reveals himself to have been a socialist in his early days. Recalling the background of "May Day," Stahr tells White that he "was an office monkey on *The New York Call.* I was there during the suppression and the raids and all us boys read the *Communist Manifesto* and swore by it." But Stahr says that he left the party because he saw no future in it for himself as "a bit shot." The moving force is still individual aspiration, just as it was in *This Side of Paradise* with Amory Blaine, who thought that a socialist revolution might land him on top.

But the most important difference between the two versions is the reversal of roles. In the earlier one, Stahr is in control and, though he reveals himself as a communist apostate, he defeats a weak and drunken communist opponent; in the later one, the drunken Stahr loses control to a strong, sober and humanly attractive communist, and defeats himself. The change is from a picture of capitalism as still capable and self-reliant before the ineffectual attacks of maudlin liberals who have been duped into communism, to one of capitalism as so sick unto death that it falls frailly before the first glancing blow from a confident, home-grown communism. This later version is so literally the party historical scenario that some parody may be suspected. Even Brimmer is a little awed at the depths of Stahr's repose, which he has created in a split second. "I always wanted to hit ten million dollars," he says, "but I didn't know it would be like this."

But despite his sympathies for both sides and his ability to project himself imaginatively into both men and understand their allegiances, neither Stahr's conservatism nor Brimmer's radicalism expresses Fitzgerald's political beliefs. Fitzgerald's secretary in Hollywood reports that while he did want to present Stahr's manner of thinking thoroughly, he did not want to justify it. "Despite Stahr's genius and artistry, he did not 'come along' politically." And by the time he was in Hollywood, Fitzgerald had decided that Marxism was incompatible with artistic freedom. "I could never be a communist," he told Sheila Graham. "I could never be regimented and told what to write." It is unlikely then, that Fitzgerald would have been sympathetic to Brimmer's attempt to organize the writers, even though he felt some of the writers' grievances against the studio system.

Another feature of *Tycoon* that indicates Fitzgerald's ambivalence between Marxism and the bourgeois-capitalist order is the constant crossing of political perspectives. Prince Agge, for example, who "had been brought up in the dawn of Scandanavian socialism," sees an actor costumed as Abraham Lincoln and "stared as a tourist at the mummy of Lenin in the Kremlin." An actor in a screen-test looks good and Stahr asks if he could be used "as the old Russian Prince in *Steppes?*" "He *is* an old Russian Prince," says an assistant, "but he's ashamed of it. He's a Red. And that's the one part he says he wouldn't play." "It's the only part he could play," says Stahr. And when Brimmer the communist, who has already been compared to Spencer Tracy and Superman by the infatuated narrator, goes down to the Trocadero for dinner with Stahr, Cecilia says he has "that look that Father O'Ney had that time in New York when he turned his collar around and went with father and me to the Russian Ballet." One side is seen in terms of the other and then back again, so that the final impression is not of clearly opposing sides but of an ideological collage.

The blurring extends to Stahr himself; the Reds see him as a conservative—Wall Street as a Red. Like his creator, Stahr tries to enter sympathetically into the world of his adversaries. He has employed a squad of writers and research men for over a year in an attempt to tell the story of the Russian revolution "in terms of the American thirteen states, but it kept coming out different, in new terms that opened unpleasant possibilities and problems." So, after all of the hopeful mixing and matching—of Lenin and Lincoln, of Reds and Princes, of Communist labor organizers and Catholic priests, of Bolsheviks and Founding Fathers—the implication is that the bourgeois idealist, sympathetic to Marxism, must begin to realize that the ideology represents finally not an extending and perfecting of his own ideals, but the formation of an order alien to many of his values. The attempts at mutual assimilation never quite succeed, as Stahr's glimpse of "unpleasant possibilities" suggests.

And yet, the very solidity and concreteness of Fitzgerald's presentation of the capitalistic Stahr show how indebted he is to Marxian methods of analysis. The convincingness of the scenes in what Cecilia calls "A Producer's Day" depends, in fact, on Fitzgerald's revealing the hidden conditions of movie production in much the same way that Marx revealed the conditions of industrial production in his chapter, "The Working Day" from *Capital*. The similarity of titles suggests that for this section Fitzgerald drew directly on Marx's model. And it happens that this particular chapter of *Capital* was the Communist writing that Fitzgerald mentioned most frequently during the time he was writing *Tycoon*. His own acquaintance with the selection, along with his understanding of it, probably comes from Edmund Wilson, who refers to it in *To the Finland Station* (1940) as "the terrible chapter on the 'Working Day.' " Fitzgerald nearly echoes this very phrase, advising his daughter Scotty to read "the terrible chapter in *Das Kapital* on 'The Working Day.' " And since "A Producer's Day" in *Tycoon* is presented as being "drawn partly from a paper" that the narrator, Cecilia Brady, wrote in college, it would seem significant that Cecilia is modeled on a combination of Fitzgerald's college student daughter and Budd Schulberg, the young Marxist screenwriter. Fitzgerald let Schulberg read the opening chapters of *Tycoon* after having read in manuscript Schulberg's own indictment of the sick extremes of capitalist individualism, *What Makes Sammy Run?* "I sort of combined you with my daughter Scottie for Cecilia," Fitzgerald told him.

One of the least theoretical chapters in *Capital* but one of the most vivid and painful, "The Working Day" lays the evidence for Marx's theory that the surplus value from which capitalism takes its profits and its existence is exacted from the surplus labor of the workers. The chapter gives account after account of English factory labor employed for twelve- and fourteen-hour days in killing conditions and paid nearly starvation wages. Fitzgerald's intuitive understanding of the ideas behind the accounts is indicated by analogies he drew with conditions in the movie industry. Where Marx writes of the "small thefts of capitalists from the laborers' meals and recreation time" and "the petty pilfering of minutes," Fitzgerald comments in the margin, "They do this at M.G.M. in a big way; so the secretaries say." But an even more striking indication of his grasp of the principles at work in the chapter is the pairing he makes in his "College of One" curriculum for Sheila Graham of "The Working Day" with Henry James's "The Aspern Papers." The protagonist of that work is an exploiter as surely as are the English mill owners, consistently using others for his purposes, resorting to anything that will aid the drive to self-aggrandizement and profit, all the way from chicanery to ruthless force. The protagonist is an exploiter of a special modern breed, one who invades the privacy of people's lives and uses it as grist for his own mill, but that Fitzgerald should see an analogy suggests how clearly he saw the dangers of morally unrestrained egotism under capitalism.

But even though Fitzgerald uses Marx's method, he comes up with a strikingly different conclusion about the nature of human production. Marx's main point in "The Working Day" is that in order to build up the value that provides its profits, capitalism has an inherent tendency to extend the working day as far beyond the natural day and as close to the physical limits of the workers as possible. But in "A Producer's Day," Fitzgerald stands Marx on his head, just as Marx claimed to have stood Hegel on his feet. In order to produce the surplus value, Stahr, the capitalist, extends his own working day to and beyond the human limits. A victim finally of his own overwork, Stahr is the capitalist-worker, the "producer" in both a Hollywood and a socialist sense, and Fitzgerald's last ambivalent insistence on the primacy of the ideal and the individual over the material and the collective as the driving forces of history. In his coordinated attention to all the details of production—a flood on the lot, a playwright's problems adjusting to screenplays, a crane-shot to establish a mood, the re-assembling of a struck set, the accounting estimates of costs and profits, and much more—Stahr provides the unity that makes the labor of others productive and profitable. And in doing so he shows all the signs of overwork that Marx notes in "The Working Day." Marx comments on "the generally injurious influence of night work": Stahr has a special night secretary, stays at the studio till eleven, goes home to read scripts for another two or three hours, and many nights simply sleeps at the studio. He has no domestic or private life, and is dying from simple overwork. He is, in fact, in love with both work and death, and follows the tendency Marx saw in capitalism toward the "greatest possible daily expenditure of labor-power, no matter how diseased, compulsory, and painful it may be."

The difference, of course, is that Stahr, even though he illustrates perfectly Marx's theory that capitalism extends the working day and shortens the worker's life, is the vampire-like, labor-sucking capitalist of Marx's theory (only in relation to himself). By using the same method to describe Stahr that Marx uses to describe the exploited proletariat, Fitzgerald expresses his belief that only a shaping vision can give value to material production. In refuting Hegel, who envisioned a *zeitgeist* as giving shape to human history, Marx tried to demonstrate that ideas emerged from the conditions of material production, not the other way around. But Fitzgerald uses Marx's own method to propose that it is an almost God-like or God-given imaginative vision, gained by Stahr in his illuminating flight above the earth that opens the novel, which then comes down to earth, shapes the material conditions of production, and gives us our visions back. As Fitzgerald writes in *The Great Gatsby*, "the rock of the world is founded on a fairy's wing." Or, as Zelda wrote in a letter of 1932, "Scott reads Marx—I read the cosmological philosophers. The brightest moments of the day are when we get them mixed up."

Fitzgerald's own humorous attitude toward Marxism cautions us not to accept his sympathies for it without extreme qualifications. The writer who complains in his *Notebooks* that "in thirty-four and thirty-five the party line crept into everything except the Sears Roebuck catalogue," and who intones with tongue-in-cheek solemnity that, "To bring on the revolution it may be necessary to work inside the communist party," is clearly writing from ironic detachment rather than commitment. And if we look at his professions of sympathy throughout his career, we see that they are usually qualified by support for a counter-ideology which espouses the concept of the superior or autonomous individual. In 1924, for example, he proclaimed himself "a communist (with Nietschean [*sic*] overtones)." If a proletarian Superman sounds paradoxical, his Jeffersonian communism of 1931 is at least explainable in terms of the Communist Party effort in the 1930s to stress the "revolutionary" and "original democratic" impulses of the Founding Fathers and their documents. In the 1931 interview with a Montgomery, Alabama newspaper, Fitzgerald said he was "a Jeffersonian democrat at heart and somewhat of a Communist in ideals." By the mid-'30s, Fitzgerald was criticizing D.H. Lawrence's attempt to synthesize the animal and emotional for leaving out politics and being essentially "pre-Marxian," just as he saw himself as "essentially Marxian." In an attempt to reconcile the animal-emotional and the political, along with apparently the spiritual, he advised young writers to "read Tolstoi, Marx, and D.H. Lawrence and then read Tolstoi, Marx, and D.H. Lawrence." In the last year of his life, 1940, he wrote to Maxwell Perkins that Spengler and Marx were "the only modern philosophers that still manage to make sense in this horrible mess." Though both Spengler and Marx share common ground in their predictions that western capitalism would fall by historical laws, Spengler's idealism comes to Fitzgerald more naturally than Marx's materialism, just as Spengler's class society appeals to him more than Marx's classless one.

All these linkings of Marx—with Nietzsche, Jefferson, Lawrence and Spengler—suggest that Fitzgerald's ambivalence put him on a quest for a non-existent kind of idiosyncratic and highly personal Marxism. During a dinner party at the house of Budd Schulberg, Fitzgerald took his host and Ring Lardner, Jr., into another room and discussed communism with them for an hour. "Nothing original," he later told Sheila Graham disappointedly; "They are content to follow the party line." Fitzgerald seems to have hoped to the end that the individual freedom he knew as a bourgeois artist could somehow be reconciled with the socio-economic critique and concern for justice that he admired in Marxism. If the plight of two friends who had managed their resources wisely, yet had been dragged down in the terrible reverses of 1932 could drive Fitzgerald "more and more toward the red flag about which I have been may-poling at a distance all through the decade," the fact is that he consistently maintained that critical distance. The combination of enthusiasm and skepticism implied in the metaphor is characteristic of his double-vision; he could incorporate Marxism into the moral standpoint from which he examined and condemned his American plutocrats, and yet not be blinded by its ideology from seeing and wondering at their beauty and heroism.

WILLIAM E. DOHERTY

"Tender Is the Night" and "Ode to a Nightingale"

Critics often express a feeling that there is something mysterious about Fitzgerald's *Tender Is the Night*, that there is something unsatisfying in the analyses we have had—a discomfort one does not feel with the more elaborately structured *The Great Gatsby*, or with the intriguing, unfinished *The Last Tycoon*. Searching the critical opinion on *Tender Is the Night*—this "magnificent failure"—one is likely to feel that something *is* missing; one seems to have, as Maxwell Geismar says, "the curious impression at times that the novel is really about something else altogether."

It seems strange that the relationship between the novel and Keats's "Ode to a Nightingale," which supplied Fitzgerald with both title and epigraph, should have received no more than passing attention from the critics. The epigraph reads:

> Already with thee! tender is the night,
>
> . . . But here there is no light,
> Save what from heaven is with the breezes blown
> Through verdurous glooms and winding mossy ways.

We know that Fitzgerald had a lifelong and deep response to Keats: "for awhile after you quit Keats all other poetry seems to be only whistling or humming." The "Ode to a Nightingale" was especially important to him; he found it unbearably beautiful, confessed he read it always with tears in his eyes.

I

It is true that the title *Tender Is the Night* was chosen late in the extended course of the book's writing; but it seems clear that Fitzgerald was conscious of the "Ode" not merely in the last stages of composition. The title is appropriate, though no one has said why. Yet, a moment's reflection will show that there is a good deal of Keatsian suggestiveness in *Tender Is the Night* in both decor and atmosphere—the Provençal summers of sunburnt mirth, the night perfumed and promising, the dark gardens of an illusory world. But I suggest that there are parallels more significant than those of color and mood. The correspondences I offer in this case, when taken individually, might seem no more than coincidental; but considered in their cumulative weight, they indicate a calculated pattern of allusion beneath the literal surface of the novel which deepens the psychoanalytic rationale and adds context to the cultural analysis the book offers. In addition, the "Ode" appears to provide us with a sort of thematic overlay which clarifies unsuspected symbolic structures, essential to the understanding of the book.

I will begin with an admission that weakens my case. Fitzgerald dropped a reference to the nightingale from his second and subsequent version of the published novel. In the *Scribner's Magazine* version he wrote of "roses and the nightingales" that had become an essential part of the beauty of that "proud gay land," Provence. Why that observation was dropped, I cannot say; but its appearance, however brief, suggests that like Keats, Fitzgerald associated the south of France with the romantic bird. There is a second and more interesting reference which remained. It too connects the bird and the south of France. To understand its significance, one most consider it in context.

The Riviera, Mediterranean France, came to be, as Maxwell Geismar has pointed out, that apogee of ease and grace, that "psychological Eden" in which Fitzgerald and his heroes took refuge. None of his characters responds more fully to this environment than does Rosemary, coming as she does from the "salacious improvisations of the frontier." At the party at the Villa Diana, no guest is more enchanted by the life that seems promised there; she feels a sense of homecoming, feels drawn as if by magnetic lights. The spell of the party is still on her as she lies awake in her room "suspended in the moonshine, . . . cloaked by the erotic darkness." She is disturbed by secret noises in the night: an "insistent bird" sings in the tree outside. She is not sure what bird it is, but the singing and the Divers seem to merge in her mind: "Beyond the inky sea and far up that high, black shadow of a hill lived the Divers. She thought of them both together, heard them still singing faintly a song like rising smoke, like a hymn, very remote in time and far away." But Rosemary is confused by it all; she cannot think as yet except through her mother's mind. Abe North identifies the bird for her:

> "What are *you* doing up?" he demanded.
> "I just got up." She started to laugh. . . .
> "Probably plagued by the nightingale," Abe suggested and repeated, "probably plagued by the nightingale."

The entire chapter, heavy with night imagery, seems to lead up to this identification. Rosemary has been brought up with the idea of work. Now she is on a summer's holiday, an emotionally lush interval between two winters of reality; and what she discovers is a world remote, romantic, something southern, a mysterious dark lure of life to which she responds—symbolized by the night bird. It is unreal; a duel will be fought; "up north the true world thundered by."

What I suggest is that the novel deals with characters who are plagued by the nightingale, those enamoured of the romantic illusion. Nicole seems to be the Nightingale.

Consider the scene in which Nicole sings to Dick. As she waits for Dick at the sanatorium, singing surrounds Nicole, summer songs of ardent skies and wild shade. The night, the woods, gardens, flowers are associated with Nicole throughout the novel. Here, the unknown seems to yield her up, "as if this were the exact moment when she was coming from a wood into the clear moonlight." Dick responds to that illusion, wishes that she had no other background, "no address save the night from which she had come." She leads him to a secret copse. In this melodious plot she has hidden a phonograph. She plays for him "thin tunes, holding lost times and future liaison." Through song the two of them are transported out of the copse into another world. The journey is chronicled in ironic song titles. Finally Nicole herself sings to Dick. She supposes he has heard all these songs before. " 'Honestly, you don't understand—I haven't heard a thing.' Nor known, nor smelt, nor tasted, he might have added." Now here was this girl bringing him the essence of a continent, "making him a profound promise of herself for so little. . . . Minute by minute the sweetness drained down into her out of the willow trees, out of the dark world." But there is danger in the promise of this "waif of disaster," in the song of this "young bird with wings crushed."

The brief transport from the world which the "Ode" details, the emotional adventure of climax and decline is suggested in this and in a number of other scenes in *Tender Is the Night*. Indeed, the pattern describes the very rhythm of the novel. The party at the Villa Diana, as Malcolm Cowley suggests, appears to be the high point in the story. The scene marks a change of mood; thereafter, the light romantic atmosphere is dispelled. We see there the Divers at their point of greatest charm—a "vision of ease and grace," commanding all the delicacies of existence. It is a high point for another reason. It is in this scene that the principals of the story make an escape from the prosaic and temporal world. In the rarified atmosphere of the party a moment is caught in which a delicate triumph over time is achieved.

The party is given out of doors in the garden, Nicole's garden. To Rosemary the setting seems to be the center of the world: "On such a stage some memorable thing was sure to happen." The guests arrive under a spell, bringing with them the excitement of the night. Dick now seems to serve Nicole as prop man, arranging the set, dressing the trees with lamps. The guests are seated at Nicole's table:

> There were fireflies riding on the dark air and a dog baying on some far-away ledge of the cliff. The table seemed to have risen a little toward the sky like a mechanical dancing platform, giving the people around it a sense of being alone with each other in the dark universe, nourished by its only food, warmed by its only lights. And, as if a curious hushed laugh from Mrs. McKisco were a signal that such a detachment from the world had been attained, the two Divers began suddenly to warm and glow and expand, as if to make up to their guests, already so subtly assured of their importance, so flattered with politeness, for anything they might still miss from that country well left behind. Just for a moment they seemed to speak to everyone at the table, singly and together, assuring them of their friendliness, their affection. And for a moment the faces turned up toward them were like the faces of poor children at a Christmas tree. Then abruptly the table broke up—the moment when the guests had been daringly lifted above conviviality into the rarer atmosphere of sentiment, was over before it could be irreverently breathed, before they had half realized it was there.
>
> But the diffused magic of the hot sweet South had withdrawn into them—the soft-pawed night and the ghostly wash of the Mediterranean far below—the magic left these things and melted into the two Divers and became part them.

When we consider the care with which Fitzgerald dresses this scene, we sense an emphasis beyond what the mere events of the party would demand. This garden, the fireflies riding on the dark air, the summer evening, the wine-colored lanterns hung in the trees—the Romantic decor is there, and the Keatsian atmosphere: "the diffused magic of the hot sweet South . . . the soft-pawed night and the ghostly wash of the

Mediterranean far below." There is no need to insist that these images have their antecedents in the "Ode"—in its "murmurous haunt of flies on summer eves," or its "warm south," its "tender night," its "charmed magic casements opening on perilous seas"; for the clearest parallel to the poem lies in the brief achievement of the precious atmosphere, achieved through the familiar Romantic formula of escape at the moment of emotional pitch—here ironically, a moment of social ecstasy, but suggesting inevitably the dynamics of the sexual event. The imagery itself reiterates the pattern: the fragile loveliness of Nicole's garden increases "until, as if the scherzo of color could reach no further intensity, it broke off suddenly in midair, and moist steps went down to a level five feet below."

It seems unlikely that the material of the "Ode" was so immediate in Fitzgerald's mind that it would come to add to the novel a dimension of allusion of which he was unaware. We are willing to concede unlimited conscious subtlety to his contemporaries in the novel; but Fitzgerald, despite the evidence of his deliberate workmanship, is too often pictured by critics as a somewhat fatuous tool of the muse, whose mind was inferior to his talent. The intricacies of *Tender Is the Night* would suggest otherwise. Not only is the pattern of the momentary climax a repeated one in the novel; there occurs, too, the *recall to reality* that marks the ending of the "Ode." In the novel it is not the sound of a bell that signals the descent from bliss—or the word "forlorn" striking like a bell, tolling the poet back to his sole self; it is another sound heard three times in the book: when Dick falls in love with Nicole, when Abe leaves on the train from Paris, and when Tommy becomes Nicole's lover. Each time a shot is heard, a loud report that breaks the illusion, signifies the end of happiness and the escape from self.

After Nicole leaves the sanatorium, Dick tries to avoid her; but she fills his dreams. Their chance meeting in the Alps ends in Dick's complete surrender of self: "he was thankful to have an existence at all, if only as a reflection in her wet eyes." As in all her love situations, Nicole is triumphant, self-controlled, cool: "I've got him, he's mine." The scene remains tender; it is raining, the appropriate weather for love in Fitzgerald's novels. But, "suddenly there was a booming from the wine slopes across the lake; like cannons were shooting at hail-bearing clouds in order to break them. The lights of the promenade went off, went on again. Then the storm came swiftly . . . with it came a dark, frightening sky and savage filaments of lightning and world-splitting thunder, while ragged, destroying clouds fled along past the hotel. Mountains and lakes disappeared—the hotel crouched amid tumult, chaos and darkness."

This is not the storm of passion. Dick has come suddenly to his senses: "For Doctor Diver to marry a mental patient? How did it happen? Where did it begin?" The moment of passion and illusion is over. He laughs derisively. "*Big* chance—oh, yes. My God!—they decided to buy a doctor? Well, they better stick to whoever they've got in Chicago." But Dick has committed himself to Nicole. His clear sight comes too late, and when the storm is over her beauty enters his room "rustling ghostlike through the curtains."

A loud shot sounds the ominous recall another time, in the Paris railway station. Here is departure and farewell; a gunshot cracks the air. Abe, on the train, waves good-by, unaware of what has happened. The shots do not mark the end of his happiness, for he has long been in misery, though they do forebode his violent death. It is the brief summer happiness of Dick—won in a desperate bargain with the gods—that is ending. It marks the end of a summer mirth for the Divers' group, the beginning of misfortune for Dick. Dick and his friends move out of the station into the street as if nothing had happened. "However, everything had happened—Abe's departure and Mary's impending departure for Salzburg this afternoon had ended the time in Paris. Or perhaps the shots, the concussions that had finished God knew what dark matter, had terminated it. The shots had entered into all their lives . . ."

The third of these recalls to reality occurs just after Tommy possesses Nicole. The entire account from the arrival of Tommy at the Villa Diana to the departure from the hotel presents a curious parallel to the ending of the "Ode." Tommy comes to Nicole like a worshipper before a mystery. His happiness intensifies: "And, my God, I have never been so happy as I am this minute." But the time of joy is brief; the point of greatest happiness is a moment outside of self, a taste of oblivion. The ecstasy passes; disappointment and foreboding follow: "the nameless fear which precedes all emotions, joyous or sorrowful, inevitable as a hum of thunder precedes a storm." After the act, things begin to look tawdry to Tommy. He is edgy and apprehensive. Outside there are disturbing noises: "There's that noise again. My God, has there been a murder?" The final recall is heard. As they leave the room "a sound split the air outside: Cr-ACK-Boom-M-m-m! It was the battleship sounding a recall. Now, down below their window, it was pandemonium indeed . . ." There is a rush to depart. Cries and tears are heard as the women shout farewells to the departing launch. The last ludicrous moments of the scene, the girls shouting their tearful good-byes from the balcony of Tommy's room, waving their underwear like flags, appear to be Fitzgerald's ironic counterpart to the adieu of the final stanza of the poem. The fading anthem of the "Ode" becomes the American

National Anthem: "Oh, say can you see the tender color of remembered flesh?—while at the stern of the battleship arose in rivalry the Star-Spangled Banner."

II

The title of the novel and the epigraph Fitzgerald offers illuminate the significance of "night" and "darkness" in the story. An enquiry reveals a complicated and careful symbolic structure in *Tender Is the Night* involving a contrast between the night and the day, darkness and light. The title of the novel declares that the night is tender. There is in it an implicit corollary about the day.

Early in the story, the sun is established as something harsh and painful, even maddening. The sun troubles the Divers and their group. They seek shelter from it under their umbrellas which "filter" its rays. At the beach the sea yields up its colors to the "brutal sunshine." Rosemary retreats from the "hot light" on the sand. Dick promises her a hat to protect her from the sun and to "save her reason." In the scene in which Nicole lapses into madness at the Agiri Fair "a high sun with a face traced on it beat fierce on the straw hats of the children." The day scenes are those of pain and fear: "the April sun shone pink upon the saintly face of Augustine, the cook, and blue on the butcher's knife she waved in her drunken hand."

On the other hand, darkness and the night are addressed in fond, in honorific terms: "the lovely night," the "soft rolling night," the "soft-pawed night," the "erotic darkness." Fitzgerald's description of Amiens reveals something of the character and virtue of the night: "In the daytime one is deflated by such towns . . . and the very weather seems to have a quality of the past, faded weather like that of old photographs. But after dark all that is most satisfactory in French life swims back into the picture—the sprightly tarts, the men arguing with a hundred Violà's in the cafes, the couples drifting, head to head, toward the satisfactory inexpensiveness of nowhere." Part of the meaning is here, but the symbolism of the night is not merely opposite in meaning to that of the day; it is more complicated and more intricately woven into the story. The night is the time of enchantment, masking the ugliness of reality that the day exposes. The night, as in the "Ode," is the time of beauty and the time of illusion. Dick and his friends prefer the night: "All of them began to laugh spontaneously because they knew it was still last night while the people in the streets had the delusion that it was bright hot morning." But the night is not entirely superior to the day. The desirable night is the all allowing darkness. It is a dimness preferred, perhaps, by those ineffective in dealing with the practical day-lit reality. If the day is harsh, it has vigor; the night is the time of ease and also weakness. Some hint of these sinister implications may be detected in the scene in which Baby Warren makes her frustrated effort to aid Dick after he has been beaten and thrown into the Roman jail. She cannot function in the real world: "She began to race against the day; sometimes on the broad avenues she gained but whenever the thing that was pushing up paused for a moment, gusts of wind blew here and there impatiently and the slow creep of light began once more." She cringes at the unstable balance between night and day. The strange creature she encounters in the embassy, wrapped and bandaged for sleep, "vivid but dead," appears an unwholesome figure of the night, incongruous with the day.

It would appear that Fitzgerald has divided his world into two parts—the night and the day. The day is reality, hard, harsh, and vigorous; the night is illusion, tender, joyful, but devitalizing.

The most significant illusion that the night fosters is the illusion of happiness. To the Romantic, happiness consists in preserving the high moment of joy. He has a dread of endings. *Tender Is the Night* is a book of endings: "Things are over down here," says Dick. "I want it to die violently instead of fading out sentimentally." Paradoxically, the Romantic dream is that the moment of joy can be embalmed forever in the final night; death then appears to be a welcome extenuation of the night, ending all endings. Both the poem and the novel deal with these lovely illusions; but what they teach is that the fancy cannot cheat so well, that disillusionment is the coefficient of time.

There is a difference in tone between the two works which is due to the fact that Keats emphasizes the swelling dimension of the ecstatic experience, while Fitzgerald deals more with its deflation. Where Keats conveys a sense of disappointment, fond regret, Fitzgerald expresses a Romantic's anti-Romantic argument; for in tracing the grim disenchantment Fitzgerald underscores the sense of deception, trickery, the sense of victimage in the martyring of the dreamer. The "immortal bird" of the "Ode" becomes the "perverse phoenix" Nicole; the deceiving elf becomes the "crooked" Nicole, one of a long line of deceivers, pretending to have a mystery: "I've gone back to my true self," she tells Tommy; ". . . I'm a crook by heritage." We suspect complicity in her father's sin; he tells the doctor, "She used to sing to me."

There are other victims of the Romantic deception—the inmates of the sanatorium where Dick labors without accomplishment. "I am here as a symbol of something", the American woman artist tells Dick. She and the others are there because "life is too tough a game" for them. Unlike the thick-ankled peasants who can take the punishment of the world on every inch of flesh and spirit, these are the fine-spun people suffering private illusions, their "compasses depolarized." They are "sunk in eternal darkness," people of the night, spirits sensitive and weak, now caught in Nicole's garden. For it is Nicole who has designed the means of holding these inmates fast. With floral concealment and deceptive ornament she has created those camouflaged strong points in which they are kept. Outwardly these houses are attractive, even cheerful, screened by little copses; but "even the flowers lay in iron fingers." Perhaps the "Ode" suggested the names: the "Beeches" and the "Eglantine."

III

These inmates are, many of them, the "victims of drug and drink." There is in *Tender Is the Night* what might be called a potion motif, involving liquor, drugs, and poison. As in the "Ode" these are associated with the illusory adventure. Dr. Diver is as much an addict as his patients. In the early parts of the novel wine is associated with the delicacy of living the Divers maintain and with the sensual qualities of their lives. The enjoyable swim in the ocean is like the pleasure of "chilled white wine." The wine-colored lamps at the Villa Diana give a lively flush to Nicole's face. Nicole is gay-spirited after the "rosy wine at lunch." There is a faint spray of champagne on Rosemary's breath when Dick kisses her for the first time. But wine quickly loses its pleasant character. As Dick's esteemed control begins to slip and he acts for the first time without his customary "repose," he stares at the shelf of bottles, "the humbler poisons of France—bottles of Otard, Rhum St. James, Marie Brizard. . . ." Dick's Roman debauch recalls Abe's disastrous drunks. At home Dick drinks brandy from a three-foot bottle. He comes to regard liquor as food, descending to the level of the rich ruins he treats. Late in the novel we see that the sinister qualities of these draughts, potions, beakersful are associated with Nicole: in falling in love with her, in marrying her, Dick "had chosen the sweet poison and drunk it." Again Nicole is characterized as the attractive evil, the sinister allurement.

The draught of vintage from the deep delved earth, the dull opiate, the hemlock of Keats's poem may not be the direct sources of Fitzgerald's images; yet the associations of drug, drink, and poison with the Romantic appetencies are interesting and suggest that Keats and

Fitzgerald were dealing with a similar psychological syndrome—the urge to "fade away, dissolve and quite forget. . . ."

This urge, as Albert Guerard, Jr., points out in his essay, "Prometheus and the Aeolian Lyre," is really the urge toward loss of self, the impulse toward self-immolation, to the drowning of consciousness—one of the hallmarks of the Romantic temperament—which accepts the myth of a vital correspondence between man and nature, a correspondence demanding the submersion of our rational, coherent selves. In the "Ode to a Nightingale," Mr. Guerard argues, Keats has written a poem about the actual submersion of consciousness, dramatizing the process itself, and presenting in the poem a symbolic evasion of the actual world:

> In one sense this ode is a dramatized contrasting of actuality and the world of the imagination, but the desire to attain this fretless imaginative world becomes at last a desire for reason's utter dissolution: a longing not for art but for free reverie of any kind. . . . This sole self from which Keats escapes at the beginning of the poem, and to which he returns at its close, is not merely the conscious intellect aware of life's weariness, fever, and fret, but truly the sole self: the self locked in drowsy numbness, the self conscious of its isolation. . . .

Mr. Guerard's analysis may be modified, perhaps, to this degree: the "Ode" seems not so much a product of the Romantic myth of a prevailing correspondence between man and nature as it is an acknowledgment that the correspondence does not prevail. This thesis is reiterated in *Tender Is the Night*. What the nightingale symbolizes and promises in the "Ode," Nicole symbolizes and promises too. The ecstatic union with the bird is a taste of oblivion in loss of self.

Dick manifests the symptoms that Mr. Guerard indicates. There is the obsessive awareness of isolation that characterizes Dick even in his student days. He feels separated from his "fathers." He has the feeling that he is different from the rest, the isolation of the scientist and the artist—"good material for those who do most of the world's work"; but it is a loneliness he cannot endure. He wanted to be good, to be kind; he wanted to be brave and wise; but, as we learn toward the end, "he had wanted, even more than that, to be loved." He gives a strange answer to Franz's criticism of his scholarship: "I am alone today. . . . But I may not be alone to-morrow." One by one he burns his books to keep warm. In marrying Nicole he abandons his work in "effortless immobility." The critics have frequently noted the self-sacrificial aspect of Dick's behavior; but too frequently that self-sacrifice has been taken as the very theme of the novel because Dick gives himself so completely in serving others that he is left with nothing in the end. Rather, this self-sacrifice should be understood as one of the paradoxical impulses which constitute the desire to submerge the self. Self-immolation seems to contradict the longing for freedom from burdens and cares, yet both urges are aspects of the desire to abandon individuality. Abe, like Dick, has a strong desire for loss of self, and forgetfulness. Abe wants oblivion and seeks it in drink; he longs for death. Tommy too has inclinations toward the moribund, following death and violence all over the world. Baby Warren "relished the foretaste of death, prefigured by the catastrophes of friends." Dick looks fondly at death in his decline. At the railing of Golding's yacht he comes close to suicide and to taking Nicole with him. The isolation Dick feels as a young man is never relieved. The entire age is alien to him. Dick mourns on the battlefields of World War I: "All my beautiful lovely safe world blew itself up here with a great gust of high explosive love." Coming home to bury his father, he feels the final tie has been broken; there is no identity with his own land; he feels only a kinship with the dead: "Good-by, my father—good-bye, all my fathers."

IV

Finally, what does the correspondence between the novel and the "Ode" reveal about the social and cultural analysis Fitzgerald offers in *Tender Is the Night?* The distinction between the night and the day that Fitzgerald establishes symbolically has its significance in the "class struggle" he presents; the social antagonisms seem to be aspects of the antipathy which arises between the Romantic and the anti-Romantic disposition.

Fitzgerald, as we have seen, divides things into opposing pairs in *Tender Is the Night*. When Rosemary arrives at the Riviera beach she finds two groups. The McKisco party is made up of McKisco, the *arriviste* who has not yet arrived, his silly ambitious wife, two effeminates, and the shabby-eyed Mrs. Abrams. They are pale, gauche people, unattractive beside the Divers' group. The Divers are rich, cultured, talented, leisured. We get a fuller understanding of what these groups may represent in the scene in which Dick and Rosemary visit the house on the Rue Monsieur. It is a place of incongruities and contrasts. Clearly there is a clash between the past and the present, suggesting, it seems, the evolving future of the Western world: "It was a house hewn from the frame of Cardinal De Retz's palace in the Rue Monsieur, but once inside the door there was nothing of the past, nor of any present that Rosemary knew. The outer shell, the masonry, seemed rather to enclose the future so that it was an electric-like shock, a definite nervous experience, perverted as a breakfast of oatmeal and hashish, to cross that threshold . . ." The people within are an odd mixture. They fit awkwardly into the environment. They lack the command over life that earlier ages managed to exert. Rosemary has a detached "false and exalted feeling" of being on a movie set. No one knew what the room meant because it was evolving into something else. It is important to recognize who these people in the room are:

> These were of two sorts. There were the Americans and English who had been dissipating all spring and summer, so that now everything they did had a purely nervous inspiration. They were very quiet and lethargic at certain hours and then they exploded into sudden quarrels and breakdowns and seductions. The other class, who might be called the exploiters, was formed by the sponges, who were sober, serious people by comparison, with a purpose in life and no time for fooling. These kept their balance best in that environment, and what tone there was, beyond the apartment's novel organization of light values, came from them.

The room apparently holds the society of the West. We find in it the McKisco group, the sponges, the hard practical people; and there are the Divers' type, the dissipated old "quality" class, the rundown Romantics who are doomed. The sober and serious exploiters set the tone for the future, and in it they will succeed. Rosemary stands between the two groups. Her youth and success separate her from the Divers' crowd, but she inclines toward them by temperament and training. She is a product of her mother's rearing, tutored in the values of the old society. "I'm a romantic too," Rosemary tells Dick. Yet, she is coldly practical, "economically . . . a boy not a girl." The first day on the beach Rosemary does not know which group is hers. She is attracted by the Divers' party; but, "between the dark people and the light, Rosemary found room and spread out her peignoir on the sand."

The people of the McKisco type are not the victims of Nicole; they are immune to the Romantic illusion. The "tough minded and perennially suspicious" cannot be charmed. McKisco is the only one at the party at the Villa Diana who remains unassimilated, unaffected by the emotional excursion. In the house on the Rue Monsieur there are others who are likewise immune. The "cobra women" discuss the Divers:

> "Oh, they give a good show," said one of them in a deep rich voice. "Practically the best show in Paris—I'd be the last one to deny that. But after all—" She sighed. "Those phrases he uses over and over and over—'Oldest inhabitant gnawed by rodents.' You laugh once."
> "I prefer people whose lives have more corrugated surfaces," said the second, "and I don't like her."
>
> "I've never really been able to get very excited about them, or their entourage either. Why, for example, the entirely liquid Mr. North?"

The incapacity for illusion gives these people an advantage in the world. McKisco, for whom the sensual world does not exist, ends successful and honored; his novels are pastiches of the work of the best people of his time. "He was no fool about his capacities—he realized that he possessed more vitality than many men of superior talent, and he was resolved to enjoy the success he had earned." McKisco's duel with Tommy symbolizes the clash between the two groups and underscores the anachronism of the soldier and hero. Tommy is a product of the older civilization, educated in forgotten values. Ironically it is McKisco who is "satisfied" in the duel. He builds a new self-respect from his inglorious performance. Tommy, Abe, and Dick are Romantic remnants, the children of another century, fettered by its illusions—"the illusions of eternal strength and health, and of the essential goodness of people; illusions of a nation, the lies of generations of frontier mothers who had to croon falsely, that there were no wolves outside the cabin door."

They are the salt of the earth—charming, gifted people, but overmatched in the struggle against the cold, shrewd frauds who are inheriting the earth. *Tender Is the Night* deals with the passing of the old order, with the passing of an attitude toward life, or rather with the last remnants of that life, "the oldest inhabitants gnawed by rodents." The specific content of the illusions which fetter them is less important than how Fitzgerald deals with the attraction to the irrational dream which marks the romantic temperament, a dream which may promise the world, the sustained ecstasy of love or the satisfactions of oblivion—symbolized by the beautiful mad woman, Nicole. She is the dream without real referent. She has no existence outside the mind of the dreamer: "When I talk I say to myself that I am probably Dick. Already I have even been my son, remembering how wise and slow he is. Sometimes I am Doctor Dohmler and one time I may even be an aspect of you, Tommy Barban. Tommy is in love with me . . ."

In the end it is Doctor Diver who is "cured" when he releases her from his mind; he returns to the terrible emptiness of the "sole self." Late in the novel Nicole sings to him again in her "harsh sweet contralto." But this time Dick will not listen: "I don't like that one."

The dream and the dreamer are, of course, Fitzgerald's subject matter in fiction; and in treating them he invariably delivers up the dreamer as victim of his own Romantic infatuations. And yet for all his insight, his self-lacerating satire, Fitzgerald leaves the dream and the dreamer somehow inviolable at the end. Gatsby, the most extravagant Romantic, leaking sawdust at every pore, is still intact at the end and dies with his dream intact. "No—Gatsby turned out all right at the end; it was what preyed on Gatsby, what foul dust floated in the wake of his dreams" that defeated him.

The best of the Romantic writers are not vulnerable to their own myths. The "Ode to a Nightingale" declares exquisitely the abandonment of faith in the imagination. It is not until *Tender Is the Night* that Fitzgerald abandons that last comfort of the Romantic, the notion that the botching, the disappointment of the imagination's most cherished ambitions may be blamed on the unworthy environment of the dreamer. *Tender Is the Night* is a harder, harsher book than *Gatsby*; and it tells us that the super dream is an internal corruption, a damaging, self-begotten beauty. Dick's final return to his sole self in upstate New York—"almost certainly in that section of the country, in one town or another"—is an utterly unsentimental fade-out; the hero is gone from the stage before we can cover him with our fond sympathy, before we can murmur, "Alas."

Chronology

1896	Born September 24 in St. Paul, Minnesota, to Edward Fitzgerald, a Proctor and Gamble salesman, and Mary McQuillan Fitzgerald.
1911–13	At Newman Academy in New Jersey.
1913–17	At Princeton University; leaves, without graduating, to enter U.S. Army.
1919	Discharged from Army in February.
1920	*This Side of Paradise*; marries Zelda Sayre.
1921	First tour of Europe; *Flappers and Philosophers*.
1922	*The Beautiful and Damned; Tales of the Jazz Age*; birth of daughter, Frances, in St. Paul; moves, with family, to Long Island.
1924	Moves, with family, to the Riviera.
1925	*The Great Gatsby*.
1926	*All the Sad Young Men*.
1927	Works as scriptwriter in Hollywood; moves, with family, to house near Wilmington, Delaware.
1930	Zelda suffers mental collapse.
1931	Works again as Hollywood writer.
1932	Moves to house in Rodgers Forge, Maryland.
1934	*Tender Is the Night*.
1935	*Taps at Reveille*. Period of "crack-up" begins.
1937	Moves back to Hollywood; starts relationship with Sheilah Graham.
1940	Dies in Hollywood on December 21; his body is buried in Rockville, Maryland.
1948	Death of Zelda Fitzgerald in fire at a sanitarium.

Contributors

HAROLD BLOOM, Sterling Professor of the Humanities at Yale University, is the author of *The Anxiety of Influence, Poetry and Repression* and many other volumes of literary criticism. His forthcoming study, *Freud: Transference and Authority*, attempts a full-scale reading of all of Freud's major writings. He is the general editor of *The Chelsea House Library of Literary Criticism*.

EDMUND WILSON, was one of the leading American literary critics of this century. Among his books were *The Shores of Light, Axel's Castle* and the novel, *Memoirs of Hecate County*.

LIONEL TRILLING, University Professor at Columbia, also was one of the most eminent critics in American literary history. His works include *The Middle of the Journey*, a novel, and *Sincerity and Authenticity*.

MARIUS BEWLEY was Professor of American Literature at Rutgers University. He was the author of *The Complex Fate* and *Masks and Mirrors*.

MALCOLM COWLEY is one of our most eminent men-of-letters. His best known books are *Exile's Return* and *A Second Flowering*.

ROBERT ORNSTEIN is Professor of English at Case Western Reserve University, and has published widely on Shakespeare and on other Elizabethans.

MICHAEL MILLGATE, Professor of English at the University of Toronto, has written a critical study of William Faulkner and a biography of Thomas Hardy.

ROY. R. MALE is Professor of English, Emeritus, at the University of Oklahoma. He is the author of *Hawthorne's Tragic Vision*.

ARTHUR MIZENER is Professor of English, Emeritus, at Cornell University, and the author of *The Far Side of Paradise*, a critical biography of Scott Fitzgerald.

JAMES GINDIN, Professor of English at the University of Michigan, has written books on John Galsworthy and on post-World War II British fiction.

MARY E. BURTON teaches at the University of California, La Jolla. She has written on Wordsworth's *Prelude*.

DAVID PARKER is Professor of English at the University of Malaya. He has published essays on Chaucer and on Shakespeare.

ROBERT ROULSTON teaches at Murray State University, Kentucky, and writes on Southern literature.

RONALD J. GERVAIS is Associate Professor of English at San Diego State University, and has published many articles on ninteenth and twentieth-century literature.

WILLIAM E. DOHERTY writes extensively upon modern literature.

Bibliography

Barrett, William. "Fitzgerald and America." *Partisan Review* 18 (May–June 1951): 345–53.

Bishop, John Peale. "The Missing All." *Virginia Quarterly Review* 12 (Winter 1937): 107–21.

Bruccoli, Matthew J. *Profile of F. Scott Fitzgerald*. Columbus, Ohio: Merrill, 1971.

———. *Some Sort of Epic Grandeur: The Life of F. Scott Fitzgerald*. New York: Harcourt Brace Jovanovich, 1981.

Buttitta, Tony. *After the Good Gay Times: A Season with F. Scott Fitzgerald*. New York: Viking Press, 1974.

Byer, Jackson R., ed. *The Short Stories of F. Scott Fitzgerald: New Approaches in Criticism*. Madison, Wisc.: University of Wisconsin Press, 1982.

Callaghan, Morley. *That Summer in Paris: Memories of Tangled Friendships with Hemingway, Fitzgerald, and Some Others*. New York: Coward-McCann, 1963.

Callahan, John F. *The Illusions of a Nation: Myth and History in the Novels of F. Scott Fitzgerald*. Urbana: University of Illinois Press, 1972.

Coleman, Tom C., III. "Nicole Warren Diver and Scott Fitzgerald: The Girl and the Egotist." *Studies In The Novel* 1, vol. 2 (1971): 34–43.

Cowley, Malcolm. "Fitzgerald: The Double Man." *Saturday Review* 34 (February 24, 1951): 9, 10, 42–44.

Cowley, Malcolm, and Cowley, Robert. *Fitzgerald and the Jazz Age*. New York: Scribner, 1966.

Eble, Kenneth Eugene. *F. Scott Fitzgerald*. Rev. ed. Boston: Twayne Publishers, 1977.

———, ed. *F. Scott Fitzgerald: A Collection of Criticism*. New York: McGraw-Hill, 1973.

Fahey, William A. *F. Scott Fitzgerald and the American Dream*. New York: Crowell, 1973.

Friedrich, Otto. "F. Scott Fitzgerald: Money, Money, Money." *American Scholar* 29 (Summer 1960): 392–405.

Greenfield, Howard. *F. Scott Fitzgerald*. New York: Crown Publishers, 1974.

Hindus, Milton. *F. Scott Fitzgerald: An Introduction and Interpretation*. New York: Holt, Rinehart and Winston, 1968.

Kazin, Alfred. *F. Scott Fitzgerald: The Man and His Work*. Cleveland: World Publishing Co., 1951.

LaHood, Marvin J., ed. *Tender is the Night: Essays in Criticism*. Bloomington: Indiana University Press, 1969.

Lehan, Richard Daniel. *F. Scott Fitzgerald and the Craft of Fiction*. Carbondale: Southern Illinois University Press, 1966.

Lubell, Albert J. "The Fitzgerald Revival." *The South Atlantic Quarterly* 1, vol. 54 (January 1955): 95–106.

Merrill, Robert. "Tender Is the Night as a Tragic Action." *Texas Studies in Literature and Language* 4, vol. 25 (Winter 1983): 597–615.

Miller, James E., Jr. *F. Scott Fitzgerald, His Art and Technique*. New York: New York University Press, 1964.

Mizener, Arthur. *The Far Side of Paradise: A Biography of F. Scott Fitzgerald*. Boston: Houghton Mifflin, 1951.

———. *F. Scott Fitzgerald: A Collection of Critical Essays*. Englewood Cliffs, N.J.: Prentice-Hall, 1963.

Schulberg, Budd. "Old Scott: The Mask, the Myth and the Man." *Esquire* 55 (January 1961): 96–101.

Stallman, Robert W. "Conrad and *The Great Gatsby*." *Twentieth Century Literature* 1 (April 1955): 5–12.

Stern, Milton R. *The Golden Moment: The Novels of F. Scott Fitzgerald*. Urbana: University of Illinois Press, 1970.

Trower, Katherine B. "Visions of Paradise in *The Great Gatsby*." *Renascence* 1, vol. 25 (Autumn 1972): 14–23.

Turnbull, Andrew. *Scott Fitzgerald*. New York: Scribner, 1962.

Way, Brian. *F. Scott Fitzgerald and the Art of Social Fiction*. London: Edward Arnold, 1980.

West, James L. W. *The Making of 'This Side of Paradise.'* Philadelphia: University of Pennsylvania Press, 1983.

West, Rebecca. *Ending in Earnest*. Garden City, N.Y.: Doubleday, 1931.

Wilson, Edmund. *The Shores of Light*. New York: Farrar, Strauss and Giroux, 1952.

Acknowledgments

"F. Scott Fitzgerald" by Edmund Wilson from *The Shores of Light* by Edmund Wilson, copyright © 1952 by Edmund Wilson, 1980 by Helen Miranda Wilson. Reprinted with permission of Farrar, Straus and Giroux, Inc.

"F. Scott Fitzgerald" by Lionel Trilling from *The Liberal Imagination: Essays on Literature and Society* by Lionel Trilling, copyright © 1945 by Lionel Trilling. Reprinted by permission.

"Scott Fitzgerald and the Collapse of the American Dream" by Marius Bewley from *The Eccentric Design* by Marius Bewley, copyright © 1957 by Columbia University Press. Reprinted by permission.

"Fitzgerald: The Romance of Money" by Malcolm Cowley from *A Second Flowering* by Malcolm Cowley, copyright © 1956 and 1973 by Malcolm Cowley. Reprinted by permission.

"Scott Fitzgerald's Fable of East and West" by Robert Ornstein from *College English* 2, vol. 18, (November 1956), copyright © 1956 by the National Council of Teachers of English. Reprinted by permission.

"Scott Fitzgerald as Social Novelist: Statement and Technique in *The Last Tycoon*" by Michael Millgate from *English Studies* 1, vol. 43, (February 1962), copyright © 1962 by Swets and Zeitlinger B.V. Reprinted by permission.

" 'Babylon Revisited': A Story of the Exile's Return" by Roy R. Male from *Studies in Short Fiction*, vol. 2, (1964–65), copyright © 1964 by Newberry College. Reprinted by permission.

"*Tender Is the Night*" by Arthur Mizener from *Twelve Great American Novels* by Arthur Mizener, copyright © 1967 by Arthur Mizener and New American Library, Reprinted by permission.

"Gods and Fathers in F. Scott Fitzgerald's Novels" by James Gindin from *Modern Language Quarterly*, vol. 30, (1969), copyright © 1969 by *Modern Language Quarterly*. Reprinted by permission.

"The Counter-Transference of Dr. Diver" by Mary E. Burton from *English Literary History* 3, vol. 38, (September 1971), copyright © 1971 by The Johns Hopkins University Press. Reprinted by permission.

"*The Great Gatsby*: Two Versions of the Hero" by David Parker from *English Studies* 1, vol. 54, (February 1973), copyright © 1973 by Swets and Zeitlinger B.V. Reprinted by permission.

"Whistling 'Dixie' in Encino: *The Last Tycoon* and F. Scott Fitzgerald's Two Souths" by Robert Roulston from *South Atlantic Quarterly* 4, vol. 79, (Autumn 1980), copyright © 1980 by Duke University Press. Reprinted by permission.

"The Socialist and the Silk Stockings: Fitzgerald's Double Allegiance" by Ronald

J. Gervais from *Mosaic: A Journal for the Interdisciplinary Study of Literature* 2, vol. 15, (June 1982), copyright © 1982 by *Mosaic*. Reprinted by permission.

"*Tender Is the Night* and 'Ode to a Nightingale' " by William E. Doherty from *Exploration of Literature*, edited by Rima Drell Reck, copyright © 1966 by Louisiana State University Press. Reprinted by permission.

Index